MIRACLE BY DESIGN

MIRACLE BY DESIGN

THE REAL REASONS BEHIND JAPAN'S ECONOMIC SUCCESS

FRANK GIBNEY

Times
BOOKS

Published by TIMES BOOKS, a division of
Quadrangle/The New York Times Book Co., Inc.
Three Park Avenue, New York, N.Y. 10016

Published simultaneously in Canada by Fitzhenry
& Whiteside, Ltd., Toronto

Library of Congress Cataloging in Publication Data

Gibney, Frank, 1924-
  Miracle by design.

  Includes bibliographical references and index.
  1. Industrial management—Japan. 2. Industrial
management—United States. 3. National
characteristics, Japanese. 4. Japan—Industries. 5.
Businessmen—Japan.
I. Title
HD70.J3G52   1982   658'00952   82-50043
ISBN 0-8129-1024-9

Manufactured in the United States of America
10 9 8 7 6 5 4 3 2 1

For Hiroko, Elise, and Jody

Acknowledgments

Particular thanks is due to Maurice B. Mitchell, who very kindly reviewed this manuscript at several stages in its writing; I am indebted to him for his sound advice and effective editing help. Shigeki Hijino, another old friend, thoroughly read the manuscript, also at different periods, and contributed his usual wise counsel. Thomas Blakemore was of particular help to me on several chapters on which I consulted him. Herbert Passin made helpful comments and suggestions after reading the first four chapters. I am grateful also to Jerrold and Leona Schecter, who first suggested this theme and helped me refine it. Needless to say, any errors of omission or commission which may have crept into print here are my own.

In my reading and talks about various subjects covered here, I profited greatly from the counsel of Yamamoto Shichihei, Chalmers Johnson, and Kawashima Takenori, in person and in print. Their three books *Nihon Shihonshugi no Seishin (The Spirit of Japanese Capitalism)*, *MITI and the Japanese Miracle*, and *Nihonjin no Hōishiki (The Consciousness of Law Among the Japanese)* I found extremely valuable as support and back-

ACKNOWLEDGMENTS

ground. At several points in this book I have quoted from "K.K. Nippon Shindan" ("Japan, Inc. Examined"), a series of perceptive articles by the editorial staff of *Asahi* newspaper in Tokyo.

My wife, Hiroko, has been of constant assistance both in assembling research and in reviewing my findings. Much thanks is also due to the helpful editing of Ned Chase and Jean Pohoryles at Times Books.

I owe much, also, to the support and example of my colleagues, too numerous to mention, at Encyclopaedia Britannica, Inc. and TBS-Britannica, Ltd., the two companies I worked for during my Tokyo residence. It should not be inferred, however, that the various examples of business practice in Japan which I cite all relate in some way to my personal experience with Britannica. Quite to the contrary, I have drawn my samples and abbreviated case studies from a wide variety of sources, both observed and experienced, in different companies and industries. Examples used by way of illustrating various points have been deliberately rearranged so that real people portrayed cannot be identified. Where I refer to actual occurrences at my own companies, they are stated as such.

Preface

In the late spring of 1966, I took the elevator to the eighth floor of the Eiwa Building in the burgeoning Tokyo submetropolis of Shinjuku and walked out to say a few words, in rusty Japanese, to the employees at the company of which I had just become president. The name of the company was Encyclopaedia Britannica (Japan), Inc., the recently founded Tokyo subsidiary of the prominent educational publisher in Chicago. My employers had provided me with a new black Nissan Cedric as my company car, just enough money to rent a house in the overpriced "foreigners' market" in Tokyo, spirited words of encouragement, and a warning not to increase the sales commissions.

E. B. (Japan) was then doing a tidy business selling sets of the English-language *Britannica* to Japanese customers, who had developed a surprising interest in buying it. I was expected to run the company along guidelines supplied me from headquarters in Chicago, keep up the collection rate, and wherever possible expand the profits. My past experience in Japan and some knowledge of the language and people, it was felt, might just conceivably outweigh my inexperience in the encyclopaedia business.

PREFACE

For me, too, past associations with Japan were the key factor. Having used Japanese as a Navy language officer during and after World War II and having spent a stimulating two years in Japan later as a correspondent for *Time* magazine, I was interested in going back there to live. I was also planning a book about the Japanese side of the Pacific war and hoped to research it in my off-hours.

I never did finish that book. (It took nine years before I found the time to write another one.) Instead of writing about the Japanese, I lived their life—insofar as a foreigner can—caught up in the insistent rhythm of Japanese business and fascinated by the society that nurtures it. My work was not unsuccessful. In 1975, when I left my last full-time job in Japan as president of the joint-venture company TBS-Britannica, the small sales subsidiary of a decade before had proliferated into four distinct companies; the English-language *Britannica*s had given way to language courses, children's books, and the large Japanese-language *Britannica International Encyclopaedia*. Total annual sales of all the Britannica companies in Japan were running well over $100 million annually, roughly seventeen times what they had been in 1966. The correspondingly increased profit figures meant a great deal to both my American and my Japanese employers.

What meant even more to me was the liberal education I had received during those years—not without some pain—in the ways of Japanese business and the real reasons for its successes—reasons often only marginally related to matters of work habits or management technique. At almost every point in this learning process comparisons and contrasts with American ways of doing business kept occurring to me. If I learned a great deal about Japanese business in this time, I learned even more about the American variety. You often find a better perspective on your own business world—and your own society—by looking at it from the vantage point of a far planet.

No nation's "business" can be viewed apart from its politics and society. There are deep-seated social and historical as well as economic reasons for the way Japanese banks work, or the way Japanese companies develop products, for the way executives are paid, or the way union members feel themselves a part of management. There are good cultural explanations for paradoxes like that of a business society, professedly and proudly hierarchical and indeed "elitist" in its structure, that sets such store by the dignity and opinions of its humbler members. There are also, however, strong influences on any country from the outside—and Japan's case is no exception. In this century no other society has made such an impact on the Japanese as has the American. Tokyo may seem like the capital of a far-off planet. Yet almost everywhere in its business world an American hears loud, resounding echoes of his own. Whether we call it borrowing, adaptation, improvement, or distortion, there is a lot of American in Japan's success story.

The perspective from which I write this book is thus an unusual one. It is one I share with that small number of Americans who have made their living in Japan, over a period of years, working in Japanese business or with it. The United States is fortunate in having a similarly small but very competent body of diplomats and scholars who know Japan, its language, and its people very well—and have also spent many years there. Without them (and their counterparts from Japan) the relationship between the two countries would be in far worse shape. Yet, as any member of the American Chamber of Commerce in Japan will gladly tell you, it is one thing to visit Japan and live there as a State Department officer or a tenured professor from an American university. It is quite another thing to make your living in Japan, living under Japanese laws and customs (written and unwritten) and dependent on a Japanese work force, Japanese bankers, and Japanese customers.

Over the years I was there, most of this business community—the survivors, at least—came to feel almost comfortable with a life-style drastically different from our own—stubborn, supportive, exasperating, admirable, narrowly insular, yet surprisingly generous. We enjoyed the comforts of great cities where crime is minimal and friendly neighborhoods still exist. We admired the beauties of a classic countryside and sensed the powerful appeal of a great, concentrated culture. And by way of compensation we also learned to live under constant pressures from two opposite directions.

Within Japan, inside our own companies, we had to come to terms with a unique work society. Our daily round included wide varieties of more or less programmed group activity—formal conferences, informal discussions, sudden personal visits, mass demonstrations, organized enthusiasm sessions, and the frustrations of watching promotions on merit get swamped in a miasma of seniority and "sincerity." Even where we were buoyed up by the sense of community within a Japanese company, we had to cope with a business world around us which was at least subliminally "anti-foreign." We genuflected before xenophobic bankers to whom ten yen's worth of security in Japan was ipso facto worth a million elsewhere. We tried to cope with the regulations of an often equally xenophobic bureaucracy, which had taken the mandarin's art of subtle restriction to a new dimension. It was hard, on occasion, to escape feeling like a hostage in the headquarters camp of an economic garrison state.

Nonetheless we came to admire much in Japan's business society, and we found much to adopt. We developed tremendous respect for the sheer competence of Japanese individuals and the power of their councils. Living in a world based on mutual trust instead of an allegedly healthy adversary-and-confrontation principle was for most of us a revealing and rewarding experience.

Which is where our second set of pressures came in: how to explain all this to our betters at the home offices in Providence or Peoria. How could these "Japanese" ideas (the word itself was used as a pejorative) be worth adapting? ("You've obviously been over there too long, Armbruster" was a refrain to which we grew accustomed.) It was hard enough to explain to the visiting international vice-president from the hinterland the worth of funny little Japanese practices like lifetime employment or hiring the "whole person" right out of college for your company instead of picking up used specialists from somebody else's company—or how to center your goals on long-term market share over immediate bang-bang profitability. It was even tougher going to acclimate the newly arrived M.B.A. from New York, who failed to understand how a company can exist anywhere without heavy adversary-type control systems, well-policed independent profit centers, finely drawn PERT charts, and a constant eye for next quarter's big bottom line.

While we were talking, however, the balance was shifting. It was during my ten years in Japan that the full impact of Japan's economic high-growth period began to make itself felt across the Pacific. The 1965 statistics which I read on arriving in Tokyo were the last in which the balance of trade between Japan and the United States was heavier on the American side. The color television sets, the cameras, and the cars had already begun to make their dent in the American market, but Sony and Matsushita had not yet taken over virtually the entire American consumer electronics industry; and Honda was selling motorcycles in California, not yet putting up automobile plants in Ohio. American steelmakers were still worried about European competition, not Japanese. What bones of contention existed between the United States and Japan were political, not economic.

In 1966 the days of massive economic diplomacy, with protectionism and "trigger prices," automobile "summits" and "reciprocity,"

were ahead of us. The Japan Productivity Center and similar organizations were still sending out their reconnaissance-in-force groups of
Japanese managers and business bureaucrats to discover the vaunted
secrets of American "know-how," which most piously believed to lie
in the vaults of almost every corporation in the United States.

The ten years to 1976 changed all this. And in the more than
half-decade following there have been further changes. Many have
not been pleasant. In Japan I have watched the uncertainties of
Japanese businessmen give way to confidence and then arrogance in
many. The American market is *theirs,* they reckon. "Forget about
American unemployment or politicians denouncing Japan in Congress or captious critics who cite Japan's long past record of protectionism and threaten to invoke countermeasures from Washington.
Just let Toyota keep selling as many cars to Americans as it can—
free trade is everything." So ran one popular refrain. And as for the
arguments about Japan not sharing America's burden of Japan's
defense—not even pulling its own weight in foreign aid programs—
they are irrelevant, we were told. After all, politics and economics
are separate things.

Conversely, the attitude of American businessmen was changing,
too. No longer contemptuous of Japanese business innovation and
successes, many found it easy to denounce all Japanese competition
as "unfair," by nature part of some sinister "Japan, Inc." strategy
agreed upon between government and industry. While assuming this
adversary posture in public, the same corporation chairmen and
presidents who once scoffed at Japanese business methods were now
rushing to "install" them in their own plants at home, reading a
whole new literature of Saran-wrapped Japanese management studies and paying consultants handsome sums to explain them, even
buying up obscure treatises about Zen swordsmen to learn the "secrets" of the Japanese.

In Washington, confrontation became the order of the day. It has
only intensified as economic issues have become frozen into political
attitudes. Grievances are codified. And the two free enterprise de-
mocracies that have the most to give each other are becoming es-
tranged when they should be working together.

I have written this book, as an American who has lived and
worked in Japan, in an effort to defuse a little of this controversy by
showing just what Japanese business is about and how its successes
are so relevant to our own situation. I am well aware of the flaws in
the Japanese economic miracle—the often heedless disregard of oth-

PREFACE

ers in its international marketing, its past history of crass protectionism at home, its failure to combine international business success with a sense of international political and social responsibility. At the same time I can only urge my fellow Americans to look more closely at what the Japanese have *achieved*—and also to reflect on how their achievement underscores so many of our own oversights and shortcomings.

It was not Japanese managers and shareholders who crippled some of America's key industries through poor planning and greed for immediate profits. The Japanese did not poison relations between American management and American labor in one bitter confrontation after another. The Japanese did not break up the American community into a pit of quarreling special interests. We did that ourselves. Criticize them where they deserve it. But let's not blame them for *our own* failures.

On the contrary let us see what their example teaches us. For a look at Japan gives us insight into a method of doing business in many ways far more compatible than our own with both the innovations and the pressures of modern technology and modern society. The lessons of Japan's work society may not be wholly applicable to our situation. The Japanese have paid a heavy price for their success which we may well not want to pay ourselves. But we will pay a far higher price later if we ignore what the Japanese are telling us today.

Frank Gibney

Tokyo
March 17, 1982

Contents

MIRACLE BY DESIGN

1·The Twenty-First Century Capitalists

Within the next five years, my country is expected to become the third greatest industrial power in the world, after the United States and the Soviet Union. And this spectacular advance has been brought about less than twenty years after the first foreign businessman admitted to postwar Japan found little to buy apart from bamboo garden rakes, folkcraft items and souvenirs.
—Yoshida Shigeru, 1967

Why Japan? How did it come to be that this historically self-seclusive country, characterized as adapter rather than inventor, has made itself the wonder of the economic world? The advances of Japanese business, avowedly capitalist and free enterprise in nature, would make Adam Smith proud, if surprised—and send Ricardo, Marx, and Schumpeter alike back to their studies. The concurrent success of Japan's postwar economic policies—and the social stability accompanying them—are the envy of politicians almost everywhere else.

The growth history of Japan's postwar "miracle" is still unfolding.

MIRACLE BY DESIGN

The economy it built has weathered OPEC oil shocks, foreign export restrictions, and domestic recessions; and its statistics are business history. In 1960, Japan's $39.1-billion gross national product was not quite 8 percent of America's. Japan's $1-trillion GNP in 1980 was almost 40 percent of America's—in per capita GNP, Japan will probably pass us within the decade. Twelve billion dollars' worth of Japanese exports in 1968 had become $140 billion by 1980. Nowhere has the rate of productivity risen so fast or so steadily. If the 1960 level of Japanese productivity in manufacturing is set at 100, the 1980 level had passed the 450 mark. Japanese steel, Japanese cars, Japanese TV sets, ships, cameras, and chemicals—and now Japan's semiconductor chips, computers, and overseas factories—have made consumers all over the world satisfied and dependent. No other nation's private entrepreneurs have carried off such brilliant marketing strategies.

Nowhere have people worked harder either, to implement those strategies. In the process the Japanese have raised their standard of living greatly, with all the attendant creature comforts of a dynamic mass consumption society. Remarkably dedicated and efficient, their work force is better motivated and more secure than any other. Yet these modern Japanese are not automatons. They enjoy the rights and benefits of a working democracy. Their freedoms and civil rights are guaranteed as securely as ours. And they do not hesitate to lobby vigorously and successfully for consumerism, pollution-free environments, and enlargement of labor's rights and benefits. However did they do it?

How did they do it, indeed, at a time when the firmament of the American economic dream seems to be cracking and the failing productivity of the United States has become a matter of worldwide concern? One major American industry after another drifts into deep trouble—some finished off by competition (mainly Japan's), but others collapsing of their own weight. "Alienation" of the labor force has become a commonplace complaint, while American management is also criticized for concentrating on the quick paper profit instead of the lasting quality product. In business, as in other areas of our national life, we seem to experience a chronic lack of motivation, a failure of will. What is wrong with us? And what are we doing to remedy it?

The answers to these two sets of questions are related far more closely than is generally thought. They go beyond matters of work ethic or management techniques or government-business cooperation, although these are part of the whole. Still less can they be found by repeating the caricature criticism of a "Japan, Inc." peopled by grim "workaholics"—although there *are* some unlovely factors in Japan's economic success behind these caricatures which we would be foolish to ignore. We can neither understand the nature of Japan's economic success nor learn from it unless we see it in its social as well as economic context.

Much of Japan's business society is strange to us. Everyday words such as *law, contract, board of directors, labor union, manager,* and *shareholder*—down to basic terms like *company* and *employee*—hold different meanings for the Japanese than they do for us. Their standards are different. Where our business society grew from the Christian ethic of individuals, theirs grew from the Confucian ethic of relationships. Their people have different priorities from ours—different views of wealth, of sufficiency, and of satisfaction. Yet the philosophy of their business as well as its techniques—indeed their modern version of free enterprise democracy—resembles our own more than it does anyone else's, and owes much to ours. If our Yankee sharpshooter could be said to have beaten the British grenadier at his own game in 1776, the Japanese trading company man has been doing the same thing to the Yankee trader two centuries later.

Both countries are militant defenders of capitalism. (In fact, Japan and America are probably the only two nations where the word *capitalism* is widely used in a non-pejorative sense.) But the Japanese, in applying the theory of free enterprise capitalism to their own circumstances, have done some drastic remodeling. To use a currently painful metaphor, the old American big-fin model of capitalism, once the pride of the road, has been rebuilt and restyled almost beyond recognition. All concede that the new Japanese compact adaptation is achieving sensational performance.

To begin with, the Japanese were for our time the original practitioners of supply-side economics. They accumulated capital and used it in the classic way—for plant modernization and technology development. They saved prodigiously to provide ever more investment funds. But then they took the standard idea of capital one step further. Western economists tended to think of capital in terms of money, plant, material, and technology. This means investing in plants, patents, and processes, which will bring a good return when used well. To this, however, the Japanese capitalist adds people. The most conspicuous characteristic of Japanese capitalism is its belief that long-term investment in people—which includes training them, partly educating them, and developing them within a company—is fully as important as long-term investment in plant.

We in the West have worried about the individual's self-fulfillment or alienation. We have shaken our heads at "soulless" corporations that treat workers as virtually interchangeable parts—by definition separated from the management and ownership of their companies. The Japanese, partly from old tradition and partly, as we shall see, from modern necessity, simply infused human values into the corporation. They made the company a village. And in so doing they have not only given the worker a sense of belonging, they have also given the company a constituency that speaks up for it: its own workers. The system of lifetime employment used by Japan's major corporations, the seniority system, the companywide bonuses or "base-ups" founded on profits and paid out to blue collar and white collar alike —all add up to a "people-centered" capitalism that rebukes both the Marxist idea of helpless labor as "variable" capital and the American capitalist principle of hiring a person for a specific function only, in a connection that can be easily and quickly severed by either party.

This thinking has roots deep in Japan's tradition. Historically, the greatest exponent of the "people" philosophy was a sixteenth-century feudal leader named Takeda Shingen. At a time when plots and betrayals were as common as battles, Shingen was famous for the loyalty he received from his retainers. He reciprocated their trust by constantly asking for their opinions. And no decision was made unless it had general support. Even today, Shingen's courteous seeking out of other people's opinions—the epitome of the so-called consensus philosophy—is cited by Japanese business leaders as fine management technique. His most famous slogan is known and quoted everywhere in Japan. When asked why he did not build in his native province of Kai the fortresses that other feudal magnates were busy building elsewhere, Shingen replied that for him this was not necessary. "People are the castle, people are the walls, people are the moat," he said.

The age of mass production industry, in which American business grew great, was dominated by the capitalism first of the individual entrepreneur and the workers, then of the large corporation and the national unions, which set terms and limits of their work by contract. As we enter the closing decades of this century, this classic version of free enterprise seems to be showing its age, a bit hard put to cope with the changes and challenges of computers, automation, the knowledge industry, and an ever-widening service sector. In Japan's newer capitalism, the emphasis is on commitment rather than on contract, on training rather than perpetual hiring and firing. If people are the company's strength, the company is the people's castle, too—not a property temporarily let out by faceless shareholders.

It may not be true, as Schumpeter wrote, that capitalism will fail of its own success, as the entrepreneur becomes something of an endangered species.[1] But it seems likely, as we shall try to demonstrate, that the Japanese variety is better equipped to deal with the next century and can in many ways be adapted to the needs of a twenty-first century America. The two kinds of free enterprise society differ sharply, however, in their approach to doing business. As Yamamoto Shichihei noted in his book *The Spirit of Japanese Capitalism (Nihon Shihonshugi no Seishin),* a best-seller among Japan's young businessmen, "In both countries the label on the outside says 'capitalist,' but when you open it and look at the contents, they are very, very different."[2]

Consider some contrasts between the two versions:

• Where the typical American corporation is a functional economic organ, seeing itself primarily as a means of doing a job, the Japanese company is a functional organization, which also very consciously thinks of itself as a community of *people.* Many things follow from this difference. Unlike the American corporation, which hires and fires freely as it needs the particular kinds of skills that abound in the outside labor force, the Japanese community-company prefers to grow its own labor force, recruiting "the whole man" out of school or college and training him within the company, with a maximum of job security. Lifetime employment practices and the age seniority system are followed wherever the size and strength of the company permits.[3] As Yamamoto says, "Achievement in the functional organization is naturally transformed into seniority in the community-company."

• Where American management typically raises its money by issuing and selling shares, the Japanese company still relies heavily on bank financing. Thus the American manager has to worry about his quarterly P&L and the effect current results will have on the company's stock. That is his report card. The Japanese manager, once he has satisfied his board and his banks about his long-range business plans, is relatively free to work them out, without the need either to push for short-term results or to constantly explain his situation to his board, not to mention the friendly securities analyst next door. In addition, his board of directors generally has a majority of management officers. Ask an American manager where his duty lies and he will answer, "To the shareholders." The business community—not to mention the Securities and Exchange Commission—would be disturbed if he said anything different. The Japanese manager, by contrast, generally feels at least an equal obligation to the workers in the company. If he keeps their work community flourishing and intact, he does his job. The profits can come either way, but the way they are planned and realized is very different.

• Although there is a greater percentage of union members in Japan than in the United States (31 percent as against 23 percent), most are not tightly organized on a national level. Even among those who belong to a national federation, the single-enterprise union is more likely than not a law unto itself. Although the Japanese "company" union can be a tough negotiator, belying the pejorative implied in that American term, its interest centers in the progress of the one company, not that of the union at a national level. Union executives quite normally go on to management roles.

• Although legalistic in their exasperating fondness for proper forms and procedures, the Japanese are resolutely not litigious. The public adversary procedures now riveted into American business are frowned on in Japan, both inside the company and out. Discussion and consultation are paramount. Open confrontation is strenuously avoided, as befits a country with only 12,000 lawyers. The courts are appealed to only as a last and often desperate resort. This is characteristic of a society that prizes harmony among people rather than a winner-loser type of justice.

• The Japanese government, as Chalmers Johnson put it in his recent book *MITI and the Japanese Miracle,* plays a "developmental" role in its relations with business, as opposed to the "regulatory" function of government in the United States. The Japanese economy, he noted, is "plan-rational," whereas the American is "market-rational."[4] Which is to say that the government is a supportive force helping business attain various long-term goals and actively planning for them. This is in sharp distinction to the traditional "cops-and-robbers" relationship between business and government in the United States. Yet the pushing and tugging between government ministries and business in Japan—and among both sides—reflect competitive differences of view belying the simplistic caricature of "Japan, Inc."

• The Japanese executive tends to think of himself as a community-builder as much as a profit-maker. Prestige considerations can weigh as heavily with him as monetary reward. His idea of community service is a narrow one, however, concentrating on a single industry or a single company—often to the exclusion of everything else. The American executive's idea of community service may be far wider; his particular company is only *one* of its components. Functionally, he might think of himself as a kind of Lone Ranger, his six (figure)-gun ready for hire in the service of efficiency and profitability. (*Whose* profitability may be a secondary consideration.) Once in charge of a corporation, he will want to make the big decisions himself and lead his people after him. The Japanese businessman's ideal is to encourage those under him to formulate decisions. Although there are "dynamic leader" types in Japan and "consensus" types in America, the ideals of the two capitalisms differ. A Japanese economist contrasted them this way: Our system is rather like an electric train, with each car having its own motor, whereas your system is more like a long train drawn by two or three strong locomotives, with no motors in the other cars. You tell your workers to follow. We like people to have their own motivation—and move together.[5]

The metaphor, like most metaphors, is a bit too neat. Japanese workers are motivated by their leadership, often more than Americans; but, if the destination is charted for them, the process of getting there is where the real difference lies. The sense of participation itself can be a very important factor in good management-labor relations.

The unity of the Japanese work force is also fostered by an almost universal system of sound education in basic learning disciplines. Although generally uninspired and over-given to memory and rote learning, it produces high school graduates who are not only far better at basic disciplines—particularly science and mathematics—than their American counterparts, but who have also been educated to participate gladly in group projects.

This kind of people-centered business thinking and the society that developed it is constructing not only a new kind of capitalism, but the kind best suited to take the capitalist system into the strains and conflicts of the twenty-first century. Certainly the Japanese variety, lacking anything like our own massive natural resources and stored technological capital, has proved itself far more flexible in avoiding our peculiar problems of the past decade or two: stagflation, the decline of productivity, chronic unemployment, the factionalism of constantly warring special interest groups, the tug of adversary processes tearing at the heart of our polity, rising apathy and mistrust

9

MIRACLE BY DESIGN

among the work force, while the gap between the elite manager or capitalist and the worker or middle manager grows rather than lessens. Japanese capitalism, to be sure, has the advantage of working with a tight, homogeneous society. Nonetheless, its achievement is impressive. Japan has proved that a democracy can coordinate central economic planning without sacrificing basic freedoms. It has shown that free workers, if properly organized and informed, can perform voluntarily all the feats of communal derring-do that Marxists and others contend can be done only by government order. It is the Japanese capitalist worker, more than the Chinese or Soviet Marxist, who is at once the real-life embodiment of many socialist ideals of spontaneous fraternal cooperation, and a living rebuke to modern socialism.

This is a bitter mix of facts for Americans to swallow. The United States is widely regarded as the model for free enterprise democracy. Our name has been a synonym for efficiency. The massed assembly lines of World War II and our later direction of the Western world's recovery—and Japan's—were, however, quite possibly the swan song of our industrial age supremacy. We are now in a quandary about both productivity and purpose. And it is significant that the economic panaceas given us by our politicians, instead of looking forward, hark back to a disappearing past. The peculiar Reagan version of supply-side economics, supported by so many businessmen, premises a world where Horatio Alger's maxims all come true, with prosperity as unlimited as opportunity if we just give entrepreneurial free enterprise its head. Planning is anathema. Indeed, planned economy remains for many sturdy Americans a synonym for Communism. The true capitalist believer, by contrast, professes that Adam Smith's invisible hand will do the job. Unfortunately, judging from the current state of the American economy, Adam's hand seems to have a bad case of arthritis.

American liberals conversely hark back to the dreams of the New Deal or its later variants, projecting an enlightened pork-barrel paradise where government money can cure all economic problems, with education solving all the social ones and the federal courts ever ready to chart the way for bigger and better human rights for groups and individuals, with little regard for anyone's responsibilities. Both these versions of Arcady are obsolete survivals of our industrial past.

Meanwhile the Japanese are busy organizing for the postindustrial world. Having changed their own business makeup, encouraging new industries to expand and old industries to diversify and change, they are now working with robots, knowledge-intensive industry, and new international market plans. Their optimism for expansion has so far been handsomely justified by events.

The impact of Japan's new capitalism cannot be appreciated—nor the truths it tells us applied—if we continue to study separate aspects of it piecemeal, whether it be worker involvement, management dedication, the seniority system, or quality control circles. Once the analytic observer has isolated his particular segment of Japanese capitalism, he then proceeds in the best American tradition to analyze it to death. So we have variously "the keys to Japanese management" or "quality control—Japan's productivity secret" or "Japan's business ideology." Readers of the business press are assured almost weekly that some aspect of Japanese business thinking is available as a poultice to apply to each businessman's special problems.

Still less good does it do us to contemplate the image of Japan, Inc. as some kind of lockstep integrated complex of business directed by government, or vice versa. What such simplistics overlook is that Japan's twenty-first century capitalism is the product of intense competition as well as cooperation. Often, indeed, what may seem to the outsider to be superhuman skill proves to be more the product of exploited happy circumstance, desperate perseverance, and the common acceptance of realities.

Call it Confucian capitalism, communal capitalism, or people-centered business, Japan's business society must be examined in its totality for what it is: a successful effort, born out of adversity, to adjust capitalism—and to some extent the democracy that goes with it—to the pressures, needs, and challenges of the present and the foreseeable future.

To understand how this new capitalism works, we must be aware of the unique bureaucracy that presides over the government of this business country. We must be aware of the Japanese idea of what law is—and their rejection of the adversary method as a way of settling disputes. This is a logical development in people who cherish harmony rather than justice as the highest social good. We must realize also what are the underpinnings of the Japanese work ethic. This tradition goes back much further than one might think. Yet it is extraordinary how well it seems to fit into the postindustrial world.

There is no doubt something of the miraculous in the spectacle of a nation widely regarded in the days after the World War II defeat as an economic basket case transforming itself into the powerhouse of world industry in little more than three decades. But it was, paradoxically, a miracle by design. Japan's economic miracle was the product of many people and many institutions working together. They worked together not only because they are group-minded, but also because recent adversity had taught them there was no hope in disunity. A concurrent cooperation and competition among all these forces brought Japan's twenty-first century capitalism into being.

The lessons we learn from it may save us all. But they are far bigger lessons than mere designs for better quality control circles. Least of all can they be applied to the American situation through management techniques alone. If American steel companies, for example, were to set up tomorrow, by some wild stretch of the imagination, a plan for far-ranging capital investment in new plants, they would have to persuade government, organized labor, and the entire investment and financial community in the United States to assist in their effort! The idea of building a new capitalism—and its implications—reaches beyond management or business alone. Its execution is too important to be left to businessmen or bureaucrats alone.

Japan's new capitalism is not without its flaws. They are serious and considerable ones. The pressures of a society that stresses harmony above all can build up heavily on individuals, especially gifted ones. The costs of attaining superficial harmony can be great, comparable in its way to the rending of American society while its members seek out their individualistic or pluralistic goals of adversary-system justice. In Japan's case most of the damage is hidden from view. There is the loss of creativity, the stifling of an individual's own feelings, the homage paid to mediocrities with high position, the gap that often yawns ominously wide between what Japanese call the *tatemae,* the desired appearance of things, and the *honne,* the actual condition, the real thought, the motives that one really has. Living in Japan and working there, one sometimes feels like an actor in a stylized Kabuki drama, played inside a hothouse; and finally even a foreigner ever so gradually comes to live the role. There is no escape. Even the intelligentsia, avowedly freethinking and antiestablishment, display an appalling similarity of outlook and expression. Pressures inside the hothouse remain at a constant level. And the social humidity is for an outsider unbearably high. There are so many groups and subgroups to belong to. There are so many dues to pay.

Balances exist in this kind of society between individual expression and group tyranny, between personal liberties and conformist dictation. There is *just* enough of the former to keep Japan a democracy, and a very good one; but the weights are finely poised. And under the pressures of sudden crisis or catastrophe the balance could slip.

The members of this hothouse society, linked to each other by a web of mutual obligation, are apt to forget their manners when they go outside. They still communicate poorly with non-Japanese. Some are overly diffident. Their lack of response comes from a genuine perplexity at how to deal with foreigners, who are almost by definition outside their web of commitments. Some affect an extraordinary tunnel vision when abroad, which enables them to go about their single-minded job of enriching company and country back home, with blithe disregard for the feelings or interests of the foreigners they are visiting. (To anyone who has ever escaped ramming by a passing vehicle in Tokyo traffic, driven by a Japanese who stares resolutely ahead of him on the road, purposefully ignoring his near-victim, this *shiran-kao*—literally, "the unrecognizing face"—syndrome is all too familiar.)

No one recognizes these faults more than the Japanese. Their own literature of self-introspection and reflections on Japaneseness—the so-called *Nihonjin ron*—staggers the imagination. Many Japanese are real "internationalists." They will readily admit, however, that there remains about the Japanese an unfortunate "sense of separateness" in their dealings with the outside. As the 1981 report of the Japan–United States Economic Relations Group noted: "This sense of separateness, which has been reinforced by Western prejudice and discrimination against the Japanese, has made it difficult for the Japanese to fully participate in the international community in spite of the high degree of interdependence linking Japan economically and politically with other countries. . . ." Put less politely, the separateness manifests itself in a waspish kind of "reverse-slope" patriotism.[6] The Japanese, while diffident to express the old blatant nationalism they had in the China Incident and World War II days, tend to look suspiciously on foreigners, with a kind of incubated insular arrogance.

The younger generation of Japanese shows this kind of chauvinism far less than their fathers and grandfathers. There is, for all the incoherence and diffidence, something of an international viewpoint developing in Japan. Yet, while more relaxed and secure than their fathers, the young in Japan show few signs of kicking over the traces and abandoning the traditional work ethic of their parents.

In short, Japan's nation society is still all of a piece. The Horatio

Algers of Japan's economic folklore may be challenged, but they are not dishonored and ridiculed. The mystique of group cooperation and community effort remains. The society is obedient to its tradition. Even the intelligentsia, in Japan a well-defined mandarin class of academics, scholars, artists, journalists, and the ubiquitous commentators *(hyōronka),* while quick to challenge the politics of the establishment, its corruption and high-handedness, have notably shied away from attacking general social values and life-styles. They are too much a part of the national community to do this.

By contrast, the attack on traditional social values in America has been waged so successfully by the American liberal intelligentsia that some values have actually been inverted. (For example, where once not so long ago it was thought immoral to advocate an individual's unrestricted right to abortion, it is now thought "immoral" to be against it.) As Americans cut themselves off from a community sense of values, the cult of doing one's thing becomes almost sacrosanct. Moral issues are left to the individual to decide. Even in international politics, since the Vietnam war American individuals or groups have felt free to denounce actions of their government in as public a way as possible—heedless of what we used to think of as the national interest.

In his book *The Cultural Contradictions of Capitalism,* Daniel Bell, speaking about modern America, pointed out

> the radical disjunction between the social (techno-economic) structure and the culture. The former is ruled by an economic principle defined in terms of efficiency and functional rationality, the organization of production through the ordering of things, including men as things. The latter is prodigal, promiscuous, dominated by an anti-rational, anti-intellectual temper in which the self is taken as the touchstone of cultural judgments. . . .

Writing in the same context, Bell noted:

> When the Protestant ethic was sundered from bourgeois society, only the hedonism remained and the capitalist system lost its transcendental ethic; the lack of a transcendental tie, the sense that a society fails to provide some set of "ultimate meanings" in its character structure, work and culture, becomes unsettling to a system. . . .
>
> Western society lacks both *civitas,* the spontaneous willingness to make sacrifices for some public good and a political philosophy that

justifies the normative rules of priorities and allocations in the society.[7]

Such a deficiency has not occurred in Japanese society. The historic goals of Japan's working groups were not exactly transcendental, in the Western Christian sense, but these goals did transcend the individual. They have been maintained.

For behind the success of the twenty-first century capitalists two disparate influences are at work. One of them is old: a Confucian work ethic, modified and enriched by other strains of Japanese religion, which persists to this day in animating the majority of Japan's 117 million, long after our Protestant ethic, like a discarded cigar-store Indian, bit the dust. The other is a newer influence: ours. The twenty-first century capitalists could not have achieved their success without American intervention and inspiration.

CONFUCIAN CAPITALISM

Originally an inspiring philosophy that preached logical, simple maxims of brotherhood and justice, Confucianism was founded on respect for laws, ceremonies, and community relationships. It stressed harmony between people rather than belief in a transcendental God or gods. In the five basic relationships of Confucianism, there was no room for the cult of the individual. Whether between father and son, ruler and official, husband and wife, brother and brother, or friend and friend, the faith of Confucius was inseparable from a belief in community. The relationship, not the individual, was the measure of things.

Over the centuries the interpreters of Confucius in China turned his original inspiration into a frozen code of rituals and hierarchical obedience to authority, whose principal role often seemed to be keeping the lower orders down and the upper orders up. Confucianism was imported into Japan early, about the fourth century A.D., and successive waves of Chinese scholars brought in later export versions. After its last rethinking, the Chu Hsi variety of Confucianism in the seventeenth century, the Tokugawa shoguns seized on it as a useful device for stabilizing Japan and solidifying their own feudal hegemony.

Other religions hold forth in Japan, notably Buddhism and Shinto. There are great individuals in Buddhism, and the Buddhist ascetic is as powerful a figure in his right as the Christian. But Confucianism is another thing entirely. There is a world of difference between a way of thought which starts out based on keeping a harmonious relationship among people, at various levels, and a way of thought that insists on the individual, if not his God, as the ultimate arbiter of his fate. In the sense that their society is founded on a respect for relationships and a feeling for harmony that comes from good relationships, the Japanese have to be called Confucians. This "relationship" kind of thinking is the single greatest difference between the Japanese and ourselves. It threads its way throughout Japanese business society. It cannot be ignored.

Professor Morishima Michio, while teaching at the London School of Economics in 1975, made some interesting comments on "the collectivist character of Confucian capitalism." He wrote:

> Confucianism discourages individualism. It is intellectual and rational in character, rejecting the mysticism and incantation common to other religions. The ability of the Japanese to assimilate Western technology and science with astonishing rapidity after the Meiji Restoration was due at least in part to their education under Confucianism. Western rationalist thinking was not entirely foreign.

THE AMERICAN FACTOR

It is customary for the chroniclers of the Japanese economic miracle to point out the many tangible contributions made to it by the United States. Beyond doubt these are important. In the immediate postwar years the U.S. Occupation first fed the Japanese, then supplied enough technical skill, money, and direction to start the wheels of Japan's industry slowly turning again. And without the draconian "rationalization" of Japanese business and industry under the 1949 Dodge Plan, the economy could not have gone ahead. The Korean War also provided Japan with an unexpected windfall, in the form of $3 billion worth of arms, military equipment, and supplies purchased there for the American and U.N. war effort.

Through the fifties and sixties there was virtually a rush to acquire American technology. This the Japanese imported wholesale, through a variety of licensing arrangements used and adapted to great advantage. Although the Japanese have had since 1973 a favorable trade balance in technology licensing revenues, the opposite was once true. The Japanese drive to greater productivity was inspired by the Americans as part of the Occupation's efforts to make Japan more self-sufficient. The Japan Productivity Center, a pioneer in this work, was originally set up with U.S. government funds. The far-famed Japanese quality circle idea was first expounded by two American experts in statistical quality control, W. Edwards Deming and J. M. Juran, when they visited Japan in the late forties.

In the sixties, as postwar Japanese business came of age, a procession of pilgrims crossed the Pacific to worship at the shrines of American management efficiency techniques, as taught by various U.S. business schools. These lessons were duly brought back to Japan, digested—and modified.

Besides these tangible contributions, there has been the effect, less measurable but immense, of American democracy, American innovation, and American optimism on the thinking of the Japanese, businesspeople in particular. The attempted U.S. "democratization" of Japan served to ventilate the closed world of Japanese capitalism and semidemocratic practice. It imposed on the Japanese—some would say restored—a feeling for wider freedoms and broader horizons. A partial voting franchise became a universal franchise; a semi-independent judiciary became an independent one; a trade union movement that existed only in name and memory became a powerful economic and social force in fact. In effect, the Occupation became the second installment of the original Meiji Restoration of 1868. American optimistic and sweeping innovation was followed by gradual Japanese assimilation and adaptation and further assimilation. A renewed enterprise spirit grew in Japan as a result. Ironically, it has remained there, while the original springs of American enterprise energy dry up at home.

In a far-ranging lecture on the Japanese economy, Hanamura Nihachiro, vice-chairman of the powerful Keidanren (Federation of Economic Organizations), labeled this influence, along with Japan's political stability, one of the two factors underlying Japan's high-growth economy. He said:

First, there was a thorough democratization by the Occupation forces in the early postwar years of all old systems—political, economic, social, cultural, and educational. The breaking up of the *zaibatsu*—giant financial, industrial, and business groups—and agricultural land reform were the core of the policy of economic democratization. As a result, every Japanese stood at the same starting point and an environment was provided in which everyone was rewarded according to the effort they exerted. This generated in every Japanese a willingness to study and work hard, just as in the frontier days of the United States. . . .[8]

It is dangerous to underrate this American inspiration on the Japanese, however much it may have been modified. The twenty-first century capitalists would not be where they are today without the gigantic boosts they received from the twentieth century capitalists of the United States.

2·The Work Ethic and How It Grew

Which requirements should be considered as most important in the present efforts of the government in building Japanese industries? It can be neither capital nor laws and regulations because both are dead things in themselves and totally ineffective. The spirit sets both capital and regulations in motion. . . . Hence, if we assign weights to these three factors as far as effectiveness goes, the spirit should be assigned five parts, laws and regulations four and capital no more than one part.
—Japanese Economic White Paper: 1884[1]

One of the ruder reverse-cultural shocks many expatriate business-men receive on returning to their New York or Chicago headquarters, after ten years in the work-charged atmosphere of Tokyo, is the emptiness of the home office at 5:01 P.M. A few stray vice-presidents may still be there after their four o'clock confrontation with the president, and one or two humbler late-goers may have waited until the lemminglike rush to the elevators has thinned out. But essentially the cupboard is bare. The workday has been firmly, definitively ended and will not be resumed until shortly before nine the following morning.

At their Tokyo company, by contrast, five o'clock is still busy. Some may be leaving, but others will stay. Planning conferences on two floors are still in session. The union executive is meeting in its company-supplied office in the basement and an orientation lecture for new employees continues in the auditorium. The flower arrangement class for O.L.'s (current slang for office ladies) is about to begin, and a meeting is scheduled at five-thirty for the spring tournament committee of the company golf club. Several ancients in the purchasing department are continuing a leisurely game of *go,* while two groups from sales and production are rounding up their people for drinks and a snack, respectively, at one of the neighborhood bars.

An unfair analogy, perhaps. Certainly there are many Americans who work hard and work late, high-priced executives conspicuous among them. American workers have their social clubs and after-hours office committees as well. Nor is keeping late hours necessarily a reliable sign of dedication and efficiency. Yet the contrast between the deadly still American offices in Chicago at 5:01 and the lively round of activity in Tokyo can fairly represent the difference between two work cultures and two work ethics. The average American worker at this point in history is still fairly well educated and may still be faithful in his fashion to a traditional work ethic; but he is increasingly interested more in his own leisure, self-development, and growth "as a person." To more and more workers, being in a company means simply doing a job at a particular workplace, a situation to be endured, not enjoyed, until something better is found. To the Japanese being in a company means belonging to it. It is, variously, family, village, and club. Working hard for the company is to work hard for oneself in a family culture that centers on the workplace rather than shuns it. The work ethic is less a sociological term to be dissected than a faith to live by.

The Japanese dedication to the company is not so widely praised or appreciated by others. "Workaholics living in rabbit hutches," "economic animals," "work-happy collectivists," or "robotlike workers" are some of the descriptions lavished on them. Yet "working harder" is given by many as the real secret to Japan's success. There was a time when Americans and Britons, driven by what Max Weber called "the Protestant ethic," worked harder because they felt that work was the Lord's and nothing was so sinful as idleness. As one of Weber's Puritan spokesmen expressed it, "You may labor to be rich for God, but not for the flesh and sin." Although this spirit remains here and there, it is not exactly uppermost in the motivations of the average American worker. For personal satisfaction, added prestige and money (with the accent on the money), Americans will work hard and work long. But for the modern generations, working represents option or necessity. The matter of virtue or duty rarely enters.

Where do Japanese workers differ? Won't they lose their old-fashioned work ethic, as we seem to have lost ours, as they grow more "individualistic" and "leisure-oriented"? As their standard of living rises, won't they want to see working hours go down and vacation times lengthen so they can extend their searches for individual fulfillment, leaving the company premises after five as desolate as their American counterparts? I believe they will not. The Japanese work ethic is not all that mysterious. Neither is it all that exclusive. Although the roots of the ethic are Japanese, the sense of participating and togetherness it gives is common to all peoples. We may begin with Confucius and the Buddha, but their ethic, as applied in Japan, resulted in a kind of people's capitalism that could be of considerable benefit to all of us—Jews, Christians, Moslems, and even liberal humanists.

Although Yamamoto Shichihei is one of Japan's most prominent social commentators and essayists, his work, with one significant exception, has never been translated into English.[2] In *The Spirit of Japanese Capitalism* he sets out, among other things, to trace the origins of the work ethic that continues to animate the modern businessman in his globe-girdling search for markets and profits. He writes:

> When a Japanese travels abroad foreigners are constantly asking about Zen. To them *Zen* is something occult, part of the Mysterious East they keep talking about. At the same time people in other countries keep calling us Japanese "economic animals." I have to tell them, in all candor, that Zen and the "economic animal" concept come from the same source. For the Japanese working is not just a matter of economic achievement. By Zen standards it amounts to something like religious training. We still believe the teaching of [the seventeenth century Zen master] Suzuki Shōzan that by doing our daily work we are doing the Buddha's work as well. Thus when a manufacturer makes good products he is showing one face of the Buddha (*ichibutsu no bunshin*) to bring profit to the world. When a salesman makes his rounds, he is on pilgrimage. Each in his own task can gain salvation

through doing work well—as long as he keeps away from the "three poisons" of greed, anger, and idle complaint.

That's what I tell the people who ask me about Zen. If they want to study how Zen works, let them look at the Japanese trading companies.

Yamamoto wrote this with tongue just a bit in cheek, but he goes on to explain his point seriously. He cited Suzuki and the eighteenth century Confucian Ishida Baigan as "the two thinkers who made modern Japan," precisely by defining a work ethic out of Buddhist and Confucian tradition. With a bow in Yamamoto's direction and acknowledgments to others,[3] let us show how these thinkers paralleled the development of our own Protestant ethic at a comparable point in history. What they wrote and taught is essential to any understanding of what modern Japanese capitalism means and how it can extend itself into the next century.

Japan's Buddhist and Confucian traditions each have contributed to the work ethic. (For the purposes of this discussion, we shall omit the third strain in Japan's latent religiosity—the peculiar mix of nature-worship and nation-society beliefs lumped under the general heading of Shinto.) The Japanese are traditionally eclectic in combining both religious teaching and practice; and the two faiths have influenced each other. Without Buddhism's lofty ideals and otherworldly dimensions, the Japanese brand of Confucianism would have become a cheerless faith of merit-seeking and ritual obediences. Conversely, Japanese Buddhism would have been the poorer without the pragmatic influence of Confucianism and its skeptical scholars.

Few Japanese Buddhists can be called pious believers in the way that pious Presbyterians, Catholics, or Jews would define the term. Yamamoto is also the first to admit that the modern "flight from religion" has gone on in Japan in the same way it has in the United States and Europe. "The image of Zen may no longer be visible in Japan," he writes, "just as the image of Puritanism can barely be glimpsed in America. Yet there is no reason to assume that the basic way of thought in these religions has ceased to influence people." In other words, modern people, whatever their own personal religious belief or lack of belief, are inescapably products of inherited ethical and moral attitudes that religion has given them.

Both Suzuki Shōzan and Ishida Baigan lived in the Tokugawa era, that extraordinary period of enforced seclusion under the shoguns from which the Japanese were to break out in 1868 to begin their modernization under the restored Meiji emperor. Suzuki was originally a samurai knight who had fought under Tokugawa Ieyasu at the Battle of Sekigahara. Baigan came of humbler merchant stock. They lived a century apart, but have some similarities. Both of them left their worldly tasks in midlife to form religious schools, where they defined and developed their thinking. Both, unlike the mainstream of Japanese thinkers before them, gave particular attention to the work of the merchant and the trader and their place in the feudal scheme of things.

Tokugawa Ieyasu won the Battle of Sekigahara in 1600. With this and his later victory at Osaka Castle, he established military and political supremacy over Japan, after centuries of destructive civil wars. To keep the country quiet and stabilize the rule of his new shogunate, Ieyasu used ideological as well as military weapons. He and his successors adapted the Neo-Confucian teachings of Sung dynasty China, to reemphasize the traditional relationships between superiors and inferiors. To preserve their kind of feudalism, the Tokugawa shoguns institutionalized Japan into a class society, based on a Confucian hierarchy of warrior (that is, the samurai nobility and gentry), farmer, artisan, and, finally, merchant (in Japanese, *shi-no-ko-sho*). At the top of this famous hierarchy the samurai feudalist was substituted for the scholar-mandarin in the original Chinese ranking. This left Tokugawa and his samurai firmly in control, with the farmers and the artisans working for them directly and the merchants *(shōnin)* handling commerce for samurai who scorned trade and money. Although socially at the bottom in this ranking, the merchant class gradually prospered. By dint of shrewdness and hard work the merchants came to possess more and more of the country's wealth. The one thing they badly needed, however, was self-respect and some kind of faith to live by other than the arid Confucianism of their social and political betters, who looked on trade the way medieval Catholicism viewed usury. This Suzuki and Baigan gave them.

It was Suzuki, the Zen master, who carried through a pragmatic strain of thinking already present in that austere faith, by which warriors, farmers, or artists were encouraged to pursue excellence in whatever they did. By following a discipline well, whether they were learning swordsmanship or painting black-and-white *(sumi-e)* landscapes, believers, the Zen masters argued, could find enlightenment as readily as through prayer or reading the sutras. Suzuki now extended this teaching to include the works of the hitherto despised merchant. "Renounce desires and pursue profits wholeheartedly," he wrote, "but you should never enjoy profits. On the contrary you should use your profits for the good of others."

The good merchant, realizing that his life is fixed and predestined to go its course through this particular incarnation, should thus not "attach himself" to the profits he may make. That would amount to a greedy worship of material things. He should, however, use the revenue from his transactions for the benefit of others, thus making the best possible use of his life on earth. As Nakamura Hajime noted, Shōzan in this way developed a "business ethic of Buddhism." According to his teaching the merchant should pursue profits, but not squander them for his own pleasure, by buying costly things. Rather he should accumulate his capital and finally invest it for good purposes. The Calvinists could hardly have said it better.

Ishida Baigan followed this idea of Suzuki's and expanded on it. He was basically a Confucian, although in the Japanese tradition he felt no contradiction in using something of all three doctrines— Buddhist, Shinto, and Confucian—if the combination would help a man find the true way. His philosophy was called *Shingaku*—literally, "learning of the heart." To live by *Shingaku*, he taught, one must purge oneself of egotism and selfishness, and learn to think and feel in harmony with others, so that the harmony of heaven and the harmony of self would be one. In practice, Baigan explained his rather complicated theory with the help of simple ethical maxims. As part of his heart-learning, he taught his followers, in the manner of Shōzan before him, that each should pursue his allotted "way," trying to perfect himself in it as fully as he could. Only in so doing could an individual attain harmony with nature and serve the state as well.

A merchant himself, who had worked in Kyoto for some years before turning to religion, Baigan felt even more strongly than Shōzan that to position the merchant at the bottom rank of society was an injustice. The merchant's work was fully as indispensable as the other functions, he argued. It was wrong, therefore, to denounce profit-making as "greed." He wrote: "Obtaining profit from sales is the Way of the merchant. I have not heard selling at cost called the Way. . . . The merchant's profit from sale is like the samurai's stipend. To take no profit from a sale would be like the samurai serving without a stipend."[4]

Baigan's simplified teachings had a far wider impact than those of his predecessor. Hundreds of thousands of townsmen *(chōnin),* the traders and manufacturers of an emerging middle class, heard his message and took comfort from *Shingaku*'s maxims about honesty, frugality, and honest profit-making. Other scholars and thinkers of the time seconded his championship of the merchant class. As Motoori Norinaga, the leader of the patriotic Shinto revival, said: "Merchants are indispensable for trade. The more merchants there are, the better for the state and the public at large." Or from Kaiho Seiryo: "There is nothing shameful about selling things. What is shameful is the conduct of men who fail to pay their debts to merchants."

Heard over the distance of several centuries, these comments may sound like platitudes. But in the context of their time they were of vast significance, almost revolutionary. The conventional wisdom of the shogunate, as expressed by the Tokugawa authorities and the clan hierarchies, regarded the town merchants as little better than parasites, however useful they might be at loaning money to their betters. Baigan and his followers did for the merchant what the eclectic Shinto sage Ninomiya Sontoku did for the farmer shortly afterward, with his often-quoted maxims of thrift, savings, and hard work ("Work much, earn much, and spend little").[5] The ethic of Baigan and Shōzan before him became the ethic of Japanese business and in the next century after him offered a rationale for the samurai to become businessmen themselves.

In 1868, with the fleets of European powers at their ports demanding admittance and free trade for their manufactures, samurai of the Japanese lower nobility, led by the two powerful southern clans of Satsuma and Choshu, united to depose the last of the Tokugawa shoguns and restore the emperor, in the extraordinary self-modernization of the Meiji Restoration. The immediate purpose of Japan's Meiji modernization was defensive. The Japanese had to save themselves from the semicolonial status to which the Western powers, by virtue of their superior armament and industrial abilities, were reducing China. But there were far wider issues involved. During the two hundred fifty years of the Tokugawa shogunate, the Japanese had lived in guarded seclusion from the outside world. Within their islands, backward as they were in technical matters, the Japanese had developed a bustling, energetic, and venturesome small business and trading society, based on the trading houses and merchant bankers of Osaka, Tokyo, and Kyoto. Chafing under the rule of the shogunate, some of the clan domains, notably Satsuma and Choshu, had built up not only commercial networks of their own but also small fledgling industries, started with forbidden imports from the West. It was clear to the young Meiji reformers that Japan must now build its own steel mills and textile factories on a nationwide scale so that there would be a business and industrial foundation for the *fukoku kyōhei* (a prosperous country and a strong army) ideals of the Restoration.

The Meiji officials were for the most part reformers, not revolutionaries. They had no wish to disrupt the fabric of Japanese society. They much preferred to build on what they already had. They abolished political feudalism in favor of national loyalty to the emperor. But the basic Confucian hierarchies of the Tokugawa world remained in fact, if not in law. So did the loyalties that went with them. Commoners no longer need think of themselves as second-class citizens in the rigid relationships. It was the businessman's turn to manage new modern mills and trading companies as a full partner in the country's progress toward Civilization and Enlightenment, to quote another Meiji slogan. Yet naturally enough, when the Meiji people started the foundations of modern enterprise, they relied for their organization on the old apprenticeship systems of the Tokugawa merchants—and for their legitimacy on Baigan's protocapitalist ethic.

Work was seen as service of long commitment, "not purely an economic act but a spiritual and moral experience," as Yamamoto noted in his book. The tradition-hallowed ranks of apprentice, assistant clerk, clerk, and head clerk *(detchi, tedai, banto, dōbanto)* of the old Osaka trading houses (one of them, the House of Mitsui, had been founded in 1637) were translated into modern terms that have remained in Japanese business to this day. Unlike Europe, where the Industrial Revolution smashed feudal bonds and obediences (often in favor of more onerous varieties of serfdom), in Japan a semifeudal family system of doing business was simply transplanted into a modern capitalist society. The thinking about the seniority system and lifetime employment had its origins in Baigan's day, as did the idea of the clerk going into business for himself as a junior or branch house of the parent firm. The ancient system of main family *(honke)* and branch family *(bunke)* business, as formalized by the Tokugawa, are what lie behind the modern Japanese corporation's rationale for establishing subsidiaries. So is the idea of the company as a kind of large family organization, a new territorial group but nonetheless one with its own family consciousness, to be entered by a new company person, with appropriate rites and examinations, less in the manner of a worker joining a functional organization than that of a new member joining a lifetime club.

True to Baigan's philosophy, the idea of service to the community and "the empire" was ingrained in the new company structure. This was all the more necessary since most entrepreneurs of the big new businesses came from the samurai class, the same two-sworded gentry who had until the mid-1800s thought of the trader as a low species of humanity and were themselves unwilling to handle money.

Other unique features of Japanese capitalism began to surface at this time. Since no modern industry existed, the government itself had to start up the new factories and mills, then sell them off to private entrepreneurs or investors in the new joint-stock companies. So emerged the close cooperative relationship between government and business. Almost no capital was available for starting major modern industries. Hence the government had to set up a national taxation system, then establish a national bank, the Bank of Japan, to supply money and control it, through the new city banks. The heavy dependence of Japanese companies on bank financing and their high leverage policies started almost with their origins. Like the ties of development and cooperation between government and business, these were part of a new capitalist tradition, developing from necessity as much as invention.

The administrative bureaucracy of the Meiji government was staffed by the samurai class. Most of them had gained valuable administrative experience working as clan or shogunate officials. Journalists and educators also came from this class. So did many entrepreneurs of the new state businesses, who received their working capital in the form of government subsidies or concessions. Iwasaki Yataro, the founder of the Mitsubishi group, was a young samurai from the southern clan of Tosa when the Restoration took place. He got his start in 1874, when the government gave him thirteen ships to ferry troops in the Formosan expedition. Sixteen years later the government sold off its Nagasaki shipyards to Mitsubishi and in the same year some large tracts of land in Tokyo not far from the Imperial Palace, the beginnings of Mitsubishi's vast real estate empire. Similarly, Furukawa Ichibei, a young merchant from Kyoto, received a government charter in 1877 to develop the copper mines at Ashio. He parlayed this original investment into a network of electric companies, cable companies, light metal companies, and others, one of which ultimately became Fujitsu, the modern computer giant.

One reason that samurai took over some of the big new companies was that the average merchant, especially if he came from the old trading houses, was generally cautious about going into new enterprises. The House of Mitsui, which had helped finance the emperor's forces, was an outstanding exception. Others, like the equally prestigious House of Ono, could not meet the new challenges. Ono went bankrupt shortly after the Restoration, thanks to an overambitious investment in a new silk-reeling mill. Many of the old-fashioned merchants expanded only modestly, content either to continue manufactures of traditional Japanese materials or to serve as subcontractors for the big new government-subsidized companies. Here is the origin of the peculiar dual structure in Japanese business—the parallel existence of big business on one track and small or medium-sized businesses on another, with greatly reduced wage levels and job security. This has continued into our day.

Nonetheless, when the new large enterprises took shape, they were almost uniformly modeled on the old family merchant houses of Tokugawa days. There were four major *zaibatsu* (money clique) enterprises—Mitsui, Mitsubishi, Sumitomo, and Yasuda—conglomerates with interests in almost every branch of industry. Mitsui's prewar interests, for example, included mining, shipping, oil, cement, automobiles (Toyota was originally a Mitsui company), chemicals, precision machinery, textiles, flour, real estate, and of course, at the center of the group's activities, the Mitsui Bank. There were about sixteen other smaller *zaibatsu* organisms, organized in more specialized areas, like Furukawa, Okura, or Asano. All of them were controlled by tight family organizations at the top. Through holding companies and interlocking directorates (a control device beloved by Japanese businessmen to this day), smaller subsidiaries were knit into the organization. Close to government and themselves governed by ponderous hierarchies, these Japanese-style conglomerates were nonetheless a far cry from the later American variety that bought and sold companies for quick profit. As with the Tokugawa protocapitalists, they were territorialists who habitually put their money into capital improvement and expansion. In *The Economic Development of Japan* the late William Lockwood summarized their activities: "They performed an essential function in large-scale enterprise which could otherwise have been performed only by the state and not necessarily with greater public benefit. If they reaped fabulous gains, as they did, they continued to plough back the larger share in entrepreneurial investment in new and expanding activity." Baigan would not have disowned them.

Most of the Meiji industrialists were sadly wanting, however, in one important respect: fair treatment of their employees. Workers in that day were poorly paid and had virtually no security. Indeed the workplaces of industrializing Japan were local variations of the "dark satanic mills" that first sprang up in Europe during the Industrial Revolution. Not until the 1920s were halfway decent labor laws enacted, which gave at least some safeguards against the exploitation of women and children.

While taking advantage of the loyalties of the Japanese worker, the new Meiji capitalists did not reciprocate. The full employment idea, which had been part of the Tokugawa trading houses, was thrown out with industrialization. It was not brought back until the years after World War I, when skilled labor shortages made Japanese employers realize that it was better economics to keep a competent worker than to let him go and try to hire another. Unlike their American and European colleagues, they could not count on a constant flow of immigrants or a large reserve of fairly skilled workers. Only grudgingly did Japanese businessmen move toward the full employment policy of which they boast today. Even then, only the big *zaibatsu* enterprises could afford to do so. The films of the twenties and thirties are full of young "salary men" from small companies being fired out of hand by a screaming boss with a clipped Charlie Chaplin mustache, yelling *"kubi da"* ("You're fired"). It took the U.S. Occupation to give Japanese workers the guarantees of working standards and bargaining rights, which in the end profited and strengthened both sides.

There were, however, some influences for the good on Japanese business to offset the single-minded empire-building of family entrepreneurs like Iwasaki, the founder of Mitsubishi. The greatest of these by far was Shibusawa Eiichi. A boy from a farming family who received samurai rank under the last Tokugawa shoguns, Shibusawa helped set up the Ministry of Finance in the early Meiji government, but he left government early to go into finance and business. His object was very specific: to "bring respectability to the businessman" and remove the old image of the half-crooked, servile "trader" still prevalent among the young samurai who staffed the Meiji government. Shibusawa, a self-styled "strategist of modern industrializa-

tion," even coined the modern word for businessman (*jitsugyoka*),
probably best translated as "a practical man of affairs." The founder
of the Dai Ichi Bank (today Dai Ichi Kangyo, Japan's largest),
Shibusawa was involved in the organization of some five hundred
companies, including giants like Oji Paper and Nihon Yūsen Kaisha,
Osano Cement, and others in textiles, breweries, railroads, gas, ferti-
lizer, and insurance. As a reaction to the family-based *zaibatsu*, he
introduced the joint-stock company to Japan. This, he felt, was a
more community-type company, which could marshall existing capital resources to better advantage.

But Shibusawa's influence stretched beyond his actual business
and financial achievements. He was the conscience of Japanese business. It was he who developed the work ethic of Suzuki Shōzan and
Ishida Baigan and applied it to the world of developing Japanese
industry. Where people like Iwasaki sought to maximize profit, for
Shibusawa profit was not the primary motive. He believed that more
profit would accrue in the end to the honest businessman who
planned wisely and justly and took the long view of development,
with the interests of the country as well as the company in mind. He
saw the modern businessman as a worker for national progress. If
anyone had explained the concept of Japan, Inc. to Shibusawa, he
would have approved it almost one hundred percent.

He was a Confucian who kept a copy of the Master's *Analects*
constantly with him and felt that business needed the Confucian
ideal of strong mutual relationships and service to keep it from
degenerating into selfish profit-making. His aim was "building modern enterprise on the abacus and the *Analects.*" To him, learning was
as much a part of business as sound morality. He had no patience
with businessmen who neglected education. So many widely praised
traits of modern Japanese business a century later—its dedication to
research and knowledge communication, its emphasis on long-range
planning, its corporate community spirit—were foreshadowed in
what he did and said.

As he wrote later in life, explaining why Confucian virtue and
business should go together:

> Morality and economy were meant to walk hand in hand. But as
> humanity has been prone to seek gain, often forgetting righteousness,
> the ancient sage, anxious to remedy this abuse, zealously advocated
> morality on the one hand and on the other, warned people of profit

unlawfully obtained. Later scholars misunderstood [Confucius's] true
idea. . . . They forgot that productivity is a way of practicing virtue.[6]

The importance of the people factor in Japanese business and its
relationship to productivity comes direct from Shibusawa. No one
had a clearer conviction than he that a Japanese business was only
as good as the work ethic perpetuated among its people.

If one wished to epitomize the modern Japanese work ethic in one
phrase, Shibusawa's would do the job well: "Productivity is a way
of practicing virtue." (It contrasts interestingly with the American
World War II slogan: "Productivity: Key to Plenty.") Behind this
idea is the thought of Shōzan and Baigan, Buddhist as well as Confucian, and the conscious if often confused efforts of the Meiji reformers a century ago to modernize their country without losing its soul
—for which read "enlightened community consciousness"—in the
process. This work ethic has always been strong in Japan, but I used
the word *modern* advisedly at the beginning of this paragraph. For
the first fruits of industrialism tasted bitter. The avarice and empire-
building spirit of people like Iwasaki and his Mitsubishi bannermen
led them to rival the storied American robber barons of the late
nineteenth and early twentieth centuries in their contempt for the
just rights and needs of their workers. Two things revived the old
work ethic and the sense of shared rights and duties implicit within
it. They were the trauma of a lost war and the sense of fairness and
democratic give-and-take contributed by the postwar American Occupation—and codified in the laws the Occupation drafted. Without
these, the old work ethic could not have revived as it did. Yet we
must say, conversely, that all the laws and ordinances of the Occupation and all the sobering disasters of sunken aircraft carriers and
firebombings could have either demoralized or colonized a people
who did not have a work ethic to steady them. Few nations in history
can boast of such a tough tradition.

To understand the Japanese worker, and the ethic which animates
him, we must set aside the American view of work and its rewards.
The Japanese worker's *ikigai*—the word means "what makes life
worth living" but has no easy translation into English—is not primarily a struggle by the individual to better himself. He does not
depend on Calvin's elect work ethic (as interpreted by Ben Franklin
and various successors) in which the primary goal is to transcend
one's present situation and get something better for oneself elsewhere

in the work society. In Japan the job is the society. The society is the job. Every man who enters a company consciously holds a moral and social share in it, irrespective of any stockholding. Whether Mr. Fujii is a representative director, department head, machine operator, warehouseman, or clerk, he is a member of the firm. So are most of his friends. He drinks with them, plays golf with them, and shares his troubles with them. He competes with them, but on a very well-ordered track, in the manner of siblings competing within a family that no one would think of leaving. Barring his relatives and a few close friends, most of them from school, his associations go on within the company's house.

Within any well-established Japanese company, there are rituals, feasts, and observances, followed with an enthusiastic rigor that the West has not known since medieval guilds in Europe celebrated the jubilations and penances of the ecclesiastical year. The morning ceremonies *(chorei)* where the company president or director-in-charge tells the staff in more or less rhetorical style what is expected of them, the spring struggle snake dances, in which the union tells the managing director what is expected of *him*, the company songs, the inevitable company outings, the constant antennae rubbing of meetings and discussions are all part of the unending ceremony with which man likes to dignify his daily task.

Such ceremonies once existed in American business, at least in the era when the vaunted Protestant ethic held sway. But they were generally not so happily participated in by the workers. They were resisted and finally abolished, since they were all too often the device of the management for capitalist owners to exert authority and keep control. The Japanese do not see it that way. Their lives are surrounded by codified courtesy. The girls wiping the spotless escalator handrails in department stores or the drivers flecking imaginary dust off the black hoods of company cars express a community concern.

In early Confucian thinking, the Master and his men used to tell their disciples that right living consisted of performing the proper rituals and ceremonies. These were by no means empty things; they were means to keep people aware of their responsibilities in family society. This feeling for ritual was also present in Japan's own Shinto and Buddhist society. The Japanese word for *administration* was originally *matsurigoto*, literally, the "management of rites" or "religion." The Japanese have kept up the rituals and ceremonies of a

Neo-Confucian world and in an odd way revived them in the latter part of this century. They are the adhesive that keeps the firmament of a company in place.

The company director may not think of himself as some kind of mandarin performing proper rituals, a Shinto priest switching his bundle of magic twigs before an altar, or a Buddhist abbot chanting the sutras, but he is in fact perpetuating these roles in his everyday working activities. The ceremonies of a company play a very substantial role in developing and ensuring its integrity.

In America you use the phrase "Are you busy?" only in circumstances in which you are uncertain whether the addressee of your question should be disturbed. In Japan the question *"o-isogashii desho"* ("I assume you're busy") is a kind of salutation. It is meant as a compliment. The answer is an obligatory "no, no, not at all," by which it is meant that the addressee appreciates your question, is really swamped with work, and is happy that his industry has been recognized.

Business is not to be regarded as an individual virtue, however. To be really busy is to be engaged in the work of the company or whatever social organism to which you might belong. The individual's identity is voluntarily identified with the company's. Yamamoto tells the story of a Japanese newspaper reporter who visited the Lockheed Aircraft Corporation at the height of that company's influence-peddling scandal in Japan, in which it was made clear that Lockheed executives had bribed Japanese political leaders to buy their aircraft. The reporter was shocked to find that California Lockheed employees not directly involved in the dubious transactions with Japanese politicians felt no "sense of shame" at the disclosure. On the contrary, they felt that they had no responsibility, no connection with what had gone on. They were simply employees, who were receiving pay for their services. Their relationship with Lockheed was purely "functional."

If this had been a Japanese company, everyone in the company would have felt involved and because of this troubled. Witness the individual "shame" of employees of Marubeni Iida, the Japanese trading company involved in the Lockheed disclosures. It was exactly as if a family scandal had been exposed and publicized. The people at Marubeni Iida felt shamed, but almost no one resigned. A family is a family. So they collectively rode out the storm. To leave a company is akin to banishment or, depending on the circumstances, self-exile.

MIRACLE BY DESIGN

One must always be busy, paying one's dues to Confucius and the sages who followed him. As Yamamoto Shichihei concluded:

> In Japanese the word for idling—being at loose ends—is always used as a pejorative. Not working means you are not paying your service to the Buddha.
>
> Americans, by contrast, keep audibly hoping for the day when they can retire. "From this day on," my American friends tell me, "I don't have to work. I can just do what I want." They are jubilant at the prospect.
>
> It is not that way with us in Japan. In the past some people said that the Japanese worked hard because they were poor. That was really not a causal relationship. If being poor made people work harder, a great percentage of the world's population would be hard-working.
>
> No, we work hard because we believe in it. To do a good job and help one's company grow and prosper—that for so many of us in Japan is our *ikigai*—what makes life worth living. Our worldly activity and achievement become part of a religious exercise. It turns into a kind of religious good. Of course we do not have a priesthood in this religion of work. In a sense, it is a priesthood of believers.

All of which may help explain why the offices in Tokyo are still quite busy at 6 P.M., while headquarters back in New York has been left to the night watchman and the cleaning women.

3·The American Factor

Boys, be ambitious.
—Professor William Clark of Massachusetts
Agricultural College, addressing his students at
Hokkaido Agricultural College in the 1870s

In Jonathan Swift's satire of eighteenth century England, Lemuel Gulliver alternately visited in his travels the little people of Lilliput and the giants of Brobdingnag, experiencing the perils and privileges of being a big man among little people and a little man among big people. For many years after the shock of World War II had ended, Japan seemed to be Americans' adopted Lilliput. Japanese students came to our colleges for learning and businessmen visited our factories and business schools for instruction in marketing disciplines like productivity, promotion, and industrial psychology. The benevolent U.S. occupiers in Japan taught democracy with zeal. And gradually American tourists came to Japan to marvel over those cute little whatevers (read teacups, temples, houses, cars, or people) in which Japan's small islands abound.

Over the past ten years, however, the idea of Japan has changed most sharply. Now when Samuel Gulliver U.S.A. goes to Japan, it is Brobdingnag he sees—a fearsome land of economic monsters, dragonlike government ministries, and clever financial trolls where progress is big and teamwork is bigger, and results are little short of gigantic.

Contrast the literature about Japan and the Japanese coming from the United States in the fifties and sixties with that of the seventies and eighties. Where before Japanese were the imitators, now we are told, they hold the secrets. Where before their constructions were rickety, now they are solid. Where before they were objects of condescension, now they are sources of threat.

Both views have some truth to them, then and now. But we must take them as exaggerations even greater than the seafarer's tales that Swift put into the mouth of Lemuel Gulliver. For size, in this fable, is in the eye of the beholder. It is not just that Japan has grown. In the interim the American Gulliver has managed to achieve a shrinking act of some proportions. The physical shrinkage is still minimal. But our view of ourselves has changed in less than a quarter-century from larger than life to shrinkable small. Over the past ten years we have experienced a failure of nerve, a loss of confidence, a growing self-doubt in our people and our institutions. Small wonder that returning travelers from Japan solemnly assure us that the economic animals there are now ten feet tall.

By contrast, the Japanese know the Americans rather well. They were studying Americans and our business long before the Americans, or at least the collective consciousness of Main Street, U.S.A. knew much about the Japanese. To the Japanese, Uncle Samuel Gulliver has been a known quantity—in the guise of visitor or teacher, enemy or friend—for close to a century and a half, since Commodore Perry's squadron of black ships first dropped their anchors in Tokyo Bay and started turning away talented would-be Japanese stowaways who were anxious to visit the United States and learn its "secrets."

The Japanese did not really enter the American newspaper reader's cast of characters until the China Incident of the thirties and the subsequent bombing of Pearl Harbor. But the American has kept a presence in Japan, almost without thinking about it, since the days of the early Meiji Restoration and before, when Japanese embassies stopped in the United States before going on the long trip to Europe, and hundreds of teachers and missionaries came from the United

States to teach the mysteries of Western technology and Protestant Christianity to their fascinated, if selectively receptive, pupils. In the days when the first Toyotas had trouble starting, Henry Ford was a hero to the Japanese, as the standard-bearer of modern technological production. Fifty years before Japanese-speaking actors appeared in the televised production of *Shogun* across the United States, Douglas Fairbanks, Mary Pickford, and Charlie Chaplin were more familiar to Japanese city moviegoers than most of their own statesmen.

Historically, as the late Yoshida Kenichi put it in one of his essays, Americans were always the "people-to-learn-from." Since the days when Professor William Clark from Massachusetts gave his Hokkaido Agricultural College students the stirring invocation, "Boys, be ambitious," and Theodore Roosevelt got the Japanese out of economic difficulties by negotiating their military victory into a peace treaty with the Russians in 1905, the Americans have enjoyed this special position with the Japanese. As Yoshida concluded: "Such people who teach are not necessarily to be loved, as witness our school-days, but they cannot be ignored. They have something. They represent a standard and we have to cope with them in some way or other if we are ourselves to make good."

In business the Japanese have learned much from us. When the young Meiji statesmen sailed forth from Yokohama to examine the institutions of the West, they found the politics of Europe more suitable for study and adaptation to Japanese realities because they were more authoritarian, traditionalist, and disciplined. This was not true of business. From the beginning the new businessmen of Japan admired the American model of capitalism and the American mastery of technological change. It was for the most part American firms that were welcomed into Japan in the early 1900s in a variety of relationships—as joint-venture partners, Japan-based subsidiaries, or license-giving owners of prized technology. But more than that was involved. Until the early thirties, trade with the United States in raw silk and silk fabrics constituted almost half of Japan's total exports, and revenue from this allowed Japan's industry to expand.

Going into the present, we find that the Japanese concern and connection with the United States has been intensified not only by a postwar American military occupation that set out to "democratize" Japan in all areas, business conspicuously included, but also by a correspondingly intensive postwar effort by Japan's businessmen to learn all the lessons American business had to give and apply them wherever possible to their own condition. This effort continues. The

American image may have shrunk back to little more than life size in the Japanese consciousness. "Coming back this time to the United States," a Japanese friend remarked recently, "I felt like someone who was visiting an old girl friend for the first time in years, only to discover that her beauty and vitality had faded." But the connection remains strong, stronger than most of us realize. Anyone who reads the daily morning papers in Tokyo in Japanese will soon see how minutely the American economy is covered. Talk to Japanese businessmen about competition and you will find that most of their analogies made, examples cited, and statistical comparisons invoked are with the United States.

In short, the Confucian capitalists of Japan could never have got where they are today without the United States. They have not swallowed our business practices whole; many have been rejected or changed. They have by no means canonized all our business theories, although they have often brilliantly adapted them to fit their own needs. But their business world is not wholly of their own making. It is a mixed-blood creature, with many recognizable American features. All too often, in studying the wonders of the modern Lilliputians, Samuel Gulliver finds out that he had the idea first—and he often cannot recall why he discarded it.

There are three big factors in Japan's new capitalism for which Americans are responsible, directly or indirectly.

OCCUPATION DIRECTIVES

The U.S. Occupation of Japan began in 1945 and ended in 1952, not quite a century after Commodore Perry's ships arrived and eighty-four years after Japan's modernizing Meiji Restoration. At the time of the Occupation, most of us who participated in it were convinced that we were "democratizing" Japan from a standing start. Now that Japanese militarism was defeated, the thinking ran, we would legislate the old "feudalistic" practices out of existence and introduce the kind of equality and freedom already found in the great Republic. Many Japanese, particularly among the intelligentsia, shared our view. "Feudalistic" became the catchall pejorative for everything from the unequal franchise to not giving an old lady a seat on a crowded bus. The flurry of Occupation directives to the Japanese government, which had to be translated into law, did indeed have a revolutionary impact. But seen from a better perspective, the revolution was more like the second stage of the Meiji Restoration.

As in the time of the young Emperor Meiji, foreign innovation was the watchword. The Occupation's officials and the experts liberally imported from the United States were the spiritual successors to the several thousand foreign experts invited to Japan in the early Meiji era to set up modern universities, foundries, tax systems, courts, and banks. Conversely, a small group of Japanese students, businessmen, and union leaders began to leave for study in the United States, in what ultimately became a heavy transpacific traffic.

Many of the laws passed under Occupation pressure were badly needed. For the original attempt of some Meiji reformers at creating a true popular democracy in Japan had given way to a cautious conservatism. The genuine marks of democracy that appeared in Japan by the twenties were indeed half-erased by the militarism, censorship, and thought control authoritarianism of the wartime thirties and forties. Yet some of the Occupation laws went too far for Japanese custom and inclination. These were gradually adapted to the point of meaninglessness or repealed outright, after General MacArthur and the occupiers had departed.

Some remained, however, and became part of Japanese life. The new Constitution, with the famous "antiwar" clause written in by MacArthur, contained basic guarantees similar in many ways to the U.S. Bill of Rights. Although its interpretations vary, the Constitution and its guarantees remain. It is doubtful whether any Japanese government could or would repeal them. The land reform law stayed on the books as well. It forever destroyed the often iniquitous system of tenant farming that the Occupation found in Japan. Coincidentally, making the small farmer independent (and grateful for it) implanted the solid rural voting bloc that helped keep the Liberal Democratic Party in political power for more than a quarter-century and remains useful to it.

The judiciary was made fully independent. Those laws stayed, although modified to suit Japanese custom and distaste for too much adversary legal procedure. Fair trade legislation endured considerable modification, to put it mildly. Japanese have friendlier feelings than American governments toward such things as industry cartels and modest restraints on trade. But the Fair Trade Practices Commission *(Kōsei torihiki iinkai)* remains and has had its authority reinforced by the rising power of the Japanese consumer movement.

The most significant Occupation-directed legislation, however, was the new body of labor law. Patterned after the New Deal's Wagner Act and similar statutes, this amounted to a bill of rights for

Japanese trade unions, which had hitherto suffered from severe re-pression. Japanese businessmen still protest the excess protection given to unions by the young New Dealers in SCAP (Supreme Com-mander for the Allied Powers) headquarters; some of the guarantees undoubtedly can be exploited by unions to their advantage. Yet the new laws led to an unprecedented growth of trade unionism in Japan, organized on the peculiarly Japanese variety of the single-enterprise union. Neither the Occupation nor the Japanese labor leaders of the time had anticipated that things would go this way. The net result was to strengthen the vitality of the Japanese company and turn it into a truly cooperative organization. The prewar guarantees of life-time employment and seniority rights had been the gifts of paternal-ism, to be withdrawn at the company's pleasure. The new rights of union people led to what one might call a complementary "filialism" in Japanese business. The average union member recognized this. For all the immediate postwar tensions between management and labor, the attempt to politicize the labor movement has largely failed. Much of the success of Japan's people-centered business and indus-try can be credited to the long-term influence of MacArthur's labor laws.

TECHNOLOGICAL IMPORTS AND EXPERTS

By way of implementing its Tokyo directives, the Occupation invited various experts from the United States to Tokyo to help put the shattered Japanese economy on its feet. Often the remedies these experts suggested—and enforced—were far more sweeping, idealis-tic, and in their impact stricter than would have been possible back home in the United States. As Edwin O. Reischauer remarked in his book *The Japanese,* commenting on this phase of the Occupation (specifically the breakup of the huge *zaibatsu* companies): "Revolu-tionary reforms are easier and more fun in someone else's country."

In some very significant cases, the strong medicine worked. Joseph M. Dodge, the Detroit banker, came to Japan in 1949 to preside as a temporary economic czar over the Dodge Plan, a rigorous rational-ization of Japanese industry. The Japanese, Dodge said, were living like a man on stilts. One stilt was extra aid from the Occupation; the other was unwise government subsidy to industry. In an exercise foreshadowing the Republican budget balancers of a later era (but executed with far greater severity and skill), Dodge ordered the stilts taken away, by insisting on a strictly balanced budget. Government subsidies to unprofitable companies were cut and credit controls intensified, with the Dodge budget as the goal. Companies went bankrupt by the thousands, and hundreds of thousands of unemployed workers streamed back (fortunately) to live with relatives in the countryside. But inflation was stopped and the budget balanced. The stage was set for Japan's later economic recovery.

In the same year Professor Carl Shoup of Columbia University, one of America's outstanding experts on taxation, came to Tokyo with a mission to overhaul the Japanese tax system. He revised the national income tax system, among other things, so that it remains today almost a model of an easily enforceable levy, without the forest of complications hedging the American tax laws. As a prominent Japanese tax expert said recently: "Shoup's ideas on the income tax were too advanced to get through in the United States; but the Occupation could get them accepted in Japan. The result was that you Americans left the Japanese income tax law in far better shape than your own."

Not all the experts were invited by the Occupation or the Japanese government. In 1950 the Japanese Union Scientists and Engineers (JUSE) invited W. Edwards Deming, the authority on statistical quality control, to visit Tokyo and again explain his craft. Deming's visit came at a time when Japanese businessmen, desperately worried about developing an export trade, were pondering how to improve quality in their products and shed the international image of shoddy Japanese goods held over from prewar days. They enthusiastically received Deming's lectures on how workers and management must constantly examine production processes and evaluate their product's market acceptance to develop consistent quality. Slogans like "You can't inspect quality into a product" became bywords in Japanese industry.

Deming was invited to return again and again. And the Japanese went him one better by turning what was basically an extension of statistical method into the famous quality control circle concept that plays a powerful role in their people-centered industry. Since 1951 the JUSE's annual Deming Award for quality has been one of the most coveted prizes in Japanese business, a kind of peacetime equivalent of the old wartime U.S. Navy "E" for excellence. Only in the last few years, however, has the quality control concept made any headway at all among businesses in America, its original home. It is now widely advocated, but often erroneously praised as a Japanese innovation.

With the experts came a drive by the Japanese government to import as much American and to a lesser extent European technology as it could, on a licensing royalty basis. Technical borrowing through the fifties and sixties was on a tremendous scale. (Between 1955 and 1970 close to $2.7 billion was paid out under licensing and royalty agreements.) It was made all the easier not only by Occupation support at the beginning, but also by the casual attitude with which many American companies entered into licensing agreements with Japanese counterparts, at rather low royalty rates, when they might have held out for establishing subsidiaries or joint ventures in Japan on their own. Few believed that the Japanese market would ever amount to much.

Sony's first great achievements, for example, were founded on securing licensing rights to the transistor, an American invention. After much bureaucratic delay in Japan, Sony was able to conclude a licensing agreement in 1954. Since the transistor developed in the United States was originally for military use, costs had been no problem in its manufacture. When the Japanese started working with the transistor, Sony had to get costs down so that it could be sold profitably on the civilian market. Their success in so doing made marketing history.

THE NEW MANAGERS

In the early days of the Occupation two events occurred that would have far-reaching consequences both on Japanese business recovery and the new shape of postwar Japanese capitalism. They were closely related, although this was only dimly seen at the time. And their consequences were quite different from those which the Occupation authorities originally expected. The first was the breakup of the Japanese *zaibatsu* (money clique) big business combines. The second was the two-stage purge of thousands of wartime shareholders and officers of the *zaibatsu* groups, as well as other leading Japanese corporations.

The purge, which went on from 1946 to 1948, was intended to remove "militarist" and presumably "feudal" influences from the top levels of Japanese leadership. Although most of the purgees were former military and naval officers, many politicians and high-level officials were included, particularly those who had served the cause of "Japanese expansion" overseas. Most significant of all were the businessmen, who were removed from their posts by Occupation directive on the theory that Japanese big business had worked hand in glove with the militarists.

In the words of the U.S. government's post-surrender directive this was "a program for the dissolution of the large industrial and banking combinations that have exercised control over a great part of Japan's trade and industry." The militarism of both the purged business executives and the *zaibatsu* themselves was highly debatable. Some of Japan's big business firms had actively assisted the military's "Greater East Asia Co-Prosperity Sphere," particularly in occupied Manchuria (where the present Nissan Motor Car Company first came into prominence, incidentally). Others had either opposed the military leadership (albeit weakly) or attempted to brake its path toward war. It was true, however, that the twenty-odd *zaibatsu* combines, led by the Big Four of Mitsubishi, Mitsui, Sumitomo, and Yasuda, had comprised the leadership of Japanese prewar and wartime business. They had undeniably worked closely with successive governments in the costly heavy industry buildups supporting the Japanese war effort. The young New Deal economists in MacArthur's headquarters were by definition dedicated trustbusters. In Japan as in America, they felt trusts, by definition, had to be bad. Trusts stood for restraint of trade, monopoly capitalism, and all the bad things. So they set out to break them.

The actual trustbusting lasted only a few years. After 1948 the United States grew more interested in building up the Japanese economy quickly than in protecting the Japanese small businessman and consumer. Some trustbusting orders were suspended and others rescinded. Some of the *zaibatsu* put themselves back together again. The old Japan Iron and Steel Manufacturing Company, for example, first split off into Yawata and Fuji Steel, then ultimately reconstituted itself twenty years later as The New Japan Iron and Steel Company (Shin Nihon Seitetsu). But the laws abolishing the holding company in Japan stuck. Even if the modern Mitsubishi or Sumitomo companies think of themselves as groups and hold constant management meetings, they remain independent companies, with ownership and management largely divided (despite an interesting pattern of interlocking stock-holding). The hold of a few family trusts on the nation's business leadership is gone, as is the family empire-building of single-minded, profit-driven tycoons like Mitsubishi's Iwasaki Yatarō.

One would think that the forcible retirement of so many key executives would have crippled Japanese business. In fact, it gave

Japanese business a new lease on life. The old *zaibatsu* hierarchies included more than their share of cautious family retainers, whose loyalties were more to the particular house than the society. In return for their dominion over Japanese business, they were indeed subservient to the government in power. (If the government-business hybrid called Japan, Inc. ever existed, it was in the days of the *zaibatsu* trusts.) Not only the *zaibatsu* leaders, but officers of many other large Japanese companies had been compromised by their cozy relationship with the pre-1945 government establishment. They were old. It would not be unjust to say they were also very, very tired.

In their place the retiring captains of industry now had to appoint younger men, generally below the director level—production managers, personnel directors, working executives in various departments. For this new management generation it was the chance of a lifetime. They were assuming top directors' jobs in their forties and early fifties, ten or fifteen years before such seniority would normally have been given them. The parallel with the young samurai bureaucrats and businessmen of the Meiji Restoration is strong and striking. The new top management taking over Japan's old companies resembled in their age and thinking the pragmatic low-ranking samurai who took over the Meiji government from the Tokugawa officials a century before, because the clan leaders *(daimyo)* and their top officials, or most of them, lacked both the energy and the imagination to deal with unprecedented problems.

Japan's situation after World War II was even more critical than it had been in 1868. Its cities were in ruins, its industry smashed, its people hungry and ill-clothed. Six and a half million soldiers and civilians had returned from the overseas islands and colonies, for the most part without jobs or livelihood. The government, especially after swallowing the tough medicine of the 1949 Dodge Plan rationalization, had no money for individual welfare or corporate subsidies. The old businesses and the new ones formed from the old combines were all equally on their own. Worst of all, the country's faith in itself had been smashed by the impact of total defeat. The vaunted "Japanese spirit" *(Nihon seishin)* that had carried Japan's people through past successful wars and modernizations was a vacuum. There was nothing left in the empty shrine.

Two things only helped. One was a Japanese sense of unity in adversity. Although the Japanese have always held to their principle of harmony *(wa)* as the adhesive of their society, it had been ill-served by factionalism and the inefficient authoritarianism of the militarists, during a war where on some islands the Army and Navy chose to die fighting each in their own positions rather than unite. Now at the point of disaster, everyone was ready to pull together. Management and labor, for one thing, had to work together, with the visible alternative of destitution if they were unsuccessful. (Interestingly enough, the enforced wartime integration of both white- and blue-collar employees into the same umbrella-type labor organization paved the way for the successful single-company enterprise union of today.) SCAP directives had sharply cut down the high executive salaries of past years. With everyone in the same boat, there were far fewer distinctions of rank and position. Everyone was poor.

The other helping hand was American. The enthusiasm of many U.S. Occupation officers for Japan's democratization, however naive and ill-informed, was inspiring and in its way contagious. The new Constitution and the new laws put through by the Occupation laid the foundations for a political and economic democratization, which neither the earlier Meiji reforms nor the so-called Taisho democracy of the twenties had achieved. Again to quote Vice-Chairman Hanamura of the Keidanren: "Every Japanese stood at the same starting point and an environment was provided in which everyone was rewarded according to the effort he exerted."

The new managers could not have behaved like autocrats if they had tried. They had to inspire, exhort, and work harder than anyone else. In this effort they were animated by an ideal of national as well as corporate service, the same enlightened version of Confucian capitalism that Shibusawa Eiichi had preached, if only half successfully, in the Meiji days. If a company were going to succeed, it had to work like a community as well as an organization. It could at least depend on the wholehearted support of an America that had resumed its position as a friend, teacher, and ally. It was the Americans who spent more than $2 billion for Japan's reconstruction. It was the Americans who helped put Japanese industry on its feet and protected its first exports. It was the Americans who signed the 1955 agreement setting up programs fostering Japanese productivity.

The first Japan Productivity Center team of Japanese business visitors to the United States came, interestingly enough, from the steel industry, which in only a few years began to overtake and far surpass its American counterpart. The next team, a group of high-ranking executives, followed shortly. As the newspaper *Asahi* reported later, quoting Noda Nobuo, then president of Seikei University: "We were amazed by everything we saw. . . . American technology was so advanced and our own so backward that we wondered whether our observations and reports would be of any use in Japan. . . . Everywhere we went the Americans briefed us with the kind generosity of parents teaching children."

Some assistance came from another quarter as well. While the militarists were destroyed and the *zaibatsu* at least temporarily discredited, the government bureaucracy remained surprisingly intact. The economic ministries at Kasumigaseki in Tokyo, including the reorganized and newly named MITI—Ministry for International Trade and Industry, which appeared in 1950—had learned much from the wartime disasters. They used the model of wartime government direction of Japanese industry, with some drastic revisions. Now they began to build for the future. With their five-year plans and blueprints for strategic economic development, they charted the path for peacetime industry's recovery. Later, through favored treatment of selected industries, they smoothed it. The relationship between the younger businessmen and the younger bureaucrats was by no means one of unmixed harmony. There were many disagreements and protests. But unlike the old days of the government *zaibatsu* regime, the managers were consulted in advance. The new relationship was based on a constant process of discussion, consultation, and mutual decision which was to set a model of sorts for government-business relationship in a fast-developing growth economy. Shibusawa would have been pleased at that, too.

Thus the defeat in war in an odd way proved a blessing in disguise to Japan. We can look to the adversities of World War II to find the seeds of Japan's postwar economic success.

Conversely, we can find in the World War II victories seeds of America's postwar economic and social difficulties. On the American side World War II was the classic demonstration of successful industrial mobilization and quantification. The United States, hitherto an economically and socially powerful nation with most of its military power a matter of potential, was able to activate the potential by mobilizing national resources into the war effort. The wartime mobilization of the United States was probably the ultimate achievement of that Western industrial civilization which reached its zenith in the mid-twentieth century. Similarly Americans found at that time that the many diverse interests in our country were ready, willing, and able, under reasonably good leadership, to sink their differences in a common effort against a common enemy to achieve a common goal.

Unfortunately, Americans were lulled into a sense of false security by the brilliant success of World War II. It became axiomatic in American business policy, as to an extent in foreign policy, that people were so many interchangeable parts, in the sense that all you need do was mobilize or hire more of them, and success after success would roll off your planning board. People were essential, but not really so important. They could be taken for granted. It was planning, industrial production, and above all new technology that mattered. Technology meant efficiency and efficiency always won.

This reasoning received its most complete setback in the Vietnam war, the American equivalent of Athens' disastrous Sicilian Expedition. The thinking of a technology-minded Pentagon suggested that whenever we found good results by using a hundred people, we could automatically multiply the results tenfold by using a thousand— whoever they were. We thought that bombing would work by making it technologically more efficient—without examining the basic strategy behind it and its failures even in World War II. The Vietnam war was among other things a disaster of quantification. As one of its leading participants once noted in a moment of candor, during a meeting I attended in Saigon: "The war effort got too big for the country." No other society could land so many Coca-Cola machines so quickly on a beachhead, but this efficiency did not win the war.

The cult of indiscriminate bigness, as one might call it, was translated into business all too readily. Having achieved prodigies by building up America's industrial potential and using it to win a war, the country's business leaders decided that what was good for General Motors et al. was not only good for the country but indeed for the world.[1] Production could be taken for granted. We had solved that problem. It was now a matter of good promotion, style, and marketing. Just expand an existing design, put more people on it, and your results could be projected with confidence. Use the same processes that have done so well with industrial production and just extend them, multiplying them. The parts, it was felt, were interchangeable.

This idea found its expression also in our politics. It was assumed that everybody could be got together, if really need be, in some major effort like World War II. Hence, why should we bother about keeping the fabric of our common heritage and identity intact? Just go ahead and fight it out, each group or company grabbing what it could, and let the chips fall where they may, to be picked up and fought over by the lawyers. It had always worked before.

America's business strategy was thus just to grow bigger by increasing efficiency. While pursuing immediate profits, on which all the energies of the nation's business minds were concentrated, one need not worry overmuch about quality, as long as money was being made. With good promotion, almost anything could be sold. Designers would decide what cars would look like, while the salesmen would persuade the public to buy them.

Some new industries, like the semiconductor industry, were conceived, and in them American technology still showed its brilliance. But the good effects of technology discovery were often vitiated as soon as a product left the laboratory, had its first marketing success, and got into large-scale production. It was then that the financial men would take out their slide rules and start projecting, based on the idea of indefinitely extensible resources and infinitely interchangeable parts.

Consider, by contrast, what happened in Japan. The Japanese before World War II had been going through a severe crisis in society, the backlash of the first successes of the Meiji Restoration and its modernization. Japan's society was only superficially united by the military during World War II under the emperor. While they achieved an awesome degree of total commitment to a goal, it is true, for all their factionalism, it was the unity of a nation caught up in a bad dream, like China later in the Great Cultural Revolution, Germany under Hitler, or almost, the United States in the McCarthy era.

After World War II ended and the Japanese were picked up and rehabilitated, to an extent, by the U.S. Occupation, they realized very clearly that they had to live by their wits and hard work. They had no frontier ethic to encourage them. They had neither enough people nor resources to play the quantification game. They saw that they could not compete with the United States or indeed with Western Europe on a sheer basis of industrial potential activated and projected, so they had to develop specific targets.

This they did by concentrating on certain industries, developing their quality and their personnel within these industries. The idea of multiplying interchangeable parts had failed them in war. Now they worked on integrating individuals into economic community commitments. Once they had a person inside the community, they proceeded to develop his skills and use them in different ways. A person was trained to be a good Mitsubishi mechanic, and if he was a good Mitsubishi mechanic for a long time, the odds were he would not do nearly so well working for Mitsui. So the old idea of internal loyalties was reinforced and the Confucian work ethic dusted off for intensive use.

Because Japanese long-range planning in World War II had been such a failure, they now concentrated on planning and strategies, almost to a fault. Everything had to be thought out well in advance, tested—and above all—adapted to the needs of the marketplace, wherever that marketplace was. Thus the Japanese businessman appeared as the first world marketer.

Politically the same principle worked. Once they started on their path of postwar success, the Japanese clung to harmony as a unifying principle. "If you can succeed this well, why rock the boat—especially since if you rock the boat at all, it might sink." That was essentially the message of Prime Minister Ikeda Hayato when he urged the country to stop worrying about politics and concentrate on his "Double-Your-Income" *(Shotoku baizō)* policy. A strengthened imperative for harmony began to develop within Japan, not easily but at least facilitated by its homogeneous society. At the same time, ironically, that the Americans were destroying the unities of the World War II victory in an orgy of special interest seeking, the Japanese strengthened their maze of unspoken rules which, while pacifying special interests, worked more for the prosperity and forward motion of the whole society.

4·Management and Human Capital

Modern capitalism is absolutely irreligious, without internal union, without much public spirit, often, though not always, a mere congeries of possessors and pursuers.
—John Maynard Keynes

At forty-six Jack Wilson is the president and chief executive officer of Behemoth Industries, Inc. in Pittsburgh. He is about as dynamic as they come—"a relentless driver," as *Fortune* magazine admiringly put it in a recent close-up. Wilson works twelve-hour days at his high-rise headquarters and vainly expects those around him to do the same. Since getting his M.B.A. at Harvard in 1960, he has been a man on the move. After a few years' consulting work at McKinsey, he was picked up by Acme Products as controller, then went to New York as a partner in an investment banking house. When a head-hunting firm finally lured him to Behemoth as executive vice-president and chief financial officer, he cut the company up into new "business strategy" profit centers, turned the ailing manufacturing department around within a year, and lopped off three unprofitable subsidiaries to give Behemoth's board its best quarterly earnings' report in a decade. Elected president a year ago, after only three years with the company, Wilson has already extended the company's product line into new marketing areas, cut costs by buying out and consolidating two of Behemoth's suppliers, and set a new tough return on investment (ROI) policy for acquisitions that is the talk of the merger circuit. There are internal problems, however. Some of his plants are dangerously obsolete and their productivity rate is falling, partly because of serious labor problems. He has assured the directors that he will soon close or sell these "losers," and his new plans for increasing profitability by taking Behemoth's hotel division into the movie and casino business have already been approved.

When not on the job or flying to Behemoth's outlying plants in the company jet to inspect their financial control systems on the spot, Wilson frequently lectures to business groups ("Expanding the Corporate Portfolio" is a favorite topic); and he has been called to Washington to serve on two presidential commissions. In his spare time he skis and scuba-dives. Divorced some years ago, he is currently dating Nancy Drew, the beautiful and dynamic twenty-six-year-old vice-president of Behemoth's ad agency. His annual income, in salary and bonus, comes to $610,000; and he and his lawyer have just arranged for a five-year contract with added incentive bonuses based on annual profits and ROI increases.

Nakamura Haruo is the president and representative director of Sunrise Industries in Osaka. He is sixty-six years old and has been president for the last four years, moving up from managing director when Sunrise's eighty-seven-year-old chairman finally retired. Nakamura has been a Sunrise man since 1947, when the company was reorganized after the war. An engineer by profession, he graduated from the University of Tokyo and served in the technical branch of the Navy during World War II (he still tells American friends, with a chuckle, that the Japanese might have won the Battle of Leyte Gulf if his new fire-control system had been approved). Nakamura's progress at Sunrise has been steady—head of the No. 1 production department, director of personnel, and finally managing director in charge of production, a post he held for six years. He has seen to it that good-quality engineering graduates come to the company and has encouraged various technological advances. One of his own adaptive processes, the high-frequency integrated widget, was developed by his engineers into a prime Sunrise product, well received in the export market.

Nakamura cut down on his working hours after becoming president, leaving the heavy work to the department heads and younger directors. A member of several committees at the Keidanren (Federation of Japanese Economic Organizations), he also serves on the Industrial Structure Council, which advises the Ministry for International Trade and Industry. A good part of his time is spent representing the company at a variety of outside functions. The company policies he helped set, however, continue to be followed. Thanks partly to his earlier efforts, Sunrise has become a world marketing company and is about to establish a small manufacturing plant in the United States. The expanded R & D section he helped reorganize in 1972 continues to grow. The company recently received the coveted Deming Award for productivity. Although profits for the past year have been down, the shareholders and the leading bank have not complained, understanding Nakamura's strategy to continue going after an ever larger share of the world market in several of Sunrise's product lines. Progress is unspectacular but steady.

The execution of these policies Nakamura leaves to his younger directors. He monitors their work at executive committee meetings and keeps in touch with his directors and bankers through continual back-and-forth visiting. (This includes attendance at a regrettably growing number of corporate funerals.) Recently he has spent considerable time brushing out scrolls with hortatory mottoes to give to faithful employees. Married while still in the Navy, he has two grown children. He and his wife live in a suburb of Osaka, only a short drive away from the exclusive golf club to which he belongs. Outside of playing *go* and reading historical novels, golf is his only recreation. His total compensation comes to $270,000 at current exchange rates. (He pays a higher tax on this income than Wilson pays on his.)

Based on these comparisons, we might expect Sunrise to be the object of an imminent takeover bid by Behemoth, as Wilson urges his firm into international markets. In fact, Sunrise is beating Behemoth on all fronts. Sunrise's loss of production from strikes or absenteeism is less than a tenth of Behemoth's figure. Productivity rates continue to grow. The Japanese firm's new American subsidiary has been moving into Behemoth's market in several areas, where product quality is clearly superior. Over the next ten years, according to the planning department's forecasts, its lead is bound to increase.

Why is the dynamic leadership of Jack Wilson actually doing so badly against the plodding, drab teamwork of Nakamura? The answer is simple: Nakamura has a company behind him while Wilson does not. The unobtrusive Japanese executive is winning the competition precisely because he does not need to spend any twelve- or fourteen-hour days on it. Wilson is losing, among other reasons, because virtually the only twelve- or fourteen-hour days put in at Behemoth are his own.

Nakamura and his company made a sizable investment in human capital and they are getting it back. The ROI figure here, if they choose to compute it, will look very good. Wilson, for all his knowledge of ROIs and earnings per share, does not have any real idea what *human* capital is. He is still living in the era of Adam Smith, Marx, and mass production, where people are one thing and the investments of capitalists are another. Half unwittingly, Nakamura has been pioneering a new era of postindustrial capitalism, in which people are as much a part of capital as machines. Wilson may be doing a good job according to his lights, trying to increase his return on investment for the next quarter. But he has been doing nothing to anticipate a future in which the aspirations and capabilities of people change as fast as technology, a world in which people can no longer be dealt with as interchangeable parts, to be hired and fired at will while their M.B.A. betters work in the financial department over the numbers. Sunrise's organization, with its slogans, songs, and company smocks, might look to Wilson and his bright new M.B.A. assistants like a survival of the paternalism that American industry had long left behind. But its workers enjoy a security, a sense of community, and an idea of where they are going that Behemoth's workers can only envy.

Both these executive word-portraits are of course exaggerations, if not caricatures, of successful American and Japanese corporate leaders. Japanese managers are not all that smart, and American managers are by no means all this shortsighted. Taken as *individuals,* the world's brightest group of managers still resides in the United States. Seen in the context of their business societies, however—and this is what ultimately counts—I would have to concede that the Japanese may already have a slight edge on us. They have been gaining for some time.

Japanese managers have suffered their share of failures, miscalculations, and blunders. Early postwar car exports to the United States, for example, were rickety disasters. (One of the first Toyotas to arrive lacked the power to get up the hill to the California showroom where it was being premiered.) And some other successes were less the result of long-term planning than a stubborn refusal to admit failure in situations where pure economics argued that the project in question should be shut down. Nonetheless the Japanese have shown a pragmatic ability to learn from mistakes and an enviable persistence in keeping at a project until they get it right. They are good students —they have selectively remembered a great many things that Americans managed to forget—and they set great store on educating their people. Their approaches to business often differ widely and can resist distillation into a set of handily packaged principles. (*Case-by-case* is a magic word with Japanese businessmen.) But one general observation can be made: they are *political* businessmen.

Political businessmen tend to see their businesses or industries in political terms, whether as a single community or *polis,* or as parts of a small world of business communities, some warring, some allied. Where Americans tend to see business more in terms of straight economic opportunities and relationships designed to secure them— what Yamamoto called the "functional" organization—Japanese tend more to think of *their* corporations as political organizations— the company as "community." They are thus far more interested in organization, organic territorial growth, status within and outside the company, and the development of relationships among the company community's people.

This way of thinking can be exasperating, as anyone can witness who has had to cope with the maddening intricacies of rank and position shadings devised by personnel directors in a Japanese organization, and often slows down development in the short run. But in the long run the political businessman proves extraordinarily effective. He is not just trying to get a good price for his widgets. In the manner of "politicals" over the centuries, he is trying to enlarge and perpetuate his particular *polis* community. This objective is often more important to him than purely economic matters, such as immediate profitability.

Historically the Japanese have been a highly *political* people, far more so than their neighbors the Chinese and the Koreans. With World War II centuries of political power struggles within Japan stopped, as did the dynamic, if ultimately disastrous, impulses to lead armies and dominate neighboring countries either by statecraft or force. At one swoop the proconsuls and the generals had their job categories abolished. Business became the principal outlet for political energies. Business expansion became in a sense a substitute for empire. Over the past three decades Japan's political businessmen came into their own.

If I were to select three descriptive words for Japan's political managers in action, I should say: (1) people-centered; (2) community-conscious; and (3) development-oriented. Let us look at these three marks of Japanese management and see what they mean.

PEOPLE-CENTERED

At the Pacific Basin Institute in Santa Barbara, we sometimes host conferences of young Japanese middle managers or union committee members, as part of the study tours which the Japan Productivity Center continually sends out from Tokyo. Invariably, we have an American personnel expert in to lecture and exchange opinions with the Japanese middle managers. Invariably, he is asked about hiring practices in the United States. As the American explains how companies in the United States hire people for specific job openings when they are needed, through newspaper ads or other media, and how workers come and go as better opportunities develop elsewhere, a look of puzzlement and disbelief comes over his Japanese listeners. "But why don't you hire the whole man?" they will ask. "Without long interviews and thorough study of a person's school record and family background, how do you know what you're getting?"

The difference is a fundamental one, going back to the Japanese sense of the corporation as a community as well as a functional organization. Workers entering a Japanese company expect to begin a lifetime relationship. Hired on the basis of school or college records —and sometimes examinations—they are first screened intensively, then taken in hand by the personnel department to begin their company indoctrination. They first learn the particular company's principles—"service," "sincerity," and "cooperation" are the most frequently stressed—through lectures and careful study of company precepts and guidelines, before going on to any work assignments. For the next three or six months, they are carefully watched, not merely to see how well they work but to make sure that they have a positive and "sincere" attitude about their work. Some may leave. But after the apprenticeship period is over, they are in the company for life. Corporate divorce is still rare in Japan. Even after reaching the mandatory retirement age of fifty-five or sixty, employees may sign on again as "contract employees" doing less work at lower pay; or perhaps move on to a company subsidiary, to act as cadres for a new work force.

As the whole person moves up in the company, he or she may be rotated to a number of different jobs, with often sharply different functions. If special skills are needed, company training will supply them, even if long education periods are required. (Some Japanese companies give college or graduate school educations to particularly competent students as part of their recruitment.) Seldom are specialists recruited from the outside. Moving along guidelines set by the personnel department, they advance on set paths, with pay supplemented by allowances based on age, seniority, family status, and, to a greater or lesser degree, merit. Orchestrating promotions, job changes, and transfers—poor performers are generally shuffled around until a suitable spot is found for them—is the all-powerful personnel department. The importance of this division, far greater than in most American companies, is indicative of the stress a Japanese company puts on human investment. The investment itself is significant. For a steelworker receiving just under $1,000 monthly, for example, his company will spend $1,200 a month in housing, benefits, on-the-job training, and various sports, education, and development facilities.

There are no formal contracts in this relationship, but the commitment by both company and worker is a serious one. A Japanese company will go to almost any lengths to avoid firing or even layoffs. If such commitments were broken on a large scale, the firmament of Japanese business might break in turn. Thus far companies have only rarely resorted to "the firing ax."

During various crises of the seventies, caused either by the sudden OPEC oil shock or the bends in the market for Japanese steel or ships, some companies in trouble would turn their surplus labor into salesmen or devised temporary service companies, for example, cleaning up pollution, to use their skills. Toyo Kōgyō, the automobile company in Hiroshima, was a case in point. When rising gas prices in Japan and the United States cut sales of the rotary-engine Mazda almost in half, Toyo Kōgyō and its leading bank, Sumitomo, started their own rescue operation. Yoshi Tsurumi, a leading scholar of Japanese management systems, described this in a 1980 article in *Fortune* magazine: "The dividend was slashed by three-quarters and all paychecks were trimmed (with the heaviest cuts at the top of the ladder). Because of the tradition of lifetime employment, layoffs were out of the question, but through normal attrition and by paying bonuses for early retirement, Mazda reduced its work force from 37,000 to 27,000. . . ."

In the crash program to redesign the Mazda cars which followed, employees played a key role, offering their ideas for improving quality control and eliminating unnecessary jobs. Some went out to work as salesmen for Mazda cars, as had workers from Matsushita and other electronic companies when their assembly lines had to be closed or reduced during recession periods in their business. The degree of cooperation was hard for an American to comprehend. Even after the crises of 1980 and 1981 had rocked Detroit, the carmakers and the UAW-CIO were still arguing over *how* to cooperate.

Blue-collar workers in Japan get the same security as white-collar workers, just as they belong to the same unions. They are all part of the community or, if you will, human capital. The security that this gives the average Japanese worker is hard to underestimate. And security furthers cooperation of a spontaneous sort.

What, by contrast, are the ultimate incentives to do a good job in American business? We may say what we wish about achievement for its own sake, the pursuit of excellence, or the desire for one's skills to be appreciated in the marketplace. Yet from the factory sweeper to the vice-presidents on the executive floor, the basic job incentive is the same: fear of losing it, fear of being fired, fear of falling, fear, fear, and more fear. Fear is present everywhere under a reigning business philosophy which holds that incompetents—or depending on the circumstances, people who displease management, or who are embarrassing to it, or who are *too* competent for their own good—can be fired as quickly and as dispassionately as you remove a defective part from a machine before replacing it with another. "Do you have a problem? If so, fire him." Typically present-day firings are coated with a variety of euphemisms—"termination," "severance," "relocation," "resignation for personal reasons," even "de-hiring." But the meaning is the same.

In a unionized plant or factory, workers cannot, of course, be disposed of so readily. Indeed, in many well-unionized situations, a variety of grievance procedures often makes firing next to impossible. If there is no protection from the union, a worker who is liberally endowed with perseverance and money can always hire a lawyer. Among the many duties assumed by the American judiciary in recent years is the reinstatement of employees whom the courts hold have been fired wrongfully. But such processes take time, and turning a judge into a personnel manager can be costly and counterproductive.

The Fear of Firing clutches most fiercely at the hearts of the middle and top-ranking executives in American business just at the time when they should be at the peak of their powers. It is one thing to fight for your idea, denounce incompetence, and demand that the company go for the bigger and better mousetrap. If *they* don't like it, you can quit and go on to the company next door, in the best Andrew Carnegie tradition, or so our folklore has it. This way of thinking loses much of its attraction, however, as the executive grows older. Faced with a showdown, what does he do if he loses? In Adam Smith's world, he could find a job quickly, based on the "market's" appreciation of his skills and services, but modern business life is more complex. How does he know how many wells have been poisoned by the grinning incompetent who is about to fire him? And if he is fired, who will pay the bills for the children's colleges, the country club, and his wife's new Mercedes?

There are at least two ways to deal with this dire eventuality. The first is to demand a contract with the job, a good rustproof model with ample penalty clauses and sweeteners for early termination. The second is to go quietly among other people in the industry—competitors and suppliers—and work out some fallback positions. The two ways are not mutually exclusive. But they take time. Moreover, such protective measures, widely practiced among American executives, tend to lessen a person's productivity in the job he is doing—particularly if he happens to be in the R & D sector or performing any function requiring consistent, steady planning.

Consider the contrast. While the American executive, with what the Japanese call the firing ax over his head, works out his résumé and arranges to meet secretly with the executive vice-president of the competition, just against eventualities, his Japanese counterpart is quietly doing his job, giving one hundred percent of his time to work for one company—his company.

In the large Japanese company, whose size and resources make the full-employment system possible, no union pressure is necessary to maintain full employment in the face of all but the direst of circumstances. It is an unwritten guarantee given by the employer to each member of the work community. This is not necessarily true of those second- or third-rank companies that in numbers of employees comprise almost 70 percent of Japanese industry. With these small companies—the suppliers, subcontractors, or small entrepreneurs—full employment is not so frequently guaranteed. The conditions of business life are too volatile in a world of lower wages and frequent bankruptcies. Yet even here the goal is to attain the status of a big company, with full employment built in.

Given the cushion of full employment, people could easily become time-servers, secure in the knowledge that management has deprived itself of the ultimate sanction against them. Remarkably few Japanese do. On the contrary, the sense of community which goes along with the full employment and the seniority systems—the famous *nen ko joretsu*—impels the majority of employees to work hard for mutual benefit and personal self-respect. At least it has thus far.

Within the system there are, however, penalties for incompetence or that most mortal of Japanese corporate sins: lack of proper cooperative "spirit." The most obvious is transfer. The deputy section head removed from the cozy camaraderie of the head office in Tokyo and sent to work at a branch in Gifu or Maebashi or Kokura is really facing exile, an exile quite as ominous as the "island-sequestration" *(shima-nagashi)* for troublemakers at the ancient court or, more immediately, as the expulsion from the village—the dreaded *mura hachibu*—was for the Japanese farmer in the village society of not so long ago. There are also a variety of jobs in any Japanese company where an incompetent can do little harm. When problems arise with difficult people, they are handled coolly by the personnel department, which after all was responsible for hiring the person in the first place.

The job security, the constant education process that goes on in Japanese companies, the job rotation, and the ever-present signs, badges, and slogans give even the humblest of employees a sense of participation and company fellowship. The suggestion box in a Japanese company is not there for show. Employees on every level are expected to develop ideas for improving the company's effectiveness and communicate them. On the average 54 percent of Japanese workers participate in suggestion programs, compared with 14 percent in the United States. Some 23.5 million suggestions came up from employees at 453 Japanese corporations surveyed in 1980. (Typically, there is a Japan Suggestion Activities Association to handle such matters.)

With significant exceptions, the average American company prefers to leave all such ideas to the people on the executive floor. Karatsu Hajime, managing director of Matsushita Communication Industrial Company and a leading Japanese productivity expert, put it this way in an article in *Asahi*:

In Western business enterprises, the company is run by a super elite group of executives who have ample scope to show their originality. But ordinary workers are left to do only standardized jobs which they do by the book. They do what the book says—no more and no less. Their own humanity is ignored—it's like a caricature of Chaplin's *Modern Times.*

COMMUNITY-CONSCIOUSNESS

If we use this phrase to describe an American company, it is taken to mean that the company participates wholeheartedly in civic activities. Be it local charities, fund-raisings, boys' clubs, or inner-city rehabilitations, Acme, Inc.'s check can be counted on. Several company employees may even be seconded to help with the Community Chest drive. In a Japanese corporate context, the words have a different meaning. Community-consciousness here works inward. It means a self-consciousness of the company's own role as a community. Most Japanese companies are not so strong on civic activities, except in a limited context, for the company is considered a small civic entity in itself. Community generally means the company-as-community. At least until the retirement age of fifty-five or the age sixty level at which government welfare payments begin, the company will take care of its own.

A good Japanese company is the hothouse society intensified. Its people and their families may live far outside its geographical perimeters—although likely as not the company will have had something to do with their housing accommodations—but socially speaking their concerns lie within the company perimeter. This often includes sons and daughters who go on to work in the company themselves. The sense of constant participation can be deadening to some free spirits, but the majority find it rewarding and in a sense intellectually stimulating. For it is their company as much as it is the shareholders'. They participate in shaping the company's future, to the extent that each can.

The extent can be considerable. Japanese executives very early in the game are given increasing amounts of responsibility. It is middle management that gives the push to most Japanese companies. Lower and middle management draw up the plans and projects for top management to ratify. This is generally as top management wishes. After all, it was they who selected and trained their vital "middle."

It is an oversimplification, however, to speak of Japanese management as a showpiece of "bottom-up" decision making. (To begin with, "decision making" is an American word. Except for executives who have been to business school in the United States or read widely in American business literature, it is little known in Japan.) Some Japanese companies tend to emphasize "bottom-up" input, while others are more obviously run from the top. Matsushita and Sony exemplify the first and the second sort, respectively. There are also Japanese executives who run their companies with as tight a hand as Harold Geneen ever held on ITT. They may be called *Tennō* (emperor), the favorite pejorative for a domineering boss, and their one-man decisions may be law. These are exceptions. Yet even here one finds at least the *illusion* of a kind of participatory management. They are interested in their succession, and it is part of the job to bring everybody in the plant into the picture. At the worst, everybody in the corporation is encouraged to know what is going on.

The decision-making processes of the Japanese company can be described in many ways. I should like to repeat an earlier description, distilled from my own experience running a business in Japan, which I wrote some years back:

> If it is a smoothly managed company, the key figures are not the president or directors, but the department heads, the acting department heads, the division chiefs who run any well-managed Japanese firm. Almost every foreigner who blunders into a Japanese business is, at some point, led aside to hear a gentle lecture on the virtues of bottom-up initiative, as opposed to top-down direction. The Japanese are well aware that in the American company, it is the president or the executive vice-president who plans, who initiates, who drives the company forward, in the manner of a profit-conscious engineer pouring on the coals to pull a reluctant train. When this top-down management happens in Japan, it is resolutely disguised. The department heads, generally, are the people who work out the tactical plans. They participate in the innumerable conferences and agree in the concurred decisions. In most Japanese companies, in fact, major decisions have to be recorded by the extraordinary process which the Japanese call *ringisho* (literally, "decisions in a circle by document"). In *ringi,* after some preliminary tallies, a memorandum setting forth the details of a plan is prepared by someone on the planning staff or a junior department head. Generally, basic plans are prepared far down in the organization. It is then passed from department head to department head up the ladder to secure their opinions and agreement. Its passage is, of course, preceded by long conferences. Abridgements and correc-

tions are made, so that by the time the final paper is circulated, everyone's ideas are pretty well on the table, if not in the last draft. Everyone wants to see what is written on this basic *ringisho* [document], which is one reason for the scarcity of copies of Japanese memoranda. (The fewer copies, also, the less room for considered objections.)

Ultimately, the *ringisho* gets up to the managing director level. Many seals are already upon it and it is close to final acceptance. The director concerned may well have been informed of its progress. In fact, he may have initiated it; although, if he is a good manager, he will have taken pains to keep up the appearance of the initiative having come from the lower ranks.

By the time the document reaches the president, all that is needed is his seal. The president, too, will have been kept informed of its existence, if not its progress. He generally has no reluctance about signing it, but it is his responsibility. If something goes terribly wrong with the plan that has been outlined, it is not the senior assistant in planning who is ultimately responsible. It is the president's resignation that must be in the chairman's office the next week.

Similarities between military decision making and Japanese business decision making are striking, especially to someone who learned Japanese in a wartime atmosphere. Staff officers, often at quite a junior level, work out major strategies to be initialed by the chief of staff, and then submitted to the commander, who in most cases, does little more than initial them himself. Indeed, the *ringisho* system is more understandable to a military-staff trained mind in whatever nation. Pentagon veterans would easily adjust to it. . . .[1]

The chairmen and presidents who lead Japan's community companies are, statistically speaking, a remarkably homogeneous group. Almost all are university graduates. Fully one-third of them come from the law faculty of the University of Tokyo, which dominates Japan's establishment the way old Etonians and Harrovians used to dominate Britain's. Other public universities like Kyoto and Hitotsubashi and the private universities of Keio and Waseda are proportionally represented.

Very few Japanese presidents inherited their jobs. "In Japan," Chairman Otsuki Bumpei of the Federation of Employers' Organizations (Nikkeiren) once observed to a reporter, "we have very few top executives who were born into the job, so to speak. And a good thing it is." Most worked their way up through their companies to the director level, but on the "elite" track reserved for university graduates. A few ex-bureaucrats came in close to the top, in a kind of lateral transfer at the time of their retirement from their ministry; or just before it. This "descent from heaven" *(amakudari)* is a commonplace in Japan and one of the many ways in which the top echelons of government and business keep their thinking on roughly the same wavelength. It is, interestingly enough, the converse of the American tendency for top businessmen to seek high government posts late in their careers.

Collectively Japan's business establishment does not cut a very impressive figure. Seen in groups at meetings of the Keidanren or the Employers' Association or at the lavish hotel parties commemorating company anniversaries, they exude sobriety in their well-cut, dark-blue suits, with a kind of gruff oldtime courtliness, understandable enough considering that the average age for chairmen, at least, runs well into the late seventies and eighties. Even at informal occasions they keep an aura of dignity. On one such occasion to which I was invited, a spring geisha dance recital in a famous Tokyo rendezvous restaurant, some fifty captains of industry were in attendance. Despite the rather cozy circumstances of the party, each of the performing geisha being the very close friend of one of the tycoons and bank presidents attending, the atmosphere was about as relaxed as a lunch break between sessions of the College of Cardinals. True to old traditions of good form, none of the geisha sat next to her boyfriend and none of the audience betrayed the least sign of proprietorship.

Their workplaces are heavy with the trappings of authority. The office of Mitsui and Company's board chairman overlooks the Imperial Palace and is furnished appropriately. A walk through attendants, anterooms, and aides on the way to see the president or chairman of the Mitsubishi or Fuji bank recalls the protocol of Buckingham Palace. Company protocol is generally taken very seriously, with several layers of respect language used by company inferiors approaching the corporate throne. The ritual of Japanese company life, to a foreigner most oppressive, is rigorously observed in the almost endless succession of meetings over which the officers preside. And the formal board of directors meeting, for which even the bit players are given written scripts (for example, Managing Director Yamamoto: "Agreed" or Senior Managing Director Kurosawa: "There is no objection") is an exercise in ponderous stagecraft.

Underneath the dull protective coloration of ceremony and company protocol, however, the leaders of Japanese corporations are far more individualist than they pretend to be. They worked their way up in tough times, many of them being the same directors who were given the task of picking up their companies from the wreckage of war after their elders had been purged by the Occupation.

Some of them are old-fashioned entrepreneurs who made their own first products. Honda Soichiro started Honda Motors from a small machine shop when he set out to make a motorcycle that Japan's impoverished postwar consumer could afford. Matsushita Konosuke began his vast company with an electrical goods shop in Osaka in 1918. In more recent times the Yoshida zipper company, known worldwide as YKK, and the Dai-ei supermarket chain enjoyed similar entrepreneurial beginnings. Others are more conventional front-office businessmen, but they all know how to take risks. When Nagano Shigeo and his colleagues back in the fifties took the gamble to invest in large-scale steel production, they did so in defiance of warnings from government experts (and some in the U.S. Occupation) that Japan had no course but to stick to small, light industry production. Doko Toshio, who later succeeded Nagano as chairman of the Keidanren, smashed precedent when he merged the Harima shipyards and Ishikawajima Heavy Industries to build the world's greatest shipbuilding company. Tashiro Shigeki virtually gambled his whole company when he had Toyo Rayon buy the Du Pont rayon patents, also in the early fifties. Toyoray went on to become a powerful world textile company with interesting diversification.

Different businessmen have different approaches to management. A 1981 issue of *President,* the Japanese business magazine, contrasted the crisp "rationalistic" management style of Sony's Chairman, Morita Akio, with Matsushita's old-fashioned paternalism—comparing them to two great heroes of Japan's sixteenth century civil wars—Oda Nobunaga (the brilliant strategist who ordered things and people on his own impulse) and Takeda Shingen, who constantly consulted his captains about battles and policies in the more classic "Japan-style" manner.

Japanese managers' continuing drives to expand their corporations and put them on ever more secure footing grew out of past struggles. They are all tough competitors, both on the outside and within the company. This is necessarily so. After a man becomes a director, although the salary and perquisites grow bigger, the security stops. Directors come up for appointment periodically, generally every two years. Depending on their own performance, the power structure of the company, and their position at the chairman's court, they may be retained, transferred to a subsidiary, or unceremoniously dropped. Although the last dire possibility materializes only infrequently, no director can ignore the constant in-fighting that goes on in a Japanese company, all the more vicious because it is covered by a show of harmony and community fellowship.

Outside the company, competition is equally intense. The goal of every good Japanese company citizen is to beat the immediate competition. And because of the strong company commitment of employees, it runs throughout the organization. Developing competitive spirit is one reason that so many Japanese companies sponsor their own big-league baseball teams.

In recent years many corporate arteries have been hardening because of aged chairmen and presidents who, once ensconced, were reluctant to move on. The patriarchs of Japanese industry are legendary. Doko Toshio, former chairman of the Keidanren, retired at the age of eighty-four (Inayama Yoshishiro succeeded him at seventy-nine). Yet even after retirement Doko, one of Japanese industry's statesmen in the Shibusawa tradition, chaired an important government advisory committee. At ninety-seven Chairman Hara Yasusaburo of Nihon Kayaku, a large chemical manufacturer, was still regularly appearing at the office. With so many elders on the scene, promotion naturally slowed for those next in line. Ultimately, the grand old men began to retire. In 1980, as *Asahi* reported, 136 major Japanese companies changed their presidents, more than half of them because of the old age, sickness, or death of the incumbents. Although chairmen continue to be old, presidents these days are more apt to be in their sixties.

Few presidents are forced to resign for reasons of incompetence, at least on the surface. And whether the person in question is a company president or a baseball manager,[2] nothing shocks Japanese so much as the sudden peremptory firing. This is rare. In business as in politics, Japanese set great store on the face-saving resignation; frequently every possible reason for resignation is given but the right one. Incompetent or no, it is hard even for shareholders to dismiss a popular president or chairman if he has the company behind him.

Replacement is almost always internal, except in the case of near-disasters, when it is generally the firm's leading bank that steps in to save the situation (and its investment). This is what the Sumitomo Bank did with Toyo Kōgyō. It was the bank's responsibility to save the company, in contrast to the Chrysler case, where this charitable chore fell to the U.S. government. Most banks have a small group of their own executives on hand who are capable of running companies, like pitchers warming up in a bullpen. Katsumata Katsuji, vice-chairman of Nissan Motors, originally came from the Industrial Bank of Japan. Another Industrial Bank of Japan director, Hidaka Teru, was twice sent on rescue missions, once to Nissan Chemical and later to Yamaichi Securities, when both were in severe trouble. (He later took over at KDD [Kokusai Denshin Denwa] after that company was wracked by a bribery scandal in 1978.)

Another distinguishing feature of Japan's top executives is their relatively low rates of compensation, at least compared to the tumorous expansion of corporate salaries in the United States. Prestige and power the Japanese president seeks. But money greed does not seem to be such a primary motivation, as it is so often elsewhere. If we look at the annual compensation figures of leading Japanese businessmen, they seem impressive: the top ten range from 270 million yen to almost 2 billion yen.

In 1981 there were only 88 salaried Japanese businessmen with incomes of 100 million yen or more ($400,000 at a rate of 250 yen to the dollar). The average pay for presidents and chairmen of large companies was closer to $200,000. By comparison, pay packages for the top 25 American executives in the same year started at about $1,500,000 and ascended into the troposphere, while half-million-dollar packages were virtually commonplace. When we allow for the Japanese income tax, the discrepancy becomes greater. Most of them are taxed at a total of 80 percent, without the ample allowances and tax shelters permissible to the rich under U.S. income tax laws. Thus the $800,000 that the president of Toyota received in 1979 comes out in take-home pay to a fraction of the $942,000 in salary and stock awarded in that year to the chairman of General Motors. In Japan stock options and other special income plans are far fewer than in the United States (although if a Japanese executive wants to sell off a good portion of his stock he does not have to pay a capital gains tax on it).

An interesting comparison can be made between the take-home pay of a Japanese company president and that of an employee entering the company from college. According to a survey taken by the Japan Employers' Association, the gap in 1925 was vast. The president took home roughly 100 times the salary of a first-year employee. In 1963 the figure was 12 times. In 1979, based on after-tax income, it was merely 7.8 times. By contrast American presidents' salaries generally run about 20 times those of employees on the bottom rung of the ladder.

Japanese company presidents and directors may spend a great deal on entertainment. The $500 evening on the Ginza was a fixed rubric long before Jimmy Carter began to complain about the three martini lunch. But their regular salary and allowances keep comparatively close to the ground. Few of them live lavishly. In fact, the appointments of their housing are not too dissimilar from that of most of their employees. This likeness of living standards is in itself a powerful reinforcing factor for the company community spirit. Not the least noteworthy fact about executive pay is that, when times are bad in a Japanese company, the directors cut their own pay first—before going to talk to the union. Not so in the United States. The high incidence of executives whose pay packages go up, while their companies' profits and sales go down, is becoming a national scandal.

In these and so many other respects, the Japanese manager does not merely depend on the system of the "whole man" as a lifetime employee; he is himself a product of that system. He may consider himself a very professional manager. He studies his business hard and—whether director or department head—yields to none in his fascination with management techniques and processes. (The volume of literature on this subject found on the shelves and tables of any downtown Tokyo bookstore is staggering.) But he is a manager within the context of his company. His professional skills—and to a great extent his professional curiosity—are shaped and limited by the needs of that company, its concerns and challenges, and above all, the products that it makes.

The "management professional" in the United States is something quite different. He regards business as a science, with its own tested disciplines of marketing, motivation, and financial controls, all of them governed by a set of principles that can be learned and applied to just about any business situation. Processes and techniques of a business, any business, he finds fascinating insofar as they afford him the chance to work out strategies for attaining a variety of goals. What goal it happens to be does not interest him so much as how he can arrive at it through sound and rigorous analysis. He strives not only for profitability but also for an acceptable return on investment. He is by definition a numbers man. He assumes that his competence is judged and his monetary rewards determined by the skill with which he can produce good numbers at the storied bottom line of whatever profit center he is working for. He buys or sells businesses by mathematical formulas—multiples of sales or profits, for example. He would find little to quarrel with in Keynes's definition of capitalism quoted at the beginning of this chapter.[3]

He has no particular ambition to enter any particular company, still less to stay in it for any lengthy period of time. As a professional, his interest is in sound analysis and problem-solving. By competent performance he can advance himself and move on from one good situation to another. Today investment banking, tomorrow electronics, three years from now computers, publishing, or oil. In the purest sense of the word, he is a mercenary, a hired gun. If he happens to stay in one corporation for a length of time, it had better be with continuing promise for advancement and a good contract.

The West Point for these modern-day janissaries is that uniquely American institution, the business school. More than 500 American institutions now award the coveted Master of Business Administration degree. Each year over 50,000 new M.B.A.'s march out in search of money, with what once seemed a virtually inexhaustible market for their talents. Even in a time of recession the average M.B.A. graduate from the two-year courses at major service academies like Harvard, Wharton, and Stanford can count on starting salaries of $25,000 to $30,000, while top-of-the-class cadets can pull down well over $40,000. This is one reason why applications to the best of these institutions outnumber entrants by about ten to one.

M.B.A.'s are prized for cool and tidy efficiency. Many corporation executives will not hire anyone lacking this credential for a wide variety of jobs. They have been taught rigorously efficient methods of financial analysis, cost control, and profit maximizing. Few old-line production men can argue successfully against the plans of the new M.B.A.'s in the financial department to save money by buying out a competitor instead of starting a new product line, or canceling a proposed expansion program and instead acquiring a cash-rich, if unrelated company. Figures, we are told, do not lie. And it is hard to argue with those convincing projections that would look so good on the next quarterly report to the shareholders. "A good plan," says the grateful chairman, "it limits our exposure and cuts down the risk factor. The board will like that." And so will the analysts on Wall Street when they give their verdict on the company's prospects.

It is hard to say whether the M.B.A.'s are cause or effect of what has been going on in American business. And one is reluctant to make sweeping criticisms of the business schools as such, for their contribution to our knowledge of modern economic processes is an impressive one. Yet the way of thinking which the business-school M.B.A. has come to symbolize is analyzing American business half to death.

In a memorable 1980 article in the *Harvard Business Review,* two respected professors at the Harvard Business School, Robert H. Hayes and William J. Abernathy, discussed American business's abdication of strategic responsibilities by this "management by the numbers."

> We refuse to believe that this managerial failure is the result of a sudden psychological shift among American managers towards a "super-safe," "no risk" mind set. . . . Instead we believe that during the past two decades American managers have increasingly relied on principles which prize analytical detachment and methodological elegance over insight, based on experience, into the subtleties and complexities of strategic decisions. As a result maximum short-term financial returns have become the overriding criteria for many companies. . . .
>
> What has developed, in the business community as well as in academia, is a preoccupation with a false and shallow concept of the professional manager, a "pseudo-professional" really—an individual having no special expertise in any particular industry or technology who nevertheless can step into an unfamiliar company and run it successfully through strict application of financial controls, portfolio concepts and a market-driven strategy.[4]

In their article they noted the striking increase in financial and legal experts at the top of American companies. Surveys of young M.B.A.'s reinforce the figures. Few of them seem interested in production. If they do not go into the financial department of a large corporation, they would prefer something like investment banking or that ever-popular American business by-product, the consulting firm. Most of them are smart people. And their very concentration in the financial area increases the tendency of American business leaders to neglect the long-term building program in favor of the short-term gain, the development of technological strengths in favor of immediate profitability, the building of quality products in favor of selling marginal products by skillful marketing techniques.

All of this modern business science contrasts poorly with the old-fashioned approach of the Japanese manager, company-directed and people-centered. The emphasis on financial controls has only intensified the adversary argument within the American company, while the corresponding neglect of people continues to pull our productivity down.

DEVELOPMENT-ORIENTED

Alfred P. Sloan wrote simply and eloquently that the business of General Motors or any other American company was to make profits for the shareholders. The primary objective of the company is thus to pay a good dividend. It is a money objective. I would be a rich man if I had five dollars for each time one of my business colleagues patiently and sagely explained to me, "Profits are the name of the game."

This is good as far as it goes. If an American businessman did not say this, the SEC could doubtless take action against him for denying the interest of his shareholders.

For the Japanese businessman, as we have noted, profits in themselves are not the name of the game. Nor is the pursuit of business a game. It is a community enterprise in development. Good development and organic growth will bring profits to all, shareholders among them. So runs their logic. Profits to the managers, to the workers, to the country.

Granted that there are many in Japan who do not subscribe to this philosophy. Some companies characteristically grab after immediate profits to the exclusion of other considerations; the heavy profit-making of the trading companies at times—for example, in the real estate boom of the seventies—has been notorious. Yet these are exceptions. Threading through Japanese management is a feeling for service far stronger than anywhere else. It is not enough to make money selling things. You must produce things. Produce good things, new things, and you and your company—and your country —will get credit. Not only money but credit. This is one reason for the almost obsessive cult of quality in Japan.

This felt need to produce and develop comes partly from a built-in sense of limitation in Japanese business. Americans traditionally think of their country as a boundless frontier, where anything good is possible; Japanese traditionally think of their country as a narrow place with restrictive boundaries, where anything bad might happen. This sense of limits paradoxically drives the Japanese manager to build for an uncertain future, in the hope that by his sound construction some of the limits can be overcome.

Each company community in Japan has its vital planning division, with much of its procedures and techniques adapted from American models. But unlike their counterparts in so many American companies, the Japanese planners resolutely think in long-range terms. The five-year plans and forecasts or the "blueprints" for Japan turned out by government agencies are reflected in corresponding long-range plans for individual companies and groups. Indeed, behind the tendency of Japanese companies to work in groups of enterprises lies the feeling that stronger and larger unities can plan better and longer.

A further impetus to development and long-range planning is the leadership of the Keidanren. Starting postwar as a grouping of existing business organizations to lobby for business interests, the Keidanren has grown into the acknowledged spokesman for all Japanese business. Its directors, more than 130 of them, comprise the elite of Japanese management. The organization is in the first instance a clearinghouse for the conversations that constantly go on among Japanese businesses; for however competitive they are, a certain degree of communication is maintained through the specific "trade organizations" *(gyokai)* for various businesses. Other affiliated organizations are important—notably the Japan Employers' Association, the Chamber of Commerce and Industry, and the progressive Committee for Economic Development (Keizai Dōyukai). The memberships often duplicate one another, but this disturbs no one. Communication at every level, however time-consuming, is one of Japanese management's strengths.

The Keidanren, however, is unique. There are no parallels to it in any other country. Through it, Japanese business can speak on important occasions with one voice. It is thus more than a clearinghouse. It acts as a force within Japan for continuing development, for expansion, for the Japanese brand of capitalism. Lastly, and by no means least, it channels funding support to Japan's government party, the pro-business Liberal Democrats.

5·The Integrity of the Company

One person is all persons; all persons are one person . . .
—the eleventh century Buddhist teacher Ryōnim

Du Pont takes over Conoco for a record $7.2 billion, beating out Mobil and Seagrams for its prize. U.S. Steel acquires Marathon, again frustrating Mobil, which then starts acquiring shares of U.S. Steel. American Express buys Shearson Loeb Rhodes for just under a billion and Occidental Petroleum acquires Iowa Beef Processors for more than $700 million. Standard Oil of Ohio buys Kennecott for $1.7 billion. Sears Roebuck takes over Dean Witter Reynolds, like Shearson Loeb Rhodes a securities firm; and Allegheny acquires Sunbeam for a mere half billion dollars, beating off an unfriendly offer by Illinois Central. Mobil exhibits digestive pains with its earlier acquisition, Montgomery Ward, and Exxon, facing more losses, ponders why it shelled out $1.2 billion for Reliance Electric. But the takeovers and sales and mergers go on.

One prominent banker, talking to *Newsweek,* spoke of a "feeding frenzy" in American business, while *Fortune,* ever the optimist, started a new "Deals of the Year" section in a January 1982 issue. Listing the big fifty mergers of 1981, *Fortune* concluded: "Last year was a fabulous one for big deals, for the people who helped make them and for the shareholders of companies other companies coveted."

Viewed from a less rosy perspective, the year seemed more like a monument to the survival of the fastest if not the fittest buck. Like predators confined in a small pond, big corporate fish pursued and whenever possible devoured their acquisitions. Even little fish, given enough ready cash by ichthyophagous bankers, puffed up to swallow big fellows almost twice as large as they. A specialized but highly lucrative new American growth industry developed, as investment bankers, management consultants, and the ubiquitous law firms took it upon themselves first to scout out possible acquisitions and next, in the event a corporate raid seemed likely, either to speed it along or fight it off. (The median fee for these corporate marriage brokers, in *Fortune*'s Big 50 tabulation, was something over $2 million.)

The words *unfriendly takeover* went into the financial lexicons. Which is to say: Company A, coveting the assets of Company B, arranges to carry off B by tender offers to the stockholders to buy their shares at considerably higher prices (in cash or A's stock) than what Company B's stock is now selling for. Once these tenders have been made, and sufficient pledges received, the suitor moves in for the final consummation of his deal. The president and directors of the company to be acquired, if they like the deal, prepare for the takeover and stand ready to cut the melon with their stockholders. If they do not want to be bought, merged, or traded, they huddle with their Wall Street lawyers, get the telephones humming, and then go off on frantic airborne odysseys to line up an alternate "white knight" taker-over, by one who is presumably more in tune with management's concerns. Meanwhile the board of the beleaguered company hastily passes resolutions designed to retain present management (by extended contracts) even in the event of a merger, thus ensuring loyal management's loyalty. Bidding can go up and up in such situations, with the stockholders of the acquired company in line for a windfall, whatever the outcome. Naturally, all the lawyers involved will grow richer.

The rationale behind the "feeding frenzy" is easy to see. Given the high cost of money in the United States at the outset of the eighties, organic expansion became very expensive. With the economy running at a slow speed, developing new products or new businesses on one's own can be even more risky than the treasurer has been saying. Cautious management, and its stockholders, generally find it far safer to buy a going concern than to strike out on their own. Few mergers generate added productivity. In fact, productivity is about the last thing on a merger-maker's mind. As opposed to A company's setting up a new subsidiary, hiring new people, developing a new market, or expanding its old one, A company's acquisition of B more probably results in large-scale firings, as A's accountants and efficiency experts move in to double up functions and eliminate "unprofitable" or marginal operations. Where a brand-new operation would create jobs, the merger or takeover tends to take them away. Of course there are exceptions. Sometimes a takeover gives the smaller company greater working capital and helpful management supervision. All too often, however, one of the first tasks for the new consolidated company's management is to see how many jobs, divisions, or subsidiaries can be eliminated.

Since the merged company is just as likely as not to be totally unrelated in products and markets to the corporation takeover (and top management of the original company will probably leave), decisions about the new division's fate may be left to financial men, who are not normally paid to make plans for product line development or speculate on future market potential. The important thing is to dress up the acquisition and its assets quickly, so the transaction will quicken the pulses of those reading the next quarterly report.

All this comes later. While the merger negotiations are going on, the pace is fast and frenetic. Citadels are stormed, alliances made, and enemies held at bay. What better war game could be invented to entertain and enrich red-blooded American businessmen? What better testimony to the caprices of U.S. tax laws, which have after all made the whole game so desirable?

Sitting in a Tokyo boardroom, and engaging in the small talk that follows the actual board meeting, I was recounting the experiences of one American chief executive officer in our merger wars. His company had recently resisted an unfriendly takeover and the story of how he did it was to me fascinating—a *Wall Street Journal* cliff-hanger. I had thought my Japanese listeners, all of them officers or board members of fairly large corporations, would be fascinated by it, too. Gradually I realized, however, that the story was not getting across. It was not that my Japanese was defective (this time). It was soon evident that the words were quite clear to them. It was just that the idea of an "unfriendly takeover" simply could not be comprehended.

"But surely this sort of thing could happen in Japan?" I questioned. "Can you think of any cases where it did happen? You have mergers here, I know." "Yes," said the company president, "it is theoretically possible, but I can't think of any examples." No one else could, either.

The fact is that the "unfriendly" takeover or even the friendly merger of companies, even with great benefit to the share positions of stockholders and management, is almost impossible for the Japanese to comprehend. In the big merger world of the U.S. conglomerates, companies are passed back and forth like chattels—little pieces in a real-life monopoly game. Not so in Japan. The American merger game as played in the early eighties would not be allowed in Japan, and only partly because of legal restrictions. It is just not done.

Mergers are infrequent in Japan; outside acquisitions are a rarity. When mergers occur they are generally within the same industry. Cases abound of an ailing company being taken over by a competitor, often after several nudges from the government. Two companies may combine or join forces in one way or another to get a bigger slice of their market. Or they may keep their identities and do this through a kind of cartel arrangement that is permitted in Japan, although definitely out of order under American law. When on rare occasion an unfriendly takeover has been attempted, it has been resisted and in at least one case stopped by the government.

Under Japanese law, also, a company cannot be traded or merged without the consent of more than two-thirds of its stockholders. Thus people holding one-third or more of the shares can stop a takeover or at least indefinitely delay it. Some companies in their charter require the consent of the board of directors before any change in the ownership can be approved. In this case, the composition of a Japanese board gives management an effective veto power over any unwanted amalgamation.

Conglomerates are the acknowledged princes of takeover strategies in America. Yet the postwar phenomenon of the American conglomerate—the stable of companies, as often as not totally unrelated to one another, acquired either for interesting assets, attractive tax loss possibilities, or a bargain price—is a rarity in postwar Japan. Although the four big prewar *zaibatsu* family companies might have been called conglomerates of a sort, they were broken up by the U.S. Occupation. The successor companies that sprang from *zaibatsu* roots now stick to their own lines of business.[1] It would be almost impossible for the conglomerate to develop in Japan. Japan has laws against holding companies, and there has been no movement to change them. American conglomerates like ITT, LTV, or Esmark could not have come into existence in the modern Japanese business environment.

Underlying this disinclination for merger American-style is a basic Japanese way of thinking about the company. A company's integrity in a literal sense is its most prized asset. Building the whole company is in fact an extension of the idea of hiring the whole man. The people factor is critical, where in an American context it seems all too marginal. As we have seen, the Japanese company is not merely a functional organization. It is a community, and an independent one. It does the work of a community in so many ways that it transcends the ideas and objectives of a mere economic organization.

By contrast, the American businessman views the company as a piece of property. As the property of its stockholders, it can be handled—preserved, augmented, or disposed of—more or less like any other piece of property. It is up to the proprietors, or more generally management, since shareholding in so many American companies is well enough diluted so that for practical purposes management can call the tune. Most American unions have thought the same way. Since the company is someone else's piece of property— certainly not theirs—whatever they can get out of it is good. So why not get as much as possible, whenever one can?

American business writers, some executives, and some union leaders often exhort companies in the United States to show more (or at least some) "corporate citizenship." Such appeals would seem odd to the Japanese, for the Japanese company is a corporate citizen by definition. Its role as such is taken for granted.

The Japanese worker's livelihood, as we have already discussed, is also his neighborhood. The same is true of the Japanese executive. He has settled in a particular company, like a colonist in a new country. He subscribes to that company's goals. He has helped construct them. He believes in the company's philosophy of doing business. He has helped work it out. There is no time clock counting out the limits of his company relationship. The company is part of his life. Its integrity is his integrity.

Thus the Japanese look on a merger or takeover far differently than we do. There was a time, or seemed to have been a time in

America, when similar attitudes of community and company commitment existed. But if we have not totally lost these attitudes, their remnants exist in isolation. The Japanese have thus far determinedly kept them. Any takeover would be a threat of great magnitude for both parties involved.

Partly out of instinct and tradition, partly by conscious design—as a means of diminishing the centrifugal pulls of modern, urban, technological living—the Japanese have transplanted to the corporation many social habits of the rice-growing village. The dedication to group goals, the task-sharing, the adjustments, the sense of mutual obligation are all there. From the moment the "new person" enters the company, as we have seen, he begins to develop a sense of loyalty to this particular business-social community. Over the years this intensifies and becomes distinctive, for depending on their leadership, situation, and history, companies develop their own styles and working patterns. To merge two such companies, their particular sets of people and hence two separate ideologies, is extremely difficult.

With us it is apparently different. Although there are exceptions to the rule, the American company typically worries only about merging talents and functions. Living in the storied land of interchangeable employee parts, we tend to think that anyone who can do his job well should fit into almost any company. It is largely a matter of qualifications. Not so in Japan. Dai Nippon Manufacturing Company K.K. may be in the same kind of business as Teikoku Nuts and Bolts K.K., but their people may be quite different. Where Dai Nippon's executives are virtually an old-boy network of Keio graduates, Teikoku's people are recruited from Waseda. Where one has a long relationship with the Mitsui Bank, the other may rely on Sumitomo. Where one does most of its production in-house in its own plants, the other may rely on a network of dependent subcontractors and subsidiaries. One favors tapping high-ranking bureaucrats to join its board of directors, the other does not. Such differences matter. They represent not merely a different choice of service but a different set of attitudes, in which two different sets of people have grown up. In short, even where companies perform the same functions, they will have different identities.

When a Japanese company wishes to expand or proliferate, therefore, its management typically prefers to do so "organically" *(kōzō-teki),* as the favorite expression goes, by spinning off subsidiaries or satellites. This is done in much the same way as the basic main household *(honke)* in the village spreads out into subhouseholds *(bunke),* or used to do before the farmers sold their land at high prices to a new golf course or development company. Like the household of a second or third son, the subhousehold subsidiary retains close ties with the parental hearth. It will be headed by executives spun off from the main company, chosen variously for their competence, independence, or on occasion, their failures or their opposition to the mainstream faction running the parent corporation. Some companies use subsidiaries as a kind of pasturage for tired but respected directors. Some set up subsidiaries to use the talents of surplus people in times of recession, for example, as a steel company creates a small taxi or trucking company or a specialized sales company or housing development company to run certain areas. Others will start new enterprises purely as an outlet for promising younger department heads who might otherwise be blocked and frustrated by the slow seniority rites of passage to director status.

Like all good colonies or subhouseholds, however, such subsidiaries will set up their own communities patterned on the parent, using at first the same services as the parent and indoctrinating their workers with the same home-company attitudes. Only after they have become self-supporting, generally after a long incubation period, do most such subsidiaries take on a life and character of their own. Until the late seventies, when a new law stipulated that Japanese companies must report the profits or losses of their subsidiaries on a consolidated basis, subsidiaries could be spun off with little risk of their business failure damaging the parent company's reputation or raising questions among the shareholders. Since then the approach to bearing new corporate children has been more cautious, but it is fundamentally unchanged.

As it grows and matures, the new Japanese company receives little of the painstaking scrutiny given the young American company by its leading shareholders, government regulatory bodies, national union headquarters, and the Wall Street mandarins who analyze companies' quarterly performances and regularly explain their prospects and problems to their clients, newspaper business editors, and any other concerned parties who will listen. Rarely if at all are management consultants hired to examine the Japanese company's objectives, check its efficiency, and recommend various changes, from new product mixes to the installation of vending machines for cutting down on coffee breaks. American management consultants hoping to find Japan a veritable El Dorado have found the pickings unusually slim.

There are, however, conversations, the inevitable informal *hana-shi-ai,* between parent company directors and the executives of the new subsidiary. These are supplemented by explanation session *(kondan kai)* meetings at which shareholders' representatives are informed of the company's progress, ask questions, and give advice. But this is small stuff, compared to the minute reporting demands on American corporation executives by their betters.

If the new company, after some running time, fails consistently to meet its objectives and profit prospects dim, it can be reorganized, amalgamated into another subsidiary, or simply dissolved. The Japanese are not afraid of corporate foldings or bankruptcies. Below the level of the big companies, in that 70 percent of Japanese industry comprising small businesses, local suppliers, and contract work forces for the large companies, the corporate death rate can be quite high. (In 1980, a bumper crop year for bankruptcies, there were 17,784 business failures in Japan.) But Japanese will interfere with the internal workings of another company only as a last resort.

Thus management and workers have a chance to carve out their own destiny. Having hired their quota of new "whole men," assisted by transplants from the older corporate family, the Japanese company, like the old village, sets out to solve its problems with only a minimum of second-guessers, nitpickers, and efficiency experts to help them. There is but one significant exception. That is the company's leading bank and to a lesser extent the other banks with which it does business.

The high financial leverage of Japanese companies is now legendary. I have already noted how Japanese companies tend to raise money by borrowing, as opposed to stock issues or other equity financing. Although companies like Matsushita and Toyota are significant exceptions to the rule, it is hardly unusual to have a debt to equity ratio of five to one. Equity capital still represents only about 20 percent of the total liability in Japanese manufacturing companies.

The bank is the one overseer that the company directors have to watch and heed. And here, too, comes the question of building up confidence. First, money will be loaned on a parent company guarantee or some other form of security. Gradually, assuming that the company does well—or shows promise—the local bank manager will feel more relaxed about his money. In Japan he is quite powerful.

With good prospects, the company can secure loans from other banks, encouraging what can be healthy competition. As the banks scrutinize operations, get to know the people involved, and develop a feel for the business, they grow more helpful. If a long-range plan is explained to them and in their judgment makes sense, Japanese banks will wait a long time for the profits to come. Sometimes their faith is misplaced, with disastrous results. But averaging it out, the errors of too much trust are less than the errors of too little.

One of the best ways to dramatize the difference between the Japanese whole company and its American counterpart is by examining their respective boards of directors and the philosophy behind them. Nowhere is the conflict more visible between the American adversary method of doing business and the Japanese idea of trust, organic growth, and inner-directed compromise.

Let us take two average, rather large companies, one American and one Japanese. Each is governed by a board of directors whose rubrics correspond to the general rules and practices for such bodies in both countries. On the surface they seem quite similar. Each board meeting is accompanied by appropriate rites and solemnities. There are canonical lunches, restrained greetings, and appropriate explanations, as management makes periodic accountings of its stewardship. In both companies there is no higher authority. The directors represent the shareholders and, according to well-established legal scripture, the directors make final decisions for the company. Their approval, as it is handed down, becomes a reasonable business approximation of Holy Writ. It enables management to proceed on its course, or alter it if need be, secure in the knowledge that past doings and proposals have been looked at, amended where necessary, and finally confirmed.

That, however, is where the similarity ends. The Japanese board, in accordance with long custom, is a working board. A good portion of its members are so-called working directors, people who have risen in the ranks of the company to become department heads and finally directors in charge of one or more facets of the company operations. The president of the company is, of course, an *ex officio* member. So are the vice-presidents, and the other "managing directors." For a Japanese salary man, becoming a director *(yakuin)* is the ultimate achievement. The result of good work, seniority, and connections—or a combination thereof—the director is selected and ensconced for regular terms, generally two years in length. When he becomes a director, he is exempted from the normal rules of seniority in a Japanese corporation. This can be good or bad. On the one hand, he no longer has to retire at the cutoff age of fifty-five or sixty, whatever it may be. Whether he is fifty, sixty, or eighty, he remains a director for his allotted term. At the same time he may no longer have the job security he once enjoyed as a department head. Directors can be summarily removed at the end of the term by a decision of top management, in consultation with the shareholders (or vice versa). Although nominally such a removal has to be voted on by his peers, the decision to extend his term or end it is generally taken well in advance and rarely, if ever, countermanded.

If he has grown up with the company, the Japanese director knows quite intimately the matters put to the board for discussion. He is free to express his opinion, if called on, and can do so with all the knowledge that long experience coping with the company's problems has given him. Formal expressions of opinion on important matters, however, are rarely called for at board meetings. They are heavily discussed at the monthly or biweekly executive sessions (*jōmukai*) of the working directors and only later prepared for the full board's scrutiny.

Matters on the agenda are rarely disapproved because any controversial proposal will have long since been submitted to the directors informally and the sense of the group already taken. If the sense of the group is bad, for instance, the proposals will probably never see the light of day. "Votes" as such are rarely taken.

By contrast, the board of directors in the American company includes only a few representatives of management. It is composed largely of outside directors. These are distinguished citizens who, because of their preeminence in their own businesses, their accumulated knowledge of business in general, the number of public service committees they serve on, their generally high visibility, or their friendship with present or past chairmen, have been invited to sit on the board.

In the past most American boards were composed of working directors, like the present Japanese variety, with only a minority of distinguished outsiders, most of them representing different groups of shareholders. As shareholding became, in the case of many public companies, hugely diversified, this was no longer so important. Yet by the same token too many insiders on a board could give the impression of a collusive management working in its own interest, not that of the stockholders. Public members, however, were harder to criticize. Indeed, highly visible representative faces were good for the company's reputation. A prominent lawyer on this side of the table, the chairman of a larger corporation sitting next to him, a former Cabinet member sitting across from them, with a college president (preferably, in recent years, a woman college president) next to him—what better image of probity for a company on the way up.

Originally such directorships were thought of as a great honor, not to mention a source of added income from directors' fees, which were often quite generous. Especially over the last decade, however, as the incidence of lawsuits against corporations increased, both individual, corporate, and class action, directors found themselves personally liable for the company's actions. One prominent American, a former Cabinet officer himself, expressed a general concern when he resigned from his directorship of a large airline, pointing out that to give an intelligent opinion on matters put before the board, he would have to hire his own technical staff, a separate marketing expert, an accountant, and another lawyer (he was one himself). He was obviously unwilling to assume these added burdens.

In the classic American business tradition, the outside directors come in to their board meeting several times a year, hear plans and proposals, and give their judgment. In theory, this is based on what they know about the company, and what their stored-up knowledge of business tells them is good or bad. In practice, their judgment is generally based on what the chairman and loyal management tell them. Some directors will, of course, represent other corporations or groups of shareholders with significant stock interest. Often the interests that one of these "outside-inside" directors represents will be either hostile to management and the controlling stockholders or simply interested (hostility aside) in gradually increasing its shares to the point where control of the corporation can be had.

In many companies the meetings of the board are cloaked in a kind of arcane dignity best compared to proceedings of college secret societies in the twenties. Management representatives are left cooling their heels in the corridors while the chairman and his favorite outside directors go into executive session to determine a variety of individual or corporate fates. Sometimes the chairman or the president himself will be dethroned in a quick vote of the board, without any advance warning. (When Robert Sarnoff was forced to resign as chairman of RCA, for example, he heard about it only at the time of the meeting.) In cases of sharp disagreement, the name of the game, as we are told, is to "get the votes." After lining up their votes in advance, the majority faction will then check their Renaissance cloaks and doublets in the coatroom, while they go inside the board chambers for some good old-fashioned adversary voting. Debate, face-offs, and disputes are part of the tradition. They show us that the adversary process is working and the board meeting is not just a matter of rubber-stamping approval. To hammer out policy at the highest level is after all what a board of directors is for.

This is not so in Japan. A Japanese company may have just as many tactical disputes, personality conflicts, and policy disagreements as an American company, but they are handled differently. Where the American corporate argument is premised on principle that one side must be *RIGHT* and therefore the other must be *WRONG,* the Japanese corporate argument is premised on the generally subscribed truism that proving someone "right" or "wrong" is secondary to the company's successful survival. Besides, Japanese generally feel that no disputant has a monopoly on the truth and a bit of compromise never hurt anyone.

The board meeting in Japan, therefore, is regarded as a place where decisions are ratified, not debated. What differences of view existed should have been fought out and harmonized *before* the board meeting, not during it.[2] If confrontations occur, it is a sign not that the process is working, but that it has failed.

More than the other differences, the matter of board representation underlines the widely differing ideas about business, management, and ultimate authority in the two countries. The Japanese feel, logically to their mind, that the directors should represent the people in the company as well as the shareholders. The directors representing the company's people are generally greater in number than those representing the shareholders, because it is assumed that they know more about the company and are in a better position to direct its destinies. This is almost the opposite of American thinking on this subject, which sets great store in having directors who can be "unbiased" and objective, because they are presumably disinterested. To most Japanese this American system seems very strange. When a friend of mine was elevated to a directorship in a Japanese corporation some years ago, he asked me rather casually at what point his opposite numbers in an American company would become directors. I told him that it was highly unlikely that they ever would be. He was almost incredulous. "But what happens in your company when a man has run one or more departments successfully for a while and reaches director status? Does he have to be the president or does he have to retire?"

"Neither," I said, "we Americans don't think the management, except for the president and a vice-president or two, should necessarily be on the board. We used to have a lot of inside management directors in companies, like you today. But companies were criticized for this. After all, if all the directors were officers, wouldn't they just rubber-stamp their own pet plans and projects, without anyone to watch them and blow the whistle? If we have outside directors, though, they can be relied on to give a clear, unbiased judgment of what's going on. Normally we trust them to see that management doesn't try any hanky-panky, or do anything to interfere with good dividends for the stockholders."

"That's a pretty untrusting way you have," said my Japanese director friend. "If you can't trust the management to become directors, you must not be able to trust them at all. Why don't you fire them or change your personnel practices?"

"No, that's not necessary," I explained. "We're just putting temptation out of their way by keeping them off the board. That way we'll assure clear, unbiased, objective decisions on anything."

"But you've just said that the board members don't really know much about the company. Won't they be spoon-fed something by the president or the chairman, and end up rubber-stamping proposals which they might well have examined far in advance?"

"Clearly you don't understand our adversary system," I said. "As we Americans were all products of original sin in the first place, we always felt that special laws and safeguards should be set up to be sure that no one takes advantage of anyone else—and reverts to type. That's why we need a clean, unbiased, and objective-thinking board of directors, however little they might know about the company."

"But even if I accept your premise," my Japanese friend continued, "who checks the board of directors?"

"That's an easy one," I said. "For that we have the Securities and Exchange Commission. Every director has to make periodic reports when he purchases or acquires any stock in the company on whose board he sits. The SEC is always worried that outside directors will come in, do nothing about helping the company but try to make a killing for themselves with some cute stock deals. So the SEC people watch public company directors like hawks."

"But your government has other things to do than watch directors, doesn't it?" the new Japanese director asked.

"That's true," I replied, "especially with all the Reagan cutbacks. But it's not just the U.S. government they have to be afraid of. There are state laws, too. And if a company gets into trouble these days, the directors can be individually sued. Corporate lawsuits involving directors are splashed all over the papers. They have to watch out. In fact, most new directors now insist that a company give them trustee's insurance to pay off any successful lawsuits against them. It's a big responsibility to be an outside director now."

"Your country is certainly a good place for lawyers and insurance companies," my Japanese friend commented.

"We have our problems," I conceded, "but that's the old checks and balances system—just what Thomas Jefferson and those other lawyers who wrote our Constitution had in mind. I think our system may still be better than yours, though. Think of all the dirty linen that Japanese company directors can sweep under the rug."

"But why should they hide anything?" asked my Japanese friend. "If they have spent their lives working for the company they probably want things to turn out best for the company. If their plans for new financing or expansion seem unrealistic, their leading bank will stop them anyway. And there are also the shareholders' representatives. Anyway, we can trust them."

"Trusting people can be very dangerous," I said, "that's why American businessmen are always watching each other. And since management might not really be trustworthy, they have a separate board of directors to watch them. So we're really insured from any double-dealing."

"But most of those outside directors don't know anything about the company," said my friend. "You admitted that. How can any system like this work?"

"Let's talk about something else," I said.

6·Company Unions That Work

Without conflict we cannot make any progress. Nevertheless we must maintain harmony. After all, the worker cannot improve his conditions unless the company performs efficiently enough to finance better pay and benefits.
—Takahata Keiichi, former president,
Matsushita Electric Ind. Workers' Union

In the huge body of folklore now accumulating in the United States about Japanese business and management successes, the membership of a typical Japanese enterprise union appears as an extension of Snow White's industrious dwarfs, happily whistling the Matsushita company song or some variant as they march from factory to the company basketball court and back, all the while thinking of extra ways to improve productivity that they will share with their mates at the voluntary after-hours meeting of the local quality control circle. Although they threaten to strike occasionally, we are told that Japanese unionists rarely do, because they are too loyal to their company, in accordance with a mysterious "clan" tradition. They only want security and they have it. Their quality standards are as spotless as the clean green uniforms with Sony, Toyota, Nissan, or Ishikawajima-Harima sewn on the back.

Seen within Japan, from the standpoint of a Japanese company executive, the Seven Dwarfs' Technicolor gives way to the harsh black-and-white of snake-dancing unionists making a mess of the company cafeteria, as they scream out denunciations of management, in highly personal terms, before making a rush on the directors' offices to see whom they can trap into seven-hour kangaroo courts disguised as bargaining sessions. Younger union members, especially, seem to be worrying about themselves a lot more than they might have worried about the old company; and there is even a little talk of deserting to the competition around the corner. Although long strikes are infrequent, workers are quick to take strike votes and occasionally carry them out in short but sharp temporary work stoppages. They are masters also of the slowdown or the "work to rule" technique. Their continual posting of "demands," even apart from the classic "spring struggle" and bonus struggles, can keep a sizable portion of a company's personnel staff occupied and harried.

The two views of Japanese union people surely express a logical contradiction. But Japanese have seldom been bothered by contradictions. If some people insist that holding proposition A makes proposition B untenable—and vice versa, the Japanese have historically been content with keeping both A and B, without arguing out the inconsistencies between them. This is on the tested principle that what is useful you keep and incorporate into your tradition and beliefs, while what is less useful you can just quietly leave on the temple floor.

With this caution in mind, let us now praise famous union men; and appreciate the Japanese worker and union member, faults and virtues taken together, who is at root responsible for the high-growth economy known familiarly among American and Europeans as Japan's economic miracle. There is nothing like him in the Western world, although in China, Taiwan, Korea, Hong Kong, and Singapore, at least, people understand how he operates and would emulate him more faithfully if their governments permitted.

A few statistics will dramatize his situation. Not surprisingly, he works longer hours than his opposite numbers in the United States and Europe. In 1980 the average weekly number of hours spent on the job by a production worker in manufacturing was 43.5 in Japan, as compared to 37.3 in the United States and 37.2 in the Federal

Republic of Germany. He has also done very well for himself. Between 1972 and 1980 a production worker's average hourly wage in Japan rose from 422 yen to 1,090 yen, while in the United States it increased from $4.13 to $7.96.[1] Since inflation in recent years has been controlled far more successfully in Japan, the actual increase to the Japanese worker is greater. Using 1970 as an index year (1970 = 100), the Japanese worker was getting 147 percent of that in 1980, while the American worker's real wage index for that year was only 103.6 percent. During the same period, as we have seen elsewhere, the Japanese worker's productivity continued to rise at a level far higher than that of his American counterpart, thus making his raises a relatively painless business expense, not a seriously inflationary cost.

Out of Japan's working population of roughly 40 million, some 12,369,000 souls were union members as of 1980. The unionization rate of almost 31 percent, while less than the peak 35 percent of 1970, is appreciably higher than the 23 percent unionization rate in the United States, although lower than in the United Kingdom (57.4 percent) and West Germany (41.9 percent). The union presence in Japanese life is a strong one, and ubiquitous—at least as strong as in the United States. Newspapers and other media pay serious, respectful attention to union demands and problems. Rarely a week goes by in Tokyo or other large cities without an assortment of union rallies, meetings, or demonstrations against one aspect of government or industry policy. Yet for all this, the annual number of days lost in labor disputes in Japan is only a fraction of that in the United States. In 1979, American industry lost 33 million man-days because of labor disputes, but Japanese industry lost only 930,000. In 1977 the relative figures were 35,822,000 and 1,518,000. Even in 1974, a bad year for labor peace statistics, the unusually high figure of 9,663,000 man-days lost in Japan was far below the 47,991,000 man-days lost in the United States.

This forbearance can be at least partially credited to the Japanese worker's sense of community. When an American worker is asked his morning destination, he will generally say he is going to "work." The Japanese will almost invariably say he is going to the company. As we have noted, the associations with his fellows in the company mean a great deal to the Japanese worker. He is a member of a working community—*Gesellschaft* and *Gemeinschaft* welded as Max Weber never dreamed of—and he values his membership. The company is his neighborhood. Although the bonds of schoolmates and college contemporaries are strong, and there may well be many friends in the worker's actual neighborhood, it is generally his company contacts that count most. This may not be so true now as it was for an earlier generation. But it is still true enough so that a departure from the Japanese company is less like moving than divorce.

With this primary social loyalty in mind, we may understand more readily why more than one-third of Japan's union membership belongs to enterprise unions, that is, unions that are organized within one company only. Of the remainder, about one-third are part of the General Council of Japanese Trade Unions (Sōhyō); the final third is divided among two other union groups, the Japanese Federation of Labor (Dōmei) and the Japanese Federation of Independent Unions (Churitsurōren). Of these Sōhyō's membership is largely composed of government civil servants. Denied by law the right to strike, and restricted in their negotiating demands by government budgets, Sōhyō has concentrated on political activity, almost always in support of the Japan Socialist party and against the conservative Liberal Democratic government. Dōmei is affiliated with the moderate Democratic Socialist party and Churitsurōren with no party at all. Both the latter unions tend to stick to economic demands in their struggle tactics. Sōhyō, on the contrary, has tried over the years to divert its members' attention to political demands against the government, with increasingly disastrous results for itself.

Even where a national union federation tie exists, however (Sōhyō's civil servants excepted), the action is with the enterprise union in the single company: a phenomenon peculiar to the Japanese. When an American or Englishman uses the words *company union,* it is generally as a pejorative. A company union is a creature of the company, which does what the bosses tell it. In Japan this is not the case. Some of the most violent union disputes have been the intrafamily struggles of the enterprise unions. To the workers it is *their* company just as much as management's. And, indeed, most Japanese managements would agree with them. This is a basic difference of premise between Japanese and American business. Yet the interaction of Japanese workers and managements makes sense only if this premise is accepted and understood. Dues are used primarily to support the company union; little, if any, goes to support national headquarters.

In union negotiations in the United States and, particularly, in Britain, union leaders, in constant touch with national headquarters, will tend to orchestrate the demands of individual company or factory locals to harmonize with the broader objectives of the national union. These, if fulfilled, are presumed to raise the ante for everyone. In Japan, however, the union negotiators are generally interested in one company only—their own. Their demands are made within the context of the company's current ability to meet them, with an eye toward the effect on the company's long-term prosperity. The most militant struggle directors are "company men" as much as union men. But their demands against management can be very tough.

Aggressive union leadership, in fact, is generally rewarded in Japanese companies by quick promotion. There is no better way for a rising young man to improve his position than by causing the company untold trouble, as chairman of the union's executive committee. One of my longtime Japanese friends, now a department head in a major electronics company, found quick promotion in exactly this way. An engineer by trade, he had signed on out of college as a junior engineer in the company's Osaka office. At the university, he had been a star of the debating team. He used his fluency to good purpose and quickly made a name for himself at union meetings as an alert, persuasive speaker. Within a few years he was elected to a spot on the executive committee of the factory union. (In Japanese companies white- and blue-collar employees generally belong to the same union, with no difference in their position.) In another year or two my friend became the chairman. As chairman of the executive of an assembly line union, despite his own white-collar professional status, he gave the company a difficult time. Again and again he won concessions with a combination of clever argument, significant threat, and opportune compromise. The union had not often secured such successes.

Was he singled out for reprisal by management? On the contrary, in a time-honored Japanese tradition, he was promoted to the supervisory staff ahead of his time. In this way his talent was rewarded, while his abilities were denied to his union comrades.

I could easily name about half a dozen personal friends and acquaintances who have pushed their way up in their companies through successful troublemaking in their union's "struggle." This promotion route in most Japanese companies is well established. It encourages young union activists to work hard for the union, in the knowledge that the end result of their efforts is not only a better deal for their fellows, but quite possibly a particularly better deal for themselves. Ironically, the first big job that such former union stars receive is often a responsible post in labor relations, with the task of beating back the demands of their successors on the union executive committee.

According to Keidanren statistics, at least one out of six top Japanese business leaders have earlier in their careers served as members of their local union's executive committee. In no other industrial country does such a close connection exist between management and labor responsibilities. Conversely, no other industrialized country has such weak national control over its unions by labor federations or such strong local direction from enterprise unions in single companies.

The reasons for such peculiarities are grounded in recent history. Trade unions had existed in Japan since the Meiji era and started to thrive a bit in the so-called Taisho democracy of the twenties, but hard times and the hard-shelled paternalism of prewar Japanese companies were not conducive to rapid union growth. By the late thirties, as the militarists established their control over Japan, all workers were summarily organized into one huge state-controlled organization and private unions were abolished.

At the war's end all this changed. One of the most lasting reforms of the U.S. Occupation was a sweeping series of labor standards laws and codes, drafted by the bright young men of the SCAP labor section and other economic divisions in an effort to create a dynamic trade union movement. In October 1945, General MacArthur advised the Japanese government that trade unions would henceforth be not merely allowed but actively encouraged. A basic trade union law, setting up labor's basic right to organize and bargain collectively, was rushed through the Diet that December; and over the next two years other supporting labor legislation followed. The growth of union membership which resulted was unprecedented in history. By the beginning of 1947, Japanese union membership, which had never numbered more than a few hundred thousand prewar, shot up to five million. With active encouragement from U.S. Occupation headquarters and military government teams, workers organized themselves in factory after factory and started bargaining with management. National unions were slow to organize themselves, however, partly because of the sheer difficulties of getting from one place to another in that period. Hence it became customary to concentrate union strength in the single enterprise. In any case there were few national labor issues. Each company posed its own peculiar problems, which kept the new unions quite busy.

The national federations that did grow up, at first heavily dominated by Communists and socialists, tended to seize on political demands, for example, against capitalism and for a socialist society, as a way to mobilize a national membership. This not only lost them the support of the Occupation, which suppressed the planned general strike in 1947, but began to alienate many Japanese workers, basically conservative people whose main interest lay in improving salary and working conditions. During the fifties, strikes and other disturbances, often accompanied by real violence, were the order of the day. In the huge Tokyo demonstrations against the Occupation and later, in 1960, denouncing the proposed visit of President Eisenhower to Japan, labor activists were prominent. Sōhyō gave the demonstrations much of their leadership.

Especially as the results of the Prime Minister Ikeda Hayato's high-growth policy began to appear, in the form of greatly increased wages and better job opportunities, a radical approach lost whatever fascination it might once have held for Japanese working people. Ikeda's "Double Your Income" policy was a far more effective watchword than the tired slogans on the red banners, particularly since it was obviously working out in practice. By the late sixties the annual May Day parades in Tokyo, although still billed by their sponsors as struggle rallies of workers fighting for Marxist revolution, began to look more and more like family outings. The slogans and the banners may have been militant, but it was quite clear that the people in the processions weren't cross at anybody. Sōhyō's well-heeled "proletariat," significantly enough, made up a large portion of the 90 percent of the Japanese people who regularly reported themselves in the newspaper polls as "middle-class."

The national election of 1972, in which the Socialists, backed to the hilt by Sōhyō's union leadership, won 118 seats in the Diet, was the high watermark of Japan's political unionism, at least for the next decade. As the Confucian capitalists successfully weathered the strains of the 1973 oil crisis and continued to move the economy ahead, union executives throughout the country grew increasingly nervous about tie-ups with national federations which were politically directed—in Sōhyō's case, at least nominally dedicated to achieving a Marxist revolution. Slowly but steadily, Sōhyō has been losing strength, while the enterprise unions have been expanding. A powerful reason that Japanese unions avoid close ties with a national federation is their dislike of having political activism forced on them from above.

Admittedly there are abuses of the enterprise union system. At union elections supervisors often indicate which slate the company favors, with not so subtle suggestions that members vote that way. Company managing directors, with friends or protégés on the union executive committee, have been known to use union pressure, apparently spontaneous, to sponsor policies they themselves advocate or to make trouble for their rivals. One company president of my acquaintance used to have regular meetings with a trusted subordinate, currently head of his local's executive committee, to plan union tactics for denouncing a policy that the president himself was unable to oppose publicly. Backroom deals are made to reduce the union's demands or to increase the company's offer during negotiations. Abuses aside, it is as natural for the union to push for a friendly director in charge of labor relations as it is for the company to lobby on behalf of favored candidates for the union's executive.

Despite Western conventional union wisdom to the contrary, the enterprise union in Japan works. Management and labor both realize that the other party has the company's interests as its primary concern. They work out their differences within the framework of this premise. And both sides thus far have done very well. As an article in *Asahi* editorialized: "Obviously the cooperation of the Japanese enterprise union and the company looks to outsiders like the contestants in a three-legged race. But many here prefer to think of them as two parties working *isshin-dōtai*—heart and soul together."

There is a lesson here for Americans schooled to think of labor and management doomed to a perpetual sword's point adversary relationship. As an American of moderately liberal view, I had always felt that the union and management represented a constant "we versus they." "They," if you happened to be on the union side, were an abstract entity called management, which suggested images of Republicans, big business, boards of directors, profit-making, and economic privilege. Whereas the labor "we" connoted working people's rights, the AFL-CIO, Democrats, civil liberties, and the obligation never to cross a picket line, as well as the normal bread-and-butter aspirations of higher wages and more benefits. In Japan, as a member of management, I first felt myself affronted and threatened by the obvious concern of the union not merely to get bigger wage gains, but to interfere in what I had come to feel were the sacred decision-making prerogatives of management. It took me some time to realize that the Japanese enterprise union does not think so much in terms of we and they, but rather of our stake in the company and their stake in the company. It was hard to imagine a newly organized

American union, composed largely of thirty-year-olds, making their second big "struggle" issue the extension of the retirement age from fifty-five to sixty. But they did in our Japanese company. It was their company, after all, and they wanted to stay around.

This identification of a labor union with a single company has paradoxically made the Japanese enterprise union far stronger on the average than local chapters of a national trade or craft union in Britain or the United States—and far better resistant to layoffs, lockouts, plant closures, or other recession tactics. When enterprise union members in Japan fight hard and bargain tough, even when they resort to slowdowns or strikes, they can never be denounced as aliens trying to wreck the company. Theirs is no open conflict. At the worst it is civil dispute, with both parties insisting that their view of things is better for the company. Such disputes rarely escalate into war, for the company is everybody's country.

It is this identification of union and management goals—however far apart the means suggested for realizing them—that has made it possible for Japanese companies to proceed with the drastic labor savings involved in computerization or robotization without drawing on themselves the explosive reactions that have greeted such innovations in the United States and elsewhere. Standing in the shadow of the extraordinary steelworks of Nippon Kōkan at Ohgishima, possibly the most modern steel mill in the world, I asked the obvious question of one of the plant's executives: "How did you ever get the union to put up with all of this?"

The man answered:

> We first had to talk to the union years in advance of building the new Ohgishima works and explain exactly what we had in mind. The jobs here would be far fewer, of course, but they were good jobs. We were eliminating the dirty jobs. No one wants a dirty job if he can avoid it. Union members knew that they would either be trained for the new jobs or transferred to other branches where new and better jobs awaited them. We planned for this far in advance.
>
> Of course, we know that our situation is different from that of the United States. You have new minorities continually emigrating to America or coming up in the job market—and they will do the dirty jobs for a while. But in Japan the labor market is not so big. We realize that once employed by a large company, union members must have almost total job security. Even when the recession comes, a Japanese company will go to almost any lengths to avoid outright firings.

Company Unions That Work

The executive knew whereof he spoke. Before becoming a department head, he had enjoyed a very successful tour on the union's executive committee.

Before we leave this subject, it might be useful to describe in some detail what goes on in the spring struggle *(Shuntō)*, still the visible climax of union-management negotiating. There is nothing quite like it anywhere in the world. For those foreigners who managed businesses in Japan, it was a time of inconvenience and incongruities and rare adversarial controversies, the surfacing as it seemed of the pent-up grievances and discontents of the cold, clammy winter.

The timing seemed oddly fitting, for spring is Japan's favorite and best season. Spring in Japan, according to the classic *haiku* poet Basho, means the eye feasting on new green leaves, the song of the cuckoo on the mountainside, the delicious taste of the first bonito *(katsuo)* to be caught in the ocean waters.[2]

To the harassed company director in charge of labor relations *(romutantō torishimariyaku)*, the harbingers of spring in sight and sound are less pleasant. His new green leaves are the view of hundreds of red banners flying at outdoor union rallies, and factory office walls plastered with signs and posters denouncing the meanness of management and calling on every ablebodied worker to get out and fight for the union in its lonely struggle for Japanese workers' rights. Not for him the cry of the cuckoo. Instead there are cadenced choruses of "we're against it!" *(hantai! hantai!)*, as the company's union membership, arms locked and eyes rolling slightly, scream advance denunciations of the company's "base-up" increase in wages and benefits to be offered in that year. For him the spring taste of bonito is more like the piece of the company's hide which the union plans to have with its optimal wage and benefits package.

The spring labor struggle came into being in 1955, when several national unions began a concerted drive for a general wage increase in several industries. Significantly the national federations agreed to set basic goals for wage increases and struggle timetables only. To the individual unions in companies and factories was left the actual base-up package proposal, as well as the pace and manner of negotiations. Then newer unions in the major industries acted as pacesetters for the others. But in almost every case it was the enterprise union in each single company which called the tune.

Over the years the spring struggle has grown into a national institution, quite unlike any labor drive anywhere else in the industrialized world. Typically Japanese, it has two sides to it: ritualized mass demonstration outside and meticulous, mathematical horse trading on the inside. The demonstrations are there for all to see. From the big national Sōhyō rallies in Tokyo and Osaka, filled with labor politicians on the podium, to the unionized workers of a small company, cheering out their calls for solidarity and doing their modest version of a riot snake dance between the cupboards and desks of their normal work space, Japanese union people are standing up to be counted. And with rare exceptions, everybody belongs to the same local union. White-collar employees and factory workers, drivers and technicians, skilled and unskilled, veterans and apprentices are there to demonstrate solidarity. The Japanese union has separated itself into neither crafts nor trades, and this is a source of its unity and strength. When this year's joint struggle committee steps up to talk to management, they are representing just about every union worker in the company—and whether nonunion people wish it or not, the union sets out to speak for all the employees. The agreements it negotiates hold true for everyone.

Once the struggle begins, it continues like the ritual it has become. It is an assertion of labor's right to equality. The shouted slogans, the posters that cover the walls, the denunciations of company officials at the *danko*—the Japanese abbreviated term for joint bargaining session—resemble nothing so much as a giant high school cheer rally or baseball fans yelling at the umpire. Walking past union meetings like ours at these times, I half expected to see a couple of "BEAT STATE" banners on the wall. Some years back I noted the surprise of a fellow American businessman in Tokyo, running an American-owned magazine publishing house, who offered a handsome two-year contract to his union—more than they were asking —if its members would forgo the time-consuming rituals of the spring struggle and the comparable autumnal bonus "struggle." He was turned down to the accompaniment of some indignation that he would so trifle with a cherished union "right."

Yet during "struggle" periods, actual time away from work is kept to a minimum. Most strikes, unlike those in American labor disputes, are scheduled not at the end of a bitter negotiation, as a last recourse, but at the beginning of a struggle, as a sign that the union is in earnest. They rarely last very long. A strike can be of only a half day's duration or a few hours. And such strikes are frequently held at midday or just before closing time. Slowdowns and work-to-rule strikes—the irritating *junpō*—are much in vogue. At one point my own company's unionists adopted a stratagem where only a few people in one department actually went on strike for a day, or even a few hours. Work was so interdependent that this effectively destroyed the general work schedule, although only a few were docked any salary for their strike.

While the struggle committee runs its mass meetings and workers with red headbands *(hachimaki)* and armbands to match advertise to the outside world labor's discontent, the real work is being done by the amateur mathematicians on both the union and the company side. It is they who devise and revise complex formulas for increases in basic salary, housing and family allowances, transportation allowances, with extra efficiency and incentive increments in some cases, and in almost all cases, special differentials for high school and college graduates. From the biggest unions to the smallest, the practice varies little. The first set of union struggle "demands" is high and often imaginative to the point of fantasy, with every possible asking point figured in. Not only must wages go up, but allowances must change, proposed merit raises be curtailed, the retirement age level raised, and all new company products and policies receive prior union approval. So the recital goes.

By contrast, the company's original reply suggests an economic picture of bleak, Dickensian poverty. In the course of preparing this "answer" the company personnel specialists are constantly comparing notes with affiliates or others in the same industry, to work out something like a general level of proposal. (The unions are doing the same.) While pencils are being sharpened for the calculations, the company labor relations team goes forth to battle around the bargaining table, where the union goal is to weaken them by sheer force of numbers and constant browbeating into making substantive concessions.

The company answer is promptly denounced by the union as arrogant effrontery. A ritual of mutual recrimination continues. Another union demand, another answer. More checking to see what everybody else is doing, more sound and fury. And it happens every spring.

Outsiders are generally excluded from union-management negotiations, which to most Japanese have the status of an interfamilial dispute. Even when a particular union is part of a cohesive national federation, the experts called in from Tokyo headquarters to help out with negotiations are kept in the background. More frequently, delegations from unions in affiliated companies stop by to give their vocal support—generally at high decibel levels—to the local union objectives. This can take the form of demonstrations outside the company or at the improvised union struggle headquarters inside. Once they have brandished the local posters, handed out leaflets, and made a few speeches, the outside sympathizers go swiftly on their way (particularly since the clockers at the personnel departments in their own companies are busy estimating the amount of pay to be deducted for this unauthorized absence). Such outsiders are rarely welcome inside the bargaining room. When they do appear, they tend to make the local unionists just a bit uneasy, besides giving the company a golden opportunity for claiming that other interests are "interfering" with normal peaceful bargaining processes.

Companies for their part keep any nonstaff labor advisers (generally a lawyer or two) in the background. Even when the going gets rough and the union blockades whole floors, isolating executives in their offices for hours or sometimes a day or two at a time, management rarely calls for police help or protection. For one thing, the police in Japan are notably chary of breaking up any labor "demonstration" that stops short of actual riot. Long experience of harassment by labor lawyers and Socialist party Diet members—not to mention denunciations of police brutality in the left-leaning press—has made officers of the law notably unresponsive to company calls for help. In fact, the company prefers not to call for help. To the Japanese manager, it seems far better to assume the attitude of a patient, long-suffering parent, permissively giving unruly "children" their heads, rather than seem repressive or hardhearted. If the blockades and kangaroo court sessions of a few directors become extreme, the rank-and-file unionists gradually begin to sympathize with the company's position. The director in charge of personnel and labor relations may have a ghastly week of sleepless nights in the process, but this will be well remembered at bonus time.

Actual violence in such confrontations is surprisingly low. The bitter and often bloody labor fights of the late forties and fifties are only a dim memory. If shouting, pushing, and shoving give way to blows or if company property is damaged the least bit, however, then the rules of the ball game change drastically. For selfish reasons, both sides try to avoid this eventuality.

Our own company had its share of labor problems, notably in its early and middle days. We were a new company, with a strong American affiliation. Both factors tend to make Japanese workers worry about a company's long-term survival chances. Only rarely did an actual daylong strike take place, but, in the early days, at least, we had our share of scuffles. The union struggle committee, for example, followed by a train of supporters, might attempt to rush the directors' offices, to conduct on-the-spot "negotiations" with whatever luckless director happened to be caught there. Sometimes a thin line of supervisors and personnel department staffers, arms locked in front of the office entrance, would succeed in stopping the rush. One begins to realize why stout men with broad shoulders are useful in this function. But generally the struggle committee and their followers—banners, posters, and pamphlets at the ready—would succeed in breaking into "officers' country" to deliver their message.

Rarely do they catch any of management in residence. Intelligence networks inside the company almost always warn the directors in time to make an ignominious getaway. In my case, we would then gather at the temporary "spring struggle" command post, generally high up in the nearby hotel, to plan the company's countermeasures, leaving the union free to plaster our office area with stimulating posters urging us to participate in group negotiations. "COWARDS, COME OUT AND NEGOTIATE!" "STOP WORKER OPPRESSION NOW!" "MEET OUR DEMANDS OR THE COMPANY WILL BE DESTROYED!" "FOREIGN GORILLA, TAKE OFF YOUR PHONY MASK OF CULTURE!" were typical samples of their evocative prose.

On occasion they would trap one of the directors in his office and devote the next three or four hours to what was essentially a screaming and slogan session, in the hope that he might wilt under pressure and give up some substantive concession. Hearing about one such capture, I asked my fellow directors at our hotel suite why we simply couldn't call the police and rescue him. The answer was a sharp one. "Not a chance. Even if we called them, the police would never come. They'd be accused of interfering with the right of Japanese workers to bargain freely. That's in the law."

"A stupid kind of law to have," I said.

"Thank yourselves for that," one of my colleagues said. "You Americans wrote all these labor laws during the Occupation. You loaded them in favor of the unions and we've never been able to get them repealed."

A friend of mine who ran a small retail business with several branches around the country once had the extent of police nonintervention in labor disputes drastically demonstrated, when a group of union organizers from Sōhyō visited his Tokyo headquarters to protest his anti-union attitude. The discussion grew heated. He ordered them out, then tried to eject them, and in the scuffle was himself thrown down the stairs. By this time his secretary had managed to slip out and call the police, who promptly took the organizers down to a nearby police box for questioning. It proved inconclusive. After little more than a half hour they were released, with apologies from the police for having interfered with their peaceful organizing role. When the executive complained, the police were all in sympathy with his view. "This is a labor matter, however," they explained to him, "and as such it must be handled with great delicacy. After all, we didn't actually see them throw you down the stairs. So what can we do?

"The one thing we might suggest is that you wait for another such visit and then warn us in advance. Get some witnesses in your office. If they throw you down the stairs again, with the proper witnesses, we've got them."

Recently history was made, in a minor way, when a group of salesmen, organized into an "association" of their own, took umbrage at the union activists in an affiliate who had tried to recruit salespeople into a new union.

The angry salesmen piled into buses, drove to the unionists' company, and raided union headquarters there, in the process pushing, shoving, and otherwise manhandling the union leadership. Desperate, the union called the police for protection. The local officers responded, shaking their heads in amazement to find this union, whose members had been distinguished for their kangaroo court approach to management negotiations, calling for help in a similar situation. The salesmen were let off with a gently administered warning.

Revealing as they are of certain Japanese attitudes, such incidents should not be overemphasized. They all happened in relatively small companies. Among the big ones the interplay between union and management, even at "struggle" times, is well planned. For all its shouts of protest and formal confrontation, the "struggle" is quite different from the real adversary posture of management and labor in the United States or Britain. Both sides move according to plan, at the pace of a fast minuet. If the director in charge of labor relations and his people have done their job, they will have been in constant contact with the union, over a period of months, so that they have a good idea of what will finally be asked at "struggle" time—and what expected. Conversely, if the members of the union's executive committee have done *their* jobs well, they will have a good idea of what the company is prepared to give readily as well as what might be extracted grudgingly.

Since everyone in the company knows rather accurately how well it is doing, there is rarely much doubt about the general contours of the settlement. If it has been a bad year, management generally starts by ordering a 10 percent salary cut for executives and department heads. National union headquarters rarely interfere—except in the case of Sōhyō, whose "public sector" workers are essentially negotiating with the government. It would be unthinkable in Japan to have a national headquarters countermand their local's acceptance of wage concessions, as has happened in the United States.

After all, everybody is in the same company; they all know one another very, very well. And such struggles are rarely seen by anyone as a fight to the finish. They are all won on points. Although excesses on one side or another have occurred in the past, it is striking how closely the "base-up" wage increase tracks the ups and downs of the commodity price increase. In 1976, for example, the increase was 8.8 percent, while the consumer price index went up 9.3 percent; in 1977, 8.8 percent as against 8.1 percent; in 1978, 5.9 percent to 3.8 percent; in 1979, 6.0 percent to 3.6 percent; and in 1980, 6.9 percent to 8.0 percent. Both sides know their mathematics and do it well. This is the reality behind the sound and fury of the spring struggle.

7·How to Be Law-Abiding
Without Lawyers

In a quarrel, both sides are at fault (kenka ryōsei bai).
                                                    —*Japanese proverb*

Fundamental to an understanding of Japan's business society is some knowledge of how Japanese use the laws they make, how disputes are settled, and how law and lawyers function in Japanese life. Much has already been said about Americans' fondness for the adversary system in managing institutions as well as finding solutions to its problems—and the opposite tendency in Japan to discuss rather than debate, to conciliate or "adjust" views rather than determine the precise "rights and wrongs" of a matter. In Japanese attitudes toward law and its practitioners, the differences between our two ways of doing business show up most sharply.

By latest head-count, there are well over 500,000 lawyers at work in the United States.[1] The figure has soared over the years in exponential progression. Where in 1960 there was one lawyer for every 700 Americans, we now are blessed with one in 400. There are 70,000 lawyers, give or take a few, in the state of California alone; and by

1984 they will probably number 100,000. In Washington, D.C. the labor-intensive law industry now boasts almost 30,000 practitioners —government and private counselors included. The nearly $25-billion annual total of legal fees across the nation represents almost one percent of our gross national product. Litigation has established itself as one of America's few consistent growth industries. As the Chief Justice of the United States, Warren Burger, noted some years back: "We may well be on our way to a society overrun by hordes of lawyers, hungry as locusts, and brigades of judges, in numbers never before contemplated."

Each year more than 150,000 new laws are plastered onto the books by federal, state, and local legislatures. Almost half the members of Congress are lawyers by trade, a percentage matched roughly at many local legislative levels. More than 10 million cases are on the docket at one time in the nation's courts, with more coming up constantly. It is a tempting and by no means farfetched generalization to assert that, at any given moment, about one-quarter of the country's population is in the process of suing or being sued.

It is not enough that judges run some school districts, decide whom employers must hire, when a human fetus becomes a person, how much of a lake a factory may pollute, and how dirty a pornographic magazine must be before local authorities may keep it off the newsstands. They are also called upon to settle problems, such as whether girl basketball players must be allowed to play on boys' teams, marine reservists may wear regulation wigs over their normal long haircuts on weekend drills, fat people are being discriminated against for receptionists' jobs, or clergymen are guilty of negligence when a person they counsel later commits suicide. Students regularly sue educational institutions, either to obtain entrance or to exit with a degree, failed examinations notwithstanding. Washington Redskins' fans once sued in federal court to have a referee's decision on a single play reversed.

Class action suits multiply. Joseph Califano has written that at one point, while he was secretary of health, education, and welfare in the late seventies, he was the target of 225 court orders as a result of suits against his department. Bartenders in the state of California must appraise their customers carefully, since courts there have ruled that a drunk causing injury or accident is the responsibility of the bar (or private home, in some cases) where he was served the liquor. Each week thousands of lawyers are suing for injuries in household or automobile accidents—"the pot of gold at the end of every whiplash," as one attorney put it. Medical malpractice suits—and countersuits—have become a commonplace. Now legal malpractice suits are coming into vogue.

American business is, of course, awash in legal actions and actions taken to head off legal actions. Battalions of lawyers were deployed to fight classic antitrust actions like the Justice Department's long attritional campaigns against Exxon and IBM. A small appliance company has to pay damages because a card-table leg support it had sold fifteen years before failed to operate, causing minor injuries to the user; yet a major Washington law firm can boast of holding off for twelve years a ruling of the Federal Drug Administration about labeling on peanut butter jars, in a case where court transcripts took up 24,000 pages and documents 75,000 more. The legal department is a heavily garrisoned stronghold in almost every large corporation, backed up by waves of $150–$250 an hour shock troops from the large law firms, who are always on call. Few American company officers would think of making a significant public statement—still less working out contracts, letters of agreement, or any dealings with the government—without the corporate counsel riding shotgun on the transaction. With many companies enmeshed in legal problems and confrontations, the distinction between legal advice and corporate direction blurs to the point where the company lawyer ends up as the president, since he may be, *ex officio,* the only one of the officers who understands the company's most complex problems.

The entire country, in fact, has come to resemble some kind of vast legal tournament arena where the rasp of writ on brief, like the medieval clang of battle-ax on buckler, is supposed to tell us all that the republic is in good shape. Whatever the excesses of the adversary system, we are assured, it is absolutely necessary if we are to remain a free society. For how else except through the pursuit of adversary legal argument—"that greatest legal engine ever invented for the discovery of truth," as the redoubtable John Wigmore, put it[2], can we discover who is right and who is wrong, who wins and who loses in any kind of dispute. If the effect on the participants increasingly resembles the sufferings of our medieval forefathers in the trial by ordeal ("I lost my hand putting it into the fire, but the baron said it proved I was not guilty"), that may be, as they say, the price we pay for freedom. Adversary proceedings are also stimulating and rather fun, as medieval knights and modern lawyers could tell us. How else can we preserve our free, democratic, and capitalist society, by hallowed definition a government of laws, not men!

How to Be Law-Abiding Without Lawyers

Arriving in Japan from Tournamentland, U.S.A., one finds the relative silence of litigation and legal action almost deafening. Some litigation there inevitably is, but it rarely gets into the papers. Major court decisions, particularly those of the Supreme Court, are given publicity, particularly when they have political overtones. But notable decisions are relatively few in number. Very few Japanese have ever had occasion to engage a lawyer's services. Most people in Japan live and die without ever seeing one. Trials when they do occur go on at a slow, humdrum pace. Japanese judges handle several cases at a time and hearings in each are staggered at often wide intervals. A Japanese judge's hearing schedule looks a bit like an orthodontist's appointment book.

Most lawyers are busy handling criminal cases and, except for some specialists in corporation law, can afford to handle only a small number of civil cases. There are some mass action suits—especially in pollution cases—and land- and building-related disputes are a major cause of litigation (understandable in a country where real estate values have risen to such an absurd degree). The courts are called on to interpret the Constitution, in a variety of cases, but the almost deliberately slow pace of their decisions, here as in other matters, is enough to dampen the spirits of those who seek political change through litigation. Appeal a decision and it may take ten years—or twenty. "You can always get justice in Japan," a Japanese lawyer friend of mine used to say, "if you live long enough."

Divorce cases, those lucrative necessary evils of the American legal profession, rarely go to law in Japan. Divorce can now be had easily and fault is rarely imputed. If complications arise, family mediation authorities exist to make necessary adjustments between the parties. Lawyers are also comparatively rare in Japanese real estate transactions. Although each side may have real estate experts on call, they are rarely members of the bar. The storied paper-shuffling "closings" that have paid the rent of so many metropolitan American law firms are strangely absent.

Even more surprisingly, personal injuries are rarely litigated, except for major cases. Some settlement is generally arrived at long before any lawyers are called in. Studies of the Japanese recourse to law in accidents involving taxicabs and railroads, for example, show how only an infinitesimal percentage is ever brought to court. American executives habitually consult lawyers in drawing up employment contracts; authors and entertainment personalities habitually use lawyers as a backup or substitute for agents. Japanese "talent" uses agents or managers, but here, too, lawyers are rarely found.

As we have seen, the total number of lawyers in private practice in Japan (judges and prosecutors excluded) in 1982 totaled slightly over 12,000. Japan is a country of 117 million people, as against the 240 million Americans. That is to say, there is one lawyer for every 10,000 Japanese as against one for every 400 Americans. The total number of civil actions brought in Japan in one year (1980) was about 500,000—about half the number of cases for that year in the state courts of California. On a per capita basis, there is one lawsuit in Japan for every twenty in the United States. While the caseload in the United States has increased appallingly over the past twenty years, the number of cases filed and fought in Japan remains almost static.

If we were comparing the number of laws and litigation in the United States with some still basically developing country like Indonesia, a newly industrializing country like South Korea, or even European states like Yugoslavia or Portugal, where the pace of modernity has been slower than most to accelerate, this discrepancy in the figures might be understandable, even if extreme. Yet the average Japanese and the average American share strikingly similar environments. Each belongs to a mass-market, mass-education, mass-communication democratic society, organized on free enterprise economic principles (although differing widely in their application), with a high degree of competition and a keen sense of popular rights within it. Both are typically city dwellers, actors in a technologically advanced and hence complex economy, with roughly the same problems of industrial development, environmental protection, and constant technological change. Both enjoy the widest possible guarantees of democratic freedoms and are alert to protect and preserve them. Both have constitutions, legal codes, and an independent judiciary—dedicated at least formally to the proposition that theirs is a government of "laws not of men." Yet to keep their societies going, we Americans have our 535,000 lawyers, the Japanese their 12,000.

There is no greater discrepancy between statistics in any one activity of these two highly urbanized business societies than in their use of law and lawyers and their attitudes toward them. No difference is more revealing or indicative of the vast gap in social priorities and premises between Japan's society and ours.

It is the job of an American court to dispense justice. The judge or jury should examine the facts of a case, as set forth by counsel, and decide, in a criminal proceeding, whether the accused is innocent or guilty; or in a civil case, which of the parties is right. Either the plaintiff is right or the defendant is right. Whoever has proved his case in the court—for whatever reason—wins. The other party loses. Justice is served, at least until the losing party's law firm can work up its brief for an appeal.

This concept of justice is rooted deep in the Western mind. Lawyers have been an honored part of our society for time immemorial. Traditionally they have held a position akin to that of the priest. Indeed, as our Western society grows more determinedly secular, the lawyer has come to appropriate more and more of the clergyman's prestige, and the judge something of his sacerdotal function. From the tablets given to Moses on Mount Sinai to Solon's Laws and Justinian's Code, the law in the West has been something to be revered. *"Fiat justitia pereat mundus"* (let justice be done though the world be destroyed) is not an exaggerated statement. It remains one of the last vestiges of our old traditional Christian European belief. In the United States, the judge is about the only member of traditional society whose function has not been thrown into disrepute. Small wonder that we have made judges arbiters of everything from how far children must be bused to school to the nature of the representation at political conventions.

Our idea of justice was nurtured by the religion of the Jews and the Christians, given its rationale by the philosophy of the Greeks, and codified in the laws of the Romans. It depends on a feeling of some transcendent universal rightness, linked to old Western beliefs in the supremacy of the individual conscience and bound up with a notion of the Natural Law. At its root is an ancient conviction, now more subliminal than expressed, that there must be some Divine Lawgiver watching over all.

Whether we believe in a Divine Lawgiver or not, most Americans have a rooted faith in the rights of the individual. The late Alexander Bickel, in his memorable book *The Morality of Consent,* defined this as the "vision of individual rights that have a clearly defined independent existence, predating society which are derived from nature and from a natural if imagined contract. Society must bend to these rights . . . they condition everything and society operates within limits they set. . . ."

The Japanese, although they are a notably moral and law-abiding people, and appreciate American ideas about air-conditioning, technology, and free enterprise competition, do not share our instincts about the transcendency of justice or the impermeability of individual human rights. They are by nature uncomfortable with the adversary proceedings in a court of law—not to mention the adversary method of fact-finding and decision making that has affected so many parts of American life outside the courtroom. With them the compromise is far more desirable than the confrontation. Since their goal is harmony *(wa)*—the principle that threads its way through their society—the process of discussion and consultation is in itself often more important than the precise kind of decision that may be reached as a result.

Some observers have been content to attribute their faith in solving matters by discussion—and their success at it—to the unitary nature of their monoracial society. One recalls Aristotle's prophetic comment in the *Ethics:* "If all men were friends, justice would not be necessary." In Japan, if all men are not necessarily friends, they are almost all of them relatives.

There is a deeper reason, however, which takes us back again to the difference between Christ and Confucius and the worlds they made. The American, in the tradition of Western culture, starts from a belief that there is a higher power—however his priests, philosophers, or psychiatrists denominate it—superior to man. If not an actual Supreme Being, there must be at least a universal truth, an instinct for abstract *justice* to which men appeal. This "justice" can be found, as our traditional phrase puts it, "under law." Without due process of law, in which judgment is rendered by a fair, objective, and preferably pitiless evaluation of the facts, justice cannot be had. All of the great Western religions have stressed this, but the Christian and the Jewish especially. Moses gave us God's laws. "Blessed be he who hungers and thirsts after justice," Christ tells us in the Sermon on the Mount. Christians, Jews, freethinkers, and atheist professors of law in the United States have been salivating after justice ever since.

The Japanese, by contrast, find this idea of justice difficult to grasp. The ideal of abstract justice is unsatisfactory and by their terms illogical. As Kawashima Takenori, the distinguished Japanese jurist and sociologist, has written: "The notion that a justice measured by universal standards can exist independent of the wills of the disputants is apparently alien to the traditional habit of the Japanese people. Consequently, distrust of judges and a lack of respect for the authority of judicial decision is widespread throughout the nation."[3] This is natural enough in a society that is based not on the inalienable rights *of* individuals, but on the harmonious relationships *between* individuals, in which the individual is incomplete outside the relationship.

One goes back to Confucius. As he was quoted as saying in Book 2.3 of the *Analects:* "The Master said, 'Govern the people by regulation, keep order among you by chastisements and they will flee from you and lose all self-respect. Govern them by moral force, keep order among them by ritual and they will keep their self-respect and come to you of their own accord.' "

Behind this is, of course, the underlying principle of harmony. The idea of the inner harmony of the person adjusting to the outer harmony of the world around him has remained strong in Japanese thought. It has received much support from Japanese versions of Buddhism, as well as the massive assimilation of the religious Confucianism of Chu Hsi through the two centuries of the Tokugawa period (1616 – 1867). Whether the Japanese consciously thinks of himself as a Confucian, a Buddhist, or for that matter a Christian, a basic feeling for harmony is strong within him.

The Japanese court, accordingly, although committed to dispense justice in the same manner as the American court, is actually more interested in restoring the harmony that has been shattered by a dispute. The real villain in the case, in the eyes of the judge—and for that matter most of the community—is the party who resists a workable compromise.

Let us illustrate. Assume that a squatter farming some land hears that the owner is about to sell out to a developer and decides to sue for possession of ten acres. An American judge—or jury—would decide after hearing the evidence who has the right in this case, the squatter or the owner. The court will rule in favor of one or the other. If the squatter is judged in the right, he gets the ten acres. He wins. The owner loses. Or vice versa.

The Japanese court would handle things differently. Ten acres are at issue—and quite a bit of land for Japan, at that. Assuming that the squatter has been shown by the evidence to have no right in the matter at all, the judge should rule accordingly. At the same time, the judge might also conclude, the squatter has occupied the land, he has thought enough about the matter to bring suit and considers himself to have a grievance. Why not, therefore, give the squatter two acres, leaving the original owner with eight. Eight acres, after all, is almost as good as ten. And two is better than nothing. This type of decision would be widely (if not publicly) praised by Japanese, although what Blackstone and Edward Bennett Williams would think of it, I hesitate to say.

Such reasoning, in fact, recalls the famous Japanese story of *Sambō ichi-ryō son*—Three Men Who Lost One *Ryō* Apiece. A dispute occurred between two tradesmen in early eighteenth century Edo (now Tokyo). One had found a purse containing three *ryō* (the basic gold unit of currency in Tokugawa Japan) and tried to return it to the owner, whose name was on the purse. The owner, ashamed of the fact that the purse had slipped out of his pocket (!), refused to accept the money. In a conspicuous extension of the Alphonse-Gaston tradition, they came to blows. A famous judge, Ooka Tadasuke, heard the case. Taking one *ryō* from his own purse, he added it to the three, then gave two *ryō* each to the finder and the former owner. "The finder," he said, "could have had all three *ryō* if he had just taken the money. Now he loses one. The owner could have had his three *ryō* back, if he had accepted the found purse. Now he gets two back, with a loss of one. I have to contribute one *ryō* myself, so I lose that. Each of us loses one *ryō*. Case dismissed."

His solution was widely applauded and the story is still told.

Before most modern court decisions are made final, however, efforts would have been made to have the dispute settled by mediation in Ooka's tradition. In this process, called *chōtei,* both parties would present their cases informally to a judge and two "commissioners," probably laymen, who would rule on the matter as much on the basis of personal relationships between the contending parties as on the law. Every effort is made to have disputes handled in this way; domestic disputes, in fact, must go through this conciliation procedure before they can be heard in a court. Even after the hearings had begun, the judge would have tried to effect an out-of-court settlement, called reconciliation *(wakai).* If the litigants accepted this, Japan's conventional wisdom runs, so much the better for all. No nation has erected more elaborate forms of mediation and conciliation to forestall the ultimate open conflict in court.

Again to quote Professor Kawashima:

Litigation presupposes and admits the existence of a dispute and leads to a decision which makes clear who is right or wrong in accordance with standards that are independent of the wills of the disputants. Furthermore, judicial decisions emphasize the conflict between the parties, deprive them of participation in a settlement, and assign a moral fault which can be avoided in a compromise solution.

Assigning moral faults, that pillar of American justice, is just what makes the Japanese most nervous. To apologize, however, is second nature to them. Even in criminal cases, the guilt of an accused is mitigated by the amount of remorse he shows for the crime. As in all sections of Japanese society, the device of the apology is widely used. Nor is it simply a "face-saving" mechanism. In determining the amount of punishment to be meted out, the judge weighs heavily in the balance the extent to which the guilty party attempts to make amends. Be it only a traffic accident, if a person has caused injury to another, he is well advised to rush to the hospital with flowers and gifts for the victim or, in more extreme cases, the bereaved. The judge will note this evidence of remorse, or the lack of it; and it will influence the severity of the sentence. The Japanese, in fact, find it odd that the apology is so underrated in the West. To them it seems merely an admission of the fact that an individual has interfered with harmony. It is not necessarily an acceptance of moral fault or an acknowledgment of goodness or badness. It is just, in the widest sense of the word, good manners.

In contrast to the semisacerdotal origins of lawyers and lawmakers in the West, the pedigree of the Japanese legal profession is modest. Before the Meiji Restoration of 1868 the nearest equivalent to a lawyer in Japan was the *kujishi,* a kind of innkeeper and general fixer or influence-peddler who lodged people bringing complaints before the magistrates of the Tokugawa days, lent them money, and otherwise performed useful services.

One of the first goals of the Meiji reformers was to set up a system of Western-style laws and courts, but not as a recognition of their own system's inadequate mechanisms for settling disputes. The speed with which the Japanese set up their own legal machinery was due solely to their desire to abolish the irritating system of extraterritorial courts which the Western powers were then setting up in Japan, as they had already in China. Once the Japanese could produce their own courts and laws, operating up to European standards, the Westerners would have to abide by them and pack up their own system of imported judges.

The French Civil Code was the legal instrument the Meiji leaders first chanced upon. They ordered its immediate translation ("Don't worry about mistakes," the Meiji statesman Eto Shimpei allegedly told the translators). What mattered was to bring out a translation quickly, with as little change as possible—ideally substituting the word *Japanese* for *French.* Of course the effort took longer, as Professor Takayanagi Kenzo has related. Almost twenty years were required. In the process the Japanese became interested in German law, and chunks of *Zivilprozessordnung* (Code of Civil Procedure) were added. The revised Civil Codes of Japan turned out to be mostly German, with French survivals, and some bits and pieces of British and American law thrown into the mixture. Not surprisingly, such a strong brew took a long time for Japanese lawyers and their clients to get down. Down it they did. Finally, the foreign extraterritorial courts were withdrawn, leaving the descendants of the Sun Goddess to ponder on the prefabricated legal structure they had erected for themselves.

Over the next century courts developed and laws proliferated, generally patterned on the European civil codes. (Trial by jury was rejected, after a brief experiment in the twenties, because most Japanese found it uncomfortable.) But Japanese continued to wear the harsh black-and-white of Western law like an ill-fitting tuxedo, which they were anxious to exchange or modify at the first opportunity. Most continued to prefer referring their problems to respected local intermediaries or, later, use special conciliation procedures set up by the government to cover any and all civil disputes. As the prewar Conciliation of Personal Affairs Act noted: "The main object of conciliation lies in reaching a solution to a case based upon sound morals and with a warm heart." Odd language to a Western lawyer's ears.

During the U.S. Occupation of Japan a flood of new laws, passed on American initiative, washed over the Japanese statute books. Most of them were based on Anglo-American common law. The independence of the judiciary was established. The Supreme Court was remodeled after American precedent. The protection of the law was extended to a variety of human rights which had not been covered before (women's franchise included). Over the years those new grafts of American legal thought were altered to Japanese taste. The new generation of Japanese is much more familiar with the reality of litigation than their fathers and grandfathers. In certain areas—labor disputes in particular—Japanese are resorting to the courts far more than the Meiji lawmakers would have thought either possible or desirable. The idea of human rights is understandable to modern Japanese, however their reading of these words may differ from their contemporaries in Europe and the United States. Japan's clean environment and antipollution laws, for one thing, would not be on the books today if it were not for a succession of legal actions brought by citizens' groups against private companies and, directly or indirectly, the government, because of government's failure to take action on environmental problems.

The court calendars nonetheless are far from bulging. Over the postwar years, despite a slowly rising litigiousness among contemporary Japanese, the number of cases brought to court overall has not significantly increased.

Now comes the catch. For there is an added explanation for the small amount of litigation in Japan: the government and the bar association both work hard to hold down the supply of lawyers. Hitherto we have looked only at the relatively small demand for legal services. To ensure, however, that harmony remains the goal of good Japanese and too much fabric-ripping justice is not sought, the Japanese establishment—bureaucrats, politicians, and lawyers together —have made it very, very difficult for anyone to practice law there. To be accredited as a practicing lawyer, a law graduate must spend two years working as a legal apprentice—a kind of legal internship —under a carefully structured government program administered by the Supreme Court.

Each year there are tens of thousands of law graduates, among whom close to 30,000 take the examinations for the National Legal Training and Research Institute. They are hard tests, understandably, for there are only 500 places available in the institute each year. And from its graduates not only lawyers, but all Japan's prosecutors and judges (both of them nonelective, civil service positions) must be taken. Incidentally, admission to the training courses is now restricted to Japanese nationals, which explains why so few foreign lawyers are allowed to appear in Japanese courts.

The graduates of this course are predictably clannish about their prerogatives. The modern Japanese lawyer—a far cry from the humble *kujishi* of Tokugawa days—is more like an old-fashioned British barrister. He can be assisted by a variety of "paralegals." For tax and patent work there is indeed another category of "solicitor" whose members must also pass rigorous examinations in their specialties, in the best Confucian tradition. Their time is very limited. Their services are literally at a premium. And however many non-Japanese legal experts may be imported to advise businesses on a variety of matters—one enterprising American firm has two floors of lawyers, Japanese and American, working under the guise of a legal liaison service—they may not appear at the bar in a Japanese court.

Are 12,000 lawyers enough, even for a nonlitigious people? The Japanese would probably like to have more. But apart from the obvious concern of Japanese law faculty graduates with ambitions to pass the bar (it is not unusual for a postulant to take the examinations four or five times before passing them or giving up), there is little popular agitation for more lawyers in personal cases. Most businesses continue to do their daily round with a minimum of legal talent on the payroll.

One handy index to the effectiveness of the Japanese legal system is the crime rate. Here the evidence suggests, powerfully and overwhelmingly, that the Japanese must be doing something right. In an earlier book I noted some revealing statistics for the year 1973: 196 murders in Tokyo as against 1,680 in New York; 426 cases of rape as against 3,735; 3,550 cases of car theft as against 82,731 in New York. Over the intervening years this ratio has not changed much. In fact, the rate for serious crime in Japan has generally decreased since then, while that in the United States has increased alarmingly.

Consider the comparative crime rates for 1979, in Japan and the United States. Japan had 1.6 homicides per 100,000 inhabitants, while the United States had 9.7; 1.8 robberies as against 212.1; 953 property crimes as against 4,986. The figures on the rate of arrests for crimes showed a similar discrepancy. Japan could boast of 97.5 arrests for 100 homicides, the United States, 73.4; Japanese police had 76.3 arrests for robberies as against 24.9 in the United States; for property crimes, 54.7 as against 17.1. In all these categories, and forcible rape as well, the Japanese incidence of crime was far below that of European countries with which it was compared, as well as that of the United States—and the percentage of arrests were proportionately higher. The authorities there never rest until a crime has been solved.

Statistics are not so readily available for white-collar crimes, but here again, from my own experience, I believe the discrepancy to be significant, although not so great as in the other categories.

Japanese punishments are generally far lighter than ours, and suspended sentences are frequent (there are fewer loopholes for parole, however).

Of course the Japanese are a homogeneous society, while in the

United States, our melting pot has in recent years become rather volcanic. The Japanese police are rooted in the society. They are part of every neighborhood—as the American cop on the beat once was, too—and work by persuasion as much as by coercion. Although suspects have all the basic rights of those arrested in the United States, they tend to confess rather freely, without coercion, for there remains within most Japanese an instinctive feeling of a duty to society and a mutual responsibility between citizens. Where the American thinks in terms of *my rights,* the Japanese tends to think in terms of *our rights* as well as *my duty.*

The Japanese are also unencumbered by thousands of confusing, often contradictory laws and tens of thousands of lawyers as anxious to beat them as to enforce them. As the distinguished Harvard jurist Lawrence H. Tribe wrote some years ago: "An excess of law inescapably weakens the rule of law." The Japanese, by contrast, find it best in matters of law to obey the modern architect's maxim of "less is more."

Professor Kawashima summarized these distinctions in his classic book *The Consciousness of Law Among the Japanese (Nihonjin no Hōishiki):*

To the European or American way of thinking, what ought to be and what actually exists are set off against each other in a state of continual tension. This is not only true of the law, but of Western philosophy and religion—witness the absolute distinction between God and man, between the flesh and the spirit. According to this dualism, people must face the realities of life with the law constantly in mind. No compromise may be allowed between them. The Real and the prescribed Ideal are two different things.

By way of example, take America's Prohibition laws of 1919. Despite the obvious unreality of these laws, the U.S. government committed itself to enforce them drastically, although with conspicuous lack of success. Even recently, Japanese travelers in the United States continued to be struck by the phenomena of liquor service being cut off on trains when they crossed the borders of a "dry" state or the huge profusion of liquor stores clustered just outside the city limits of localities where Prohibition in some form was still maintained.

Of course even in the different societies of the West, law and morality have to make their adjustments to present-day realities. This is unavoidable. Nevertheless this dualism between *what ought to be* and *what really is* is constantly kept in mind. . . . Although different expedients are used to develop belief in the justice of a law, there is nothing like the Japanese way of, so to speak, enforcing [the law] in easy installments *(nashikuzushi)*. . . .

In Japan, by contrast, there is no tradition of this duality between the ideal and the actual, or at best a very weak one. There is not even a basic idea of a God transcending humanity. World War II soldiers used to talk of "meeting at Yasukuni Shrine" as semi-deities if they were killed in battle; and great personalities in our history, like Tokugawa Ieyasu, were enshrined as gods after their death and worshipped, for instance, at the great temple tomb of the Toshogu. Similarly, there is no tension posed between what ought to be law and morality on one hand and the realities of the human spirit and human society as it exists. It is a basic assumption that we must make compromises between them.

Kawashima went on to say that, while the Japanese will have laws just as in the West against traffic violations and prostitution, they will always "use discretion" in enforcing them—since, especially in the latter case, you cannot legislate successfully against human nature. That prostitution is bad is recognized, but the Japanese find that the strenuous efforts to extirpate it made by American police are really quite pointless. He added:

> In the Japanese consciousness of law, such strenuous, yet mechanical efforts to enforce an unrealistic law show an appalling lack of flexibility. It would be a very brave police force which attempted to enforce rigorously in Japan a law which ran so counter to human instincts.

He concluded:

> In Japan the law is thought of as a hereditary family sword. Handed down over generations, this treasured sword is not an instrument for striking; it is nothing more than an ornament, a prestige symbol for the house. Similarly, we think of the law as a hereditary family sword. That is to say, we think of it as an ornament rather than a means for enforcing the power of the government to control the daily life of our society.[4]

As other Japanese jurists have gone on to explain, however, the ornament concept does not imply that the law is harmless. It is rather something to be used sparingly. And if not quite so threatening as a samurai sword of Damocles, it can be wielded with great energy when found necessary.

When the Japanese decide that public safety or the welfare of the society is at stake, they will act swiftly and efficiently to protect them. Severe penalties will be imposed, and few if any compromises or loopholes will be permitted.

Try violating the strict Japanese laws on gun control or drunken driving or the possession of narcotics. An offender in these categories will find the bite of an ornamental sword quite painful.

8·Our Contracts, Their Consultations

. . .in case a dispute arises between the parties hereto with respect to their rights and obligations under this contract . . . the parties shall discuss the matter among themselves with good faith.

—*typical Japanese contract clause*

When Americans and Japanese talk of *law, lawyers,* and *rights* they may be using the same terms, in English or Japanese, but the meanings they read into these terms and the premises underlying them are often worlds apart. Without understanding this it is impossible to understand many Japanese business tactics and reactions. Nowhere else is it so apparent that the Confucian capitalists really are that. Here more than anywhere the difference of viewpoint between us is striking. At the least the minimal Japanese use of law in business suggests that an approach quite different from ours can be successful. Going further, a look at their peaceful unlawyered landscape allows us some room for reflection on the lengths to which we have distorted the original premises of Western capitalism and turned "doing business by the book"—and under law—into a snare of petty litigations and frivolous adversary proceedings which, at this point in history, threaten to rip our own business society apart.

In Japan, as I discovered, one needs little legal help. The lawyers our company had retained in Tokyo I came to value as wise counselors. They knew far more about Japanese business than I did. And given the decision-making habits of most American head-offices, it always helped the Tokyo-based American businessman to note in reports back to the United States—on matters ranging from sales figures to the latest political forecast—that he had consulted the lawyers. Lawyers were not needed, however, for normal business consultations. One of the first things an American businessman in Japan learns is the difference in attitude about lawyers. In an American negotiation, or any business dealing for that matter, you bring the lawyer with you and the party of the second part is impressed. At least, according to the conventional wisdom, he knows you mean business; indeed, if counsel were not accompanying you to a serious meeting, people might assume that your errand was frivolous. In Japan, if you bring a lawyer with you to a business meeting, the fact is apt to be used against you. It is evidence that your intent is adversary and hence hostile—and that you are not really interested in coming to an agreement, except on your own presumably unreasonable terms.

There are very few legal departments or company counsel in Japanese corporations. Insofar as they have dealings with their American or European opposite numbers, they will retain the legal talent necessary, much of it non-Japanese. (Experience has taught them that dealing with American companies without adequate legal help is a bit like taking a midnight walk in New York's Central Park without a bodyguard.) But wherever possible the normal business of checking contracts or agreements is done by the young men in the planning department, general administration, or the president's office. While some of them may have law degrees, it would be very rare to find a practicing lawyer among them; and there is relatively little specialization. In the local Japanese scheme of things, a businessman is assumed able to draft and comment on business agreements without the need to call in outsiders.

Most Japanese companies do not think of calling in the lawyers until they find themselves facing litigation. I myself was shocked to find that one of the first Japanese companies I dealt with, a large corporation of roughly $700-million annual sales, not only lacked an in-house counsel; only one or two of the top executives even knew who their lawyer was. He was used primarily, it was explained to me, in dealings with foreign firms.

It must be understood that Japanese businesses do not have to cope with the almost daily problems of antitrust proceedings or investigations, actions by the Federal Trade Commission, the Securities and Exchange Commission, and other federal regulatory agencies, not to mention the multitude of personal and class action suits brought against American businesses. Although the U.S. Occupation supplied Japan with a brand-new set of antitrust regulations, more stringent in many ways than the American originals, and the Fair Trade Practices Commission, among others, the laws setting up such rules and institutions have been watered down in practice. In addition, the custom of "administrative guidance" given by government ministries to businesses eliminates the need for the sort of adversary proceedings between government and business that provide Washington lawyers with such good livings. In any case law is used sparingly all around. What Japanese firms need is people who know their way around the government.

There is, incidentally, extraordinarily little tax litigation in Japan. Although differences between the tax office and the company on what is owed and what can be deducted are constant, they are generally ironed out in discussions between the local tax office and the company's accounting department. The result is generally a compromise. In corporate as well as personal tax matters, litigation is a rarely used resort.

Contracts, of course, are necessary in Japanese business as well as American. There are probably many Japanese scholars and lawyers who would agree *in principle* with Sir Henry Maine's classic comment that the "movement of progressive societies has hitherto been a movement from status to contract." But the way contracts are actually handled in Japan is quite different.

"Japan," wrote Yamamoto Shichihei in *The Spirit of Japanese Capitalism,* "is a society of 'consultation' *(hanashi-ai),* whereas America and Europe represent societies of 'contract' . . . the word for contract *(keiyaku)* may exist in Japanese, but in meaning and content it is completely different from the use of contract elsewhere." To the Japanese an agreement is the result of consultation and the prelude to more consultation. A contract can thus readily be changed by consultation, when both parties sit down to review the progress of their association.

With us the interpretation is vastly different. The faith of Americans in the written contract is of the stuff that once moved mountains. Sophisticated businessmen who view priests, presidential spokesmen, and securities analysts with equal skepticism will look with awe on any agreement with two signatures on it, appropriately witnessed and vetted by the lawyers. A contract is held to be as close as you can get to ultimate truth, apparently. If it is violated, you have "a clear case in court." This is about the closest to ultimate truth that many American businessmen can conceptualize. Although few businessmen recall the Gospel of Saint John, "In the beginning was the Word," it may be as close as they have to a philosophy.

Having been brought up myself on the supremacy of the written Word, I remember being shocked, on setting out to address a meeting of my employees at one point, by the advice I received from the Japanese vice-president of our joint venture. It was a particularly difficult time, since a group of hitherto docile editorial employees, feeling uncertain about the future, were about to start a union. I wanted to talk them out of it, before anything was put in writing. The vice-president felt differently. "It doesn't matter so much what you write down or they write down," he said, "but watch what you say to them. Be very cautious. What you say you can't easily take back."[1]

Yamamoto in his book explained the difference in our attitudes as basically a religious one. The Japanese, not possessing an idea of a transcendent God, have traditionally thought of an agreement as between two human parties, with any divine participation hazy at best. By contrast, the Western religions—Christianity, Judaism, and Islam—conditioned believers to swear to God or before God in concluding an agreement, thus making the primary relationship one of the individual involved to God, with the other party to the agreement coming a far-off second.

To quote again from Alexander Bickel:

> . . . A contract hearing and model is committed not to law alone but to a parochial faith in a closely defined set of values. It is weak on fragmentism, strong on theory. For it, law is not so much a process, and certainly not a process in continual flux, as it is a body of rules binding all, rules that can be changed only by the same form or method in which they were enacted. The relationship between the individual and the government is defined by law; as are the entire public life of the society and, indeed, the society itself.

MIRACLE BY DESIGN

Formally speaking, the statement in the last sentence could apply to Japan—except when we come to the last few words. They would probably trouble most Japanese. The idea of a whole society "defined by law" is at variance with Japanese consciousness of what *law* is and what *society* is. For what to the West is the essence of a polity is to most Japanese a necessary evil. When the new Meiji constitution was being considered in 1879, Yamagata Aritomo, the crusty conservative among the Meiji reformers, gave this warning: "Since the Restoration we have adopted foreign laws and the whole nation knows we must have laws to preserve society, but it has been completely forgotten that society must also be maintained by good morals and manners." Of course his warning was not forgotten. Granted there is a greater tendency to resort to law in the present generation than in the one preceding—and certainly than in Yamagata's—the instinct for harmony is still uppermost in Japanese. The *word* in consultation has at least equal value with the *writ* in print.

This attitude is exemplified in contract work. A Japanese company tends to think of a contract as the beginning of a relationship, in which the terms change more readily than the commitment. When the Japanese company wants to change the contract, it first sends an emissary to the party of the second part to begin discussions about a change. A clause to that effect—"Both parties will set out to hold discussions in good faith"—on any revisions or disputed points is a staple of Japanese contract-making. By and large the contract, as we have said, is regarded as merely the seal of an agreement between the two parties, based on circumstances existing at the time of their agreement.

When the American company wants to change a contract, the first thing the president does is to call in the legal department and have counsel undertake a thorough rereading of the document, to see if any unfulfilled portions of the agreement exist or if, not to put too fine a point on things, there are any legal loopholes through which the company could exit in proposing a renegotiation. The discussions with the other party will come *after* this, and not before. ("Let's not tip our hand, George, until Fred down in legal gets the goods on them. Then we move. . . .") For the American mind, the contract is in itself the agreement, the covenant, the particular piece of semi-Holy Writ devised for the purpose. What is said is secondary, at best. Indeed, an American contract will specifically state that no concurrent verbal agreement has any standing.

Let me illustrate these differences in contract thinking by three incidents which happened in Tokyo while I was working there. Identities and situations in all three cases have been camouflaged, to spare embarrassment to the parties concerned.

THE DISMISSED MANAGER

Joe Dear was a man I knew casually in Tokyo, a tall, thin character who made quite a good living selling the hardware of an American company in Japan and Southeast Asia. He and his family resided in Tokyo, where they had lived for a good many years. As long as sales were good, he enjoyed a pleasant and mutually profitable relationship with his company back in the States.

At one point, business took a dip; and Joe seemed incapable of handling the small sales force he had working under him. A new man arrived in Tokyo, fresh from headquarters, who fairly quickly decided that Joe was no longer fit to run the enterprise. His reasoning may have been sound, and Dear, an easygoing man, might have been amenable to a quiet resignation with a bit of severance. The new man was impatient, however, and after looking over Joe's contract with the company, decided that the best course was to fire him out of hand. Since Dear was a contract employee, there seemed no reason to offer any kind of sweetened resignation. According to the contract, the company had the right to "terminate" him with minimal notice.

The one thing Dear's alert American terminators had neglected to think about was the fact that he was a resident of Japan, as was the local branch of the American company involved. Hence both came under the jurisdiction of Japanese law. Had the firing been conducted back in the heartland, there would have been no problems. There was no union involved. Dear was a contract employee or, at best, a member of management by extension. Therefore, if he were told to clean out his desk in two hours and had the locks changed on his office door by the following morning, it was just a good clean personnel technique. He would receive a minimal amount of severance pay. Who could quarrel with a nice "exit" like that?

Dear, however, was quite disturbed. He paid a call on the area vice-president of his company in Hong Kong, an American who had spent a good deal of time in Japan. After reviewing Dear's past performance, the area vice-president worked out what he thought was a reasonable compromise. The firing would stand. Dear, however, would receive all the money in commissions he claimed was owing him; in addition, he would be given the minimum of a year's contract as office manager of his division. It remained only to get the approval of headquarters in Milwaukee.

This proved to be the big problem. In the usual conference call, the dynamic new M.B.A. international vice-president and the cautious cost-cutting president joined in a chorus of indignation. "What, pay $25,000 and possibly more just to keep that fellow quiet? You told us yourself he couldn't handle the job. So let's fire him. We've checked with legal here. He doesn't have a leg to stand on. Thirty days' notice is it! Anything more is blackmail. We don't pay blackmail here. You've got him off the premises and that's that . . . It's all down in writing right here. . . ."

Famous last words. On being told by the Far East vice-president that the compromise deal was off, Dear found himself a Japanese lawyer. Suit was brought in the Japanese courts, while the company's officers, back in the heartland, thought no more about the matter other than to agree that their Japanese lawyer should handle whatever came up. Much did. Although by the letter of the contract the manager had little or no case, the Japanese judge was bothered by what to him seemed a callous "termination" indeed. At the least, Japanese practice in such matters, if not the law, had been ignored. The case dragged on. One year passed, then two, then three. Arguments were exchanged, while the judge suggested various compromise solutions—which Dear, hopping mad by this time, refused to accept.

Finally, the judge brought everyone together for a last suggested settlement. The contract, he conceded, was crystal clear. But there were extenuating circumstances. And it was most evident that there had not been sufficient discussion between the parties. Why had not some reasonable settlement been made?

In the end the cautious president and the dynamic M.B.A. vice-president paid out roughly $75,000 in legal fees and a similar amount in a settlement to Dear. When the labor of people testifying and preparing papers and the costs of sending witnesses to Tokyo to testify are thrown in, the company's bill for resisting "blackmail" came to around $200,000. Embarrassing to pay all that money, when "contractually speaking" they were in the right.

THE DIS-JOINTED VENTURE

To cite another case history:

Consolidated Widgets, Inc. got together with Nippon Uijitto K.K. to produce a new portable variety of its product, through a joint-venture company, Kokusai Uijitto K.K. At the outset Consolidated drew up a licensing agreement that called for a handsome fee for the use of its portable widget. This could escalate to as high as 13 percent of sales, if the business achieved a certain volume. Ernest Guyjean, Consolidated's Tokyo vice-president, needed a high fee to convince his principals back in Cleveland that the risks of creating a foreign competitor were worth taking. He explained this to Yamato Dama-shi, Nippon's senior executive director. Nippon felt that the project was marginal anyway, and was undertaking the deal as a sop to the chairman, who prided himself on his international associations. So why not? They agreed. The company was duly incorporated and a licensing agreement was drafted and signed. Guyjean and Yamato moved over to the joint venture to run it.

Contrary to the expectations of both Nippon's planning office and Consolidated's new products director (a newly created post, working under the financial department), the new company was an instant success. Sales in Japan increased so fast that a new plant had to be built (and financed) just to keep up with the orders. All hands were congratulated. To develop the new joint venture's market and expand it, however, improvements had to be made on the original Consolidated widget. In addition, interest rates at Japanese banks, which were financing the project, had increased; so had construction costs. Going over the figures, therefore, it was apparent to everyone in Tokyo that the licensing fee, by then up to a hefty 12 percent because of sales volume, was too heavy a burden on a developing company. The Japanese asked that it be reduced. At least it should have been suspended for some years until the Japanese widget joint venture was better able to pay it.

After several long talks with Yamato and the joint venture's planning staff, Guyjean himself was convinced. Armed with recommendations and plans for a scaled-down licensing fee (which at current sales rates represented a much bigger sum than Consolidated's projections), he made the pilgrimage to the home office and asked for a contract revision. "Not on your life," said Rick Sharp, the executive vice-president, who was running the deal from Cleveland. "You must be crazy. A contract is a contract. There's no way they can wriggle out of it—and if they do, we'll hold their feet to the fire. We need the money anyway. Business here is lousy."

Yamato and his colleagues at Nippon were troubled by this reaction, because they found their request eminently reasonable. After all, no contract is eternal. Agreements should be changed according to circumstances. The health of the new company is what matters most. They proposed that the two parent companies have some consultation on this subject in Tokyo, the sooner the better. Besides, additional financing would probably be needed.

Reluctantly, the executive v.p. went to Tokyo to talk. In two days of conversation with the working directors of Nippon, he gave his Japanese partners no comfort. "A contract is a contract," he reiterated, "and you should have thought of the development costs before you made it." Although Guyjean and Yamato appealed to him, on behalf of the new joint venture, he made them no concessions. Indeed, he suggested to Guyjean that this "going over to the Japanese" would not help his job security in Cleveland.

The people at Nippon Uijitto heard his refusal politely. Although the shareholders' views were far apart, they suggested that one more day of consultation would be useful before they brought their visitor along to the Three Hundred Club for the obligatory round of semisocial golf.

Early the next morning, just before the meeting, an unexpected caller was announced at the executive v.p.'s temporary office in the Uijitto Building: Hayakawa, the branch manager of the local Mitsutomo Bank, the "leading bank" that supplied most of Kokusai Uijitto's financing. "I guess we'd better see him," said Sharp, "he's that nice fellow who comes in to make these funny courtesy calls on you, isn't he, Ernest . . . ? Probably take only ten or fifteen minutes. . . ." Guyjean winced.

Hayakawa's call indeed took only ten minutes, but it was not the courtesy visit Sharp anticipated. The bank, he said icily, had heard of the negotiations and was disappointed that Mr. Sharp and his associates were not amenable to some kind of compromise on the licensing agreement. The bank hoped that Consolidated Widgets, Inc. would reconsider. It was the bank's judgment that some modification of the terms of the original contract was necessary. If agreement were not reached on this matter, the bank would in all probability feel it necessary to demand immediate parent company guarantees from Consolidated on all the joint venture's financing.

This would amount to $10 million. Furthermore, in view of the tight money situation, the bank would probably feel compelled to insist (informally) on 30 percent compensating balances for all funds loaned to Kokusai. The entire lending relationship would also be "revised." Of course, Consolidated was free to seek to replace Mitsutomo's financing by borrowing from another Japanese city bank, but they might find that difficult.

The consultation that took place after this visit from the friendly neighborhood banker proved surprisingly constructive. An adjustment of the licensing agreement was quickly agreed to by both parties. And Sharp, his own feet a bit singed by the fire, went off to play golf at the Three Hundred Club and prepare his telephoned explanation for this unexpected concession to his betters back home.

THE NONTEMPORARY EMPLOYEES

An American business friend from Boston visited my office in Tokyo one day and told me about his new project. A publisher, he had signed up a group of editors and academics to produce a new series of technical books, translated into Japanese. The production time was to be three years, so he had drawn up meticulous three-year contracts for his staff. "It's a simple, straightforward deal," he explained. "They come in to do the work on a project basis. When they're finished, they leave. No permanent employees. No labor hassles. See any problems?"

I smiled and said something noncommittal. If nothing else, experience as an American businessman in Tokyo had convinced me that few people who emerge from a home office anywhere with a plan or idea can ever be talked out of it.

Roughly two and half years after our meeting, the New York publisher gave his staff formal notice that their contractual time would soon be up. In the interests of managing a "smooth transition," he suggested that everyone start to wind up matters then and there. The announcement started a wave of employee protests and meetings. Most immediately joined a publishing union and statements were given to the press. The contract may have been for three years, a spokesman for the editors said, but this was after all only a technicality. The publisher had wanted to produce a product. They were the producers and as such had equal rights in the product. And they felt, with extraordinary unanimity, that it was time not to cancel out, but to start another enterprise with the same company.

The publisher threatened to fire them all immediately. The employees made threats of their own. Other unions made demonstrations of sympathy, joining their denunciation of coldhearted and inhuman "foreign" ways of doing business. The actual contributors, who had translated and edited most of the books, now served notice that any further "lockout" tactics would impel them to withdraw their names (and their work) from the project. They had committed themselves to do this work, the authors said, under the mistaken impression that this would be an ongoing publishing enterprise. Obviously it was not. Thus they had been lured into this enterprise on false pretenses.

Had this been Boston, the protesting editors and their author friends would have been, so to speak, laughed out of court. A contract is a contract. But Japanese courts view such breakdowns in human relations as no laughing matter. I can only assume that my publisher friend was advised of this fact when he sought the opinion of counsel. In any case, the recourse to law was notably unsuccessful. The books were not published. The project dissolved in a cloud of acrimony and loss write-offs.

Just before that time my friend dropped by again to talk about his problems. He was especially disappointed, he said, because all of his editors had banded together in their anticompany attitude, lining up in fact behind the editor in chief. "What kind of people did you hire?" I asked. "Didn't you at least try to explain this matter of the contract to them personally, in advance?"

"I didn't pick any of them," he answered. "I don't know Japan. We just decided on the chief editor, then let him hire everybody." "You what?" I said, dropping my cigar. "You let him hire everybody?"

"Of course. We don't know Japan. So we told him to pick up a staff. He knew all about the contract."

I could imagine without much difficulty the editor hiring scores of friends and colleagues and explaining that although there was some talk about the work being done in a certain period, obviously they would be able to build up a real publishing house, one that would last—and everyone would be in on the ground floor. (Nor would he have had much trouble in recruiting able people, since the record of failures and bankruptcies in Japanese publishing has been rather high in recent years.) But to have delegated all the work of hiring to someone else was one way of surrendering your own options. The only face they had seen and talked to had been the editor.

How could management expect to get any of its points across? This is a people-oriented business. . . . There should have been consultation . . . I began to say all the usual things.

My friend just couldn't understand why the element of discussion —the *hanashi-ai* of Japanese business—is so important. "We had a firm contract," he kept saying. "It was a firm contract. They all signed it."

As Yamamoto Shichihei wrote, commenting on a similar case:

When someone receives a contract, it would be unfair treatment to terminate it without proper consultation. . . . In Japan, having a five-year contract or a three-year contract means that at the end of this period the parties consult about what to do next. In foreign countries it may seem natural that a contract and everything connected with it may automatically lapse at its expiration period. In Japan that doesn't go.

Many Japanese contracts are meticulously drawn with fine print clauses enough to delight an American lawyer, most particularly in fields like insurance and banking. But even here the attention to paper detail is generally far less than Americans would think proper. (In my own corporate dealings with Japanese banks in Tokyo, at that, I never once received anything in writing advising that a loan would be extended, a guarantee needed or withdrawn, or a compensating balance required. All such matters were settled orally.) Where the American's key word in contract writing is precision, the Japanese key word is flexibility *(yūzusei)*. As Professor Kawashima wrote, "Indefinite contractual provisions that give a feeling of uneasiness to Westerners give a feeling of security to the Japanese."[2]

Where a provision for arbitration by a third party is a standard clause in American contracts, the Japanese prefer their traditional agreement to "confer in good faith" or settle any disputes "by amicable consultation." As Kawashima said, "the confer-in-good-faith clause is the core of our country's contracts."

The Japanese, reasonably enough, feel that it is difficult to anticipate all the contingencies of a business relationship in a single written document. If the parties have a decent cooperative relationship, they should be able to handle unforeseen problems by talking them out and arriving at an equitable solution. If such a relationship is not contemplated, why do business with them in the first place? To most

American businessmen, reared in our adversary system, a "good faith" clause is without meaning.

The path of Japanese-American business dealings is strewn with the casualties of misunderstandings about contracts. Originally, most such casualties were Japanese. Japanese businessmen are impatient with contracts and often disdain to read the fine print. Some paid heavily for it. American businessmen often lost in the long run, however. By insisting on sticking to the letter of a contract at the outset, they either destroyed what might have been a profitable relationship or made the Japanese contracting party so suspicious of them that they were driven to play the fine-print game themselves —often with interesting results.

I am not arguing against contracts; they are a necessary element of business. There is much truth in Adam Smith's saying that "Commerce and manufactures can seldom flourish long in any state ... in which the faith of contracts is not supported by law." Although Japanese business is based on relationships of mutual trust far more than ours is, Japanese, too, make mistakes in recollection and interpretation. There is no real substitute for a written statement of an agreement, especially when quantities of orders and dates of deliveries are involved. Japanese business, too, has its share of sharpers and crooks, who are all the more dangerous because they abuse the trust on which their business society is founded. Even in the case of reputable Japanese firms, the American businessman's overfondness for legalities is all too often matched by corresponding Japanese tactics of evasion or deliberate delay—at which the Japanese are masters—designed to improve their negotiating position.

What I do protest is the American tendency to emphasize the contract as a thing in itself, disregarding the mutual trust and faith that should be behind any workable contract—and which must be maintained—if the working relationship is to continue. Our obsession to get things "buttoned-down," to get signatures on a piece of paper as much to our advantage as possible, has become with many an end in itself. And of course, among America's cautious committeemen managers, having a signed contract is "safe." All too often, however, the medium, as the late Marshall McLuhan noted elsewhere, becomes the message. It would be interesting, in assessing our national productivity figures, if we could ever count the long manhours spent drafting and approving the contract, at almost every level of management, fighting it first within the company, then outside, through negotiation and renegotiation, draft and redraft, until a document reasonably satisfactory to both sides is in shape. For in the incredibly complex contract—like the volumes of special cases, exceptions, loopholes, and plugged loopholes that have made an absurdity out of the American income tax laws—each finely nuanced clause or subclause invites another one to modify or nullify it. Are the Japanese, with their simple contracts and good-faith clauses, so naive after all?

Not all American businessmen are contract commandos, of course. One of my oldest friends has made a name for himself in joint-venture negotiations by assuming one simple premise. "There's no deal," as he puts it, "unless both sides understand it, find it acceptable and to their advantage." With this principle to guide him, he has negotiated successfully with Japanese, Europeans, and Americans by trying to eliminate points of difference rather than compound them. He has done very well for his firm. But typically, his greatest problem has been sniping from his own superiors, who keep accusing him of giving away the store.

9·How the Bureaucrats Rule

Throughout Japan's history political activities have been more important than any others.

—Nakane Chie

If the storied gnomes of Zurich, long cited in economists' folklore, are thought to possess remarkable business prescience and authority, their record pales before the exploits of the real-life gnomes of Kasumigaseki: the twenty thousand-odd resolutely anonymous civil servants who act as helmsmen and stabilizers for Japan's economic society. Their stronghold is the cluster of solidly built state buildings in central Tokyo's picturesquely named Kasumigaseki district—the name literally translates as "The Misty Gates." At No. 1 Chōme sit the Finance Ministry and Economic Planning Board; at 2 Chōme the Ministry for International Trade and Industry—the all-seeing MITI; at 3 Chōme the Foreign Office. Inside this crowded concrete lair the enlightened gnomes of Japan's civil service go about their daily round, tugging and pushing at the levers of fiscal and economic policy, planning new visions and revisions for tomorrow's economic development while placating angry foreign casualties of today's, setting and reviewing targets and projections, cutting losses, and expanding gains.

No European gnome prototypes ever guarded their treasure so zealously or invested it more creatively. Premiers come and go. Businesses and whole industries rise and fall. The shouts of occasional public outcry echo off their heavy walls. But the bureaucrats coolly perform their rituals, with the bare minimum of nods in the direction of their supposed political and economic betters. If superficially humble and self-effacing in their dark-suited working dress, they are proudly secure in their intellectual pedigrees—toss a pebble anywhere in Kasumigaseki at lunchtime and you will hit a top graduate of the University of Tokyo's law faculty or slightly less. Indeed, the gnomes of Kasumigaseki constitute the world's most dedicated, intelligent, cohesive, and competent bureaucracy. Japan's miracle would not have been much of a reality without them.

Like all good gnomes they seem ageless. Each year just about the brightest and the best (or almost best) of Japanese university graduates are accepted into the fellowship of Kasumigaseki to begin a long apprenticeship. They learn the business of government from the ground up, their perspective conditioned only by the ministry they have joined. They will remain generalists. There are no extra points given in Kasumigaseki for the possession of Ph.D.'s (as in the American bureaucracy, where a doctor's degree means both more status and more money). They develop a sense of solidarity within the ministry, although over the years this will split into various types of intramural factionalism. They can be for foreign trade liberalization or against, for tight money or in a cautious way advocate some monetary pump-priming; they can consistently push for bigger growth or hold out for more public sector spending. But these disputes will all be waged within their ministries. Conscious of their role as custodians of the nation's administrative treasure, the gnomes will labor to present a single face to the world around them.

Tradition supports them, for they belong not merely to the world's most competent bureaucracy but to its oldest. Their modern ministries may have been founded less than a century ago, or in their present form, barely thirty or forty years ago; but their tradition comes from the seventeenth century, when the Tokugawa shogunate enforced its writ on the land and turned the two-sworded samurai of the clans into administrators, magistrates, and keepers of protocol.

They are in their tradition Confucian, perhaps the most thorough-going Confucians of all the Japanese. The Tokugawa rulers deliberately used the latest wave of imports from Chinese Chu Hsi Neo-Confucianism to develop a sense of service to themselves. Warrior, farmer, craftsman, and merchant were the four categories of Tokugawa Japan, their rank arranged in descending order. The civil servants in Kasumigaseki are more than subconsciously descendants of the officialdom that emerged when the Tokugawa turned their samurai into judges and inspectors, charged with keeping everyone in his place.

When the young samurai of the mid-nineteenth century overturned the Tokugawa rule, ossifying after two centuries of isolationism, they dismantled only the top of the Confucian pyramid and substituted the emperor as a revived ruler-figure. The rites and bureaucracy they kept, but strengthened by patriotic Shinto underpinnings. The modern civil service that grew up in Japan thus traces its ancestry back to the administrative court of the Confucian shoguns. Their tradition of service is one of collective loyalty upward, with a corollary feeling of rendering service to the lower orders of society through their guidance.

Like all good brotherhoods the gnomes enforce anonymity. A career of speaking only for and through the ministry, on whatever lofty or humble level, is not conducive to untrammeled individual expression. Only when the gnomes in their fifties retire from their ministries does a transformation occur. The Japanese call it "descent from heaven" *(amakudari),* by which they mean the entrance of senior bureaucrats into private business. Here at last the veteran department head or vice-minister comes down to roost as a chairman, vice-chairman, president, vice-president, or adviser of a private company. At last he is free to share (within moderation) the accumulated wisdom of the Kasumigaseki gnomes and put it as expensively as possible at the service of free enterprise or, in some cases, the ruling Liberal Democratic party. With his new pay scale comes a certain amount of popular visibility.

If the foregoing portrait is an exaggeration, it is not much of one. It is hard to overstress the latent power of the Japanese bureaucrats in their ministries. There is no body of officials in the world quite like them; and even rough parallels do not easily come to mind. The British civil service or the higher French bureaucracy, like the *inspecteurs de finances,* are probably the closest modern comparisons, although more imaginative observers have likened the Japanese bureaucracy *(kanryo)* to the mandarinate of Han dynasty China. Comparisons have been made with the bureaucratic apparatus of the Soviet Union or other Communist countries, but there is little point to that. Modern Communist bureaucracies, despite the authority given them, have proved unwieldy, venal, and inefficient. By contrast, the salient points of the Japanese bureaucracy are its comparative high-mindedness, its smoothness of communication, and the abundantly evident fact that it works.

Far different from his opposite number in the American civil service, the Japanese bureaucrat sits at the top of the heap in his society. Competition is intense for the demanding tests for "high-level public officials." In 1980 some 50,000 young graduates applied; fewer than 1,300 were accepted. Roughly one-fourth of the University of Tokyo's law faculty graduates, traditionally the elite of Japan's state universities, each year pass the examinations. Among the ministries themselves there is a distinct pecking order. Finance is generally acknowledged to be at the top, with the Foreign Ministry and MITI close behind it. Those who do best in the examinations, in the Confucian tradition, have the best starting assignments. They are, self-consciously, an elite—in Japan, unlike the United States, elitist is not used among intellectual circles as a pejorative. True to the Japanese abridgments of Confucianism, however, they constitute an elite determined by merit. Whatever the background of a postulant, he is judged solely by his performance on the examinations, which are stiff and exhaustive. Admittedly, the University of Tokyo law faculty, which offers its young men (and recently a sprinkling of young women) courses heavy in administrative law, economics, history, and politics, has the best preparation for tests. It also has its own built-in old-boy network in the ministries. A bright fledgling official with a degree from a newly founded provincial university might find himself a bit lonesome among the graduates of Tokyo, Kyoto, Hitotsubashi, and Keio. But the system is simply built that way. Probably the best American comparison would be the Yale graduate going into Wall Street in the twenties or the Central Intelligence Agency in the late forties or fifties, or contemporary Harvard Law School products being ritually taken into the bosom of Manhattan or Washington firms.

Promotion goes slowly and according to seniority. Salaries are not high, compared to those in the private sector. A good Kasumigaseki gnome must wait for the big money until he retires, at some point in his early or mid-fifties, to enter private enterprise. For most of his working life the compensation lies partly in the prestige and respectability of the job, partly in the real power he wields, at a relatively early age handing down guidance to businessmen many years his senior and vastly richer. But there is also the element of service. The Finance Ministry section head *(kacho)* may give an occasional wistful look at his Todai classmate who enjoys higher pay and perquisites at the Dai Ichi Kangyo Bank or Mitsui Bussan. Yet they, poor fellows, are devoting their lifework merely to one bank or one company. The Kasumigaseki section head is working for Japan. His is the wider perspective and hence the senior view. He is after all in the Platonic sense one of the "guardians" of the state.

As with his fellows in business, the Japanese middle-ranking or even rather junior civil servant has far greater responsibility than his opposite number in the United States. He is not only the direct pipeline to that portion of the private sector with which he deals. He is also the person who likely as not originates the plans and policies within his ministry to be reviewed and discussed by his peers and finally criticized or ratified by his superiors. He enjoys real power, which goes a long way to compensate for his ostensibly humble status. He will, as a generalist, circulate among the different divisions of his ministry, relying for technical background and expertise on a second level of civil servants (who have lower status and indeed entered by a lower competitive examination). As in Japanese business, tap day finally comes for him when he is selected to head a leading department or ultimately becomes the vice-minister. He may not be so fortunate, in which case he will find an opportune time to resign and parachute down to as comfortable a landing as possible in private industry. It is the normal procedure, incidentally, that when a man becomes a vice-minister, the highest civil service rank, all his classmates still in the ministry must resign—to avoid any embarrassing seniority conflicts.

The bureaucrats of Kasumigaseki, again unlike their American counterparts, do not regulate, encourage, or on occasion frustrate the private sector by urging the Diet to pass a multitude of laws, which they then go about enforcing. On the contrary, they like new legislation kept to a minimum. Their most effective tool is administrative guidance *(gyōsei shidō)*, by which they set goals for various sectors of the economy, control inflation and the money supply, identify growing industries and help them expand, adjust exports in response to protests from foreign countries (and pressure from the Foreign Office), and try to divert the energies of companies in depressed industries toward diversification into other fields.

The guidance may be positive, as with the computer industry, for example. As early as the 1950s, MITI had started to encourage the Japanese computer industry through a variety of government subsidies and joint government and industry research projects. The fruit of much patient long-range planning is the high level of development reached by the Japanese computer-makers, among whom Fujitsu, for example, is now ready to compete with IBM. Much the same assistance was given to build up key industries like steel, automobiles, and electronics. Although Japan can now say with some justice that it has fewer protective tariff barriers than the United States, this was not so in the fifties and sixties—when the import of American and European automobiles, for example, was, to put it mildly, discouraged.

MITI, for example, now calls Japanese carmakers in for administrative guidance about the number of cars they should export. It is MITI that for some time has been pressuring Toyota, Nissan, and others to put up plants in the United States. The government is forever adjusting supply and demand in the steel industry, with monthly meetings held to pool information about the projected needs of big steel users. Based on these, MITI issues a quarterly "Outlook for Steel Supply and Demand" as a guideline for steelmakers to plan production.

What happens if a ministry's guidance is rejected by one or more of the parties involved? On the face of things, nothing. Indeed some companies, like Toyota, have proved singularly unresponsive to repeated nudges from MITI about setting up plants in the United States. Occasionally punitive action is taken, often indirectly. In an unusual confrontation of the sixties, the Sumitomo Metals Mining Company refused to accept a limit set on certain steel production, whereupon the ministry cut back on Sumitomo's quota of imported coal. Generally, however, a ministry's guidelines, after discussion, are obeyed—sometimes by general agreement in modified form. MITI in particular, often sets up "antirecession" cartels in temporarily hard-hit industries or urges (generally with success) the merger of companies in a crowded field. To the American business mind, it is all strange, dictatorial, if not downright illegal. If American antitrust statutes were suddenly thrust on Japan and enforced, a considerable portion of Japan's business elite, including most of the MITI high command, would find themselves in jail or close to it.

My own experience of administrative or "window" guidance in Japan (from the "window" in the particular office of the ministry to which final proposals are delivered) was an illuminating one. The two cases were with the Finance Ministry and MITI. Each time I was able to resist (barely) the classic impulse of American business management to storm the ministry involved with a small platoon of lawyers and accountants, demand massive support from the U.S. Embassy, and produce heavy supporting barrages of memos from the company headquarters back home. In each case I was successful, but the effort involved considerable time and patience.

The first move in such cases was to visit the office concerned and explain what I wanted to do. It was best not to take a lawyer along, unless he was Japanese and happened to be a classmate of someone in the ministry. The response was rarely encouraging. Difficulties were pointed out. Precedents were cited against success of the course of action contemplated. But perhaps, if I were willing to try a draft proposal, they might look at it.

The next step was the draft—more discussion, more limits set, a few compromises suggested. More drafts were prepared, suitably altered. In one case, I found a friend who knew the chief of the division involved. A brief meeting was arranged, he promised to look into the matter, but suggested, "informally of course," additional changes. I was referred back to my original "window." By this time I had come to know the section head there rather well. He gave me some rather constructive advice, also "informally." "Speaking just on my own, of course . . . ," it occurred to him that only one problem remained. With this classic phrase—essential to such talks—ringing in my ears, I went back to my own handlers at the office to prepare the final compromise. Now we were ready for the last step—which in a similar situation in Washington would have been the first one —to write up the proposal formally. Finally after these several months of private negotiation, we marched up to the "window" and formally presented my proposal. "Ah, yes," the section head replied with a smile of serendipity, "we'll have a look at it."

Both times the official response was favorable. It came through quite swiftly. I couldn't help reflecting that, had I refused the "guidance" and tried to run through my original ideas as the formally submitted plans, we would still be waiting for our answers, cobwebs collecting on our worn Brooks Brothers attaché cases. It has happened before.

After the informal talks have ended and appropriate "window guidance" given, the corporate seeker for a ministry's approval must prepare his forms and applications with scrupulous care. Although the Japanese are not a litigious people, they are intensely *legalistic*.

In a tradition that goes back to the Confucian rituals, protocol must be absolutely observed. In a sense the form of a request or negotiation is as important as its content. Sticklers for bureaucratic etiquette, the good listeners of Kasumigaseki can turn suddenly deaf if the proper rites of administration are neglected, that is, if a form is missing or a schedule is out of place. And a turndown from the economic ministries or their affiliate, the Bank of Japan, is notably hard to reverse.

"Honor the official, despise the people" *("Kanson minpi")* is an old and oft-quoted proverb in Japanese society. Its modern usage refers to the arrogance of the career civil servant, real or fancied, as perceived by outsiders. Among politicians, journalists, and especially businessmen, there is a great deal of resentment against "high-handed" bureaucrats and their arbitrary decisions. As a senior textile executive told the newspapers, commenting on a new "anti-depression" cartel formed in May 1981: "Superficially, it might seem reasonable to form a cartel and share hardships among all concerned. But this also impedes corporate efforts for self-help and only results in making managerial responsibility unclear. . . ." Senior executives in business constantly complain about their opinions being disregarded in favor of bureaucratic solutions. Feeling against the bureaucracy often runs high. "Gutter rats wearing glasses" was one politician's extreme and well-publicized comment.

Left to itself, probably any bureaucracy becomes rigid and unyielding. And the Japanese variety is no exception. With virtually all the power of economic ministries in the planned socialist economies, the bureaucrats in Kasumigaseki often find the experience of power a heady and intoxicating brew, like the prewar bureaucrats and the Tokugawa Confucians before them. In modern Japan, however, there are several moderating influences working on the citadels of Kasumigaseki, some from within the government, some from outside. The result is that a system that on its face seems to invite power abuses is forced to incorporate some checks and balances. Typically these influences on the bureaucracy are not codified. Nor are they openly adversarial. But there are enough of them to keep the Japanese bureaucrat, just barely, from falling into the *dirigisme* that has plagued so many of his counterparts in Europe, for example.

The first is the business connection. Each of the ministries receives a more or less constant input from Japanese business. Basic ministry plans at MITI, for example, are made after advice—generally in the form of a draft plan—is received from the Industrial Structure Council (Sangyō Kōzō Shingikai), the majority of whose 170-odd members come from the private business and financial sectors. Similar advisory councils exist for most ministries as a kind of pipeline between them and the business community. In addition, various ministry departments keep in close contact with representatives of the businesses they deal with. Representing business as a whole is the Keidanren, the real private sector Japan, Inc. Every major Japanese company and all the nation's industries are represented in the Keidanren, pay dues and assessments to it, and line up behind its spokesmen, when occasion demands.

The chairman of the Keidanren, like the present Inayama Yoshishiro, retired chairman of Japan Steel Company, is *the* acknowledged elder statesman of Japan's business world. He speaks *ex cathedra* for Japanese business, when necessary, from the Keidanren's headquarters in the Otemachi financial district, a power center rivaling that of Kasumigaseki. Bureaucrats are wise to listen if Mr. Inayama cautions or complains. Among other beneficiaries, the Japanese government's majority Liberal Democratic Party, that hydra-headed creature of many factions, receives a heavy share of its contributions from the Keidanren.

Which brings us to the Japanese government and the National Diet (Kokkai), the nominal political leadership of the country. In form, down to its two houses, the Diet resembles first the German Diet of the Kaiser's day (on which it was modeled), next the British Parliament. Its powers, thanks to the postwar U.S. Occupation, now extend far beyond the restricted scope of the Meiji planners, however. Like the U.S. Congress, it makes the law of the land and is subservient to no one. Elections are free and a large if decreasing percentage of the population uses its franchise—some 54 million people voted in the 1979 general elections. Japanese premiers and their cabinets are selected by the majority party in the Diet and make only perfunctory bows to the emperor, whose status has been reduced to almost totally symbolic value.

Yet in practice the Diet does not make laws, but approves them. It is the bureaucracy that prepares the plans, drafts the laws, under Cabinet supervision, and offers them up. The changes and compromise that result before a bill becomes law are less like the give-and-take of American congressional politics than the bureaucratic undulations of administrative guidance. Tanaka Kakuei, the former prime minister (who is still on trial for his part in the Lockheed bribery scandal of 1974), once described to me the political realities of Japan very neatly—and whatever his failings, his acute sense of observation as a thirty-five-year veteran of Japanese politics has remained undimmed:

> As a party man, you have about 20 percent leverage or maneuvering room. The other 80 percent you must accomplish by moving the civil service. You have to alert the country to the problems, but only after you have lined up the civil service. . . . It is surprising how quickly things can be decided once the government—that is, the bureaucracy, politicians and all—can line themselves up in favor of something.

That the bureaucracy should run Japan is in line with the Meiji tradition. The first modern constitution in the late nineteenth century was planned to keep control of the government with the bureaucrats, working in the name of the emperor. That the bureaucracy has remained in control, even after the U.S. Occupation forced on Japan a new constitution with all the democratic guarantees necessary to sustain a strong parliamentary government, is only partly an accident of postwar politics. The majority Liberal Democratic Party, which has presided over Japan's recovery and prosperity since 1955, was largely officered by prewar bureaucrats who reconstructed Japan in their own image. It was natural for them to delegate to their juniors in Kasumigaseki the job of suggesting laws and drafting them, under suitable control.

Nonetheless, the politicians in the Diet must face the electorate periodically, so they keep in touch with it. To this extent, they make the bureaucrats aware of political problems and popular pressures, sometimes very forcefully. The Office of the Prime Minister in Japan is notoriously understaffed. Its total staff of seventy-seven is a far cry from the massed battalions of the President's Executive Office in Washington. In each ministry the only political appointees are the minister and the parliamentary vice-minister, whose duties are principally liaison. Ministerial posts are distributed among the various factions of the majority party. If the Liberal Democrats ever gave way to a coalition government, doubtless the same system of rival names and compromises would be followed. This does little to encourage expertise. (When Nagai Michio, a distinguished educator and editorialist, was appointed minister of education by Prime Minister Miki Takeo in 1974, he was the first professional educator to grace that position in a quarter of a century.)

This system hardly makes the bureaucrats unhappy. The only

challenge to their leadership comes occasionally, when an old ex-bureaucrat gone political takes over a ministry. He will know the department heads, their strengths and weaknesses, and the position and dimensions of various skeletons buried in the ministry's capacious closets. He is a hard man to guide, still less to fool. Even at that, he must work through the civil service, as he finds it. I once asked an old friend, a veteran Cabinet minister, how a politician can force his will on a recalcitrant ministry. "Well," he said, "umm, you could start by firing the vice-minister, I suppose. . . ."

Of course, there are inevitably conversations going on at every level between the Kasumigaseki bureaucrats, staff members of the concerned section of the Liberal Democratic Party headquarters, and Diet members. Smooth communication is facilitated by the fact that fully one-fourth of the Liberal Democratic representatives are former officials themselves. (Of the eight prime ministers since Yoshida Shigeru, only two, Miki and Tanaka, lacked a civil service background.) The continuity of the bureaucrat premiers goes back far, surviving even the troubles of World War II. (Former Prime Minister Kishi Nobosuke, at eighty-six the party patriarch in 1982, was vice-minister of the Munitions Ministry during World War II.)

A third check on the power of the bureaucracy is the press. Japan's huge national newspapers constitute a conspicuously free press, along with the specialized papers and the host of monthlies, weeklies, and journalistic books that paper the Japanese islands almost to the point of suffocation. Japanese editors are far less constrained by law than their counterparts in Britain or France. They are as quick to defend press freedoms as their counterparts in the United States. But while their editorials tend to run left of center, they consider themselves part of the establishment. Reporters covering the ministries are organized in press clubs; they know the department heads well and report quite accurately both what is happening, what will happen, and what might. *Nihon Keizai Shimbun* (Japan Economic Journal), the *Wall Street Journal* of Japan, covers transactions and discussions at MITI and the Bank of Japan so minutely, for example, as to suggest some degree of consanguinity with ministry department heads. Yet they exercise restraint in their coverage. Editors are conscious of what the public can be expected to understand as much as what the public has a right to know. In some cases this distinction works out badly. The explosive Tanaka-Lockheed scandals of 1974 had to be uncovered by the crusading reporters of a weekly. In any case the possibility or threat of public disclosure by the media has the effect of inhibiting bureaucratic high-handedness as it never had in prewar Japan.

This is particularly true of corruption issues. Civil servants, taken as a body, are quite high-minded in this regard and respected as such. Politicians are widely distrusted. But the disclosure of a civil servant taking money or misappropriating it, as happened in the Lockheed case or the more recent scandals about the KDD (Kokusai Denshin Denwa), will send shock waves through the Japanese public as few things can. If one civil servant becomes a little less high-minded than others, the threat of disclosure is in itself enough to encourage honesty.

There are two final checks on the power of the Kasumigaseki bureaucrats. One is the fact that their track record is mixed. For every two industry promotion schemes, the finely tuned monetary controls and ambitious five-year plans that succeeded, there is at least one that failed. It is a valuable hedge against the delusory disease of omniscience.

Finally there are the inevitable disagreements among the ministries themselves. MITI and its allies are all for growth and export targeting. The Foreign Office wants to restrict exports or do whatever is necessary to avoid losing friends and disinfluencing people (Japanese diplomacy habitually operates in negative terms). The Finance Ministry, with its sibling, the Bank of Japan, is ever-worried about inflation, and cautions about economic expansion and overheating. The arguments generated by these differences of premise are real and long-lasting. As long as such differences persist—and are shared with others—there will be no totally united front in Kasumigaseki.

Having suggested, if not proved, how the economic bureaucrats' role is less than all-powerful, let us now concede that this bureaucratic interference with business has been an absolutely critical factor in Japan's postwar economic resurgence. Textiles and similar ailing industries were redirected and diversified. Chemicals and some heavy industry were aided and strengthened. The growth of the automobile industry was charted and heavily assisted. (Mergers were forced to achieve this, although some were refused.) So now is the growth of Japan's semiconductor and computer industries. Jet engines and aircraft may be the next recipients of some support, along with better energy technologies and their applications. Targets of opportunity will not be slighted. What the bureaucrats contributed to Japan's economic miracle was the long view design, a sense of what would be best and most effective in the next ten or twenty years, not the next two. They may never have met a payroll, but they added a vital extra dimension of planning and long-range foresight to Japanese business.

In *MITI and the Japanese Miracle,* Chalmers Johnson made this comprehensive statement of how some of the civil servants in Kasumigaseki did their job with business:

> I cannot prove that a particular Japanese industry would not or could not have grown and developed at all without the government's industrial policy (although I can easily think of the likely candidates for this category). What I believe can be shown are the differences between the course of development of a particular industry without government policies (its imaginary or "policy-off" trajectory) and its course of development with the aid of governmental policies (its real or "policy-on" trajectory). It is possible to calculate quantitatively, if only retrospectively, how, for example, foreign currency quotas and controlled trade suppress potential domestic demand to the level of the supply capacity of an infant domestic industry; how high tariffs suppress the price competitiveness of a foreign industry to the level of a domestic industry; how low purchasing power of consumers is raised through targeted tax measures and consumer-credit schemes, thereby allowing them to buy the products of new industries; how an industry borrows capital in excess of its borrowing capacity from governmental and government-guaranteed banks in order to expand production and bring down unit costs; how efficiency is raised through the accelerated depreciation of specified new machinery investments; and how tax incentives for exports function to enlarge external markets at the point of domestic sales saturation. . . .

Such a close relationship between government and business, it will be argued, can play no part in the American experience. Yet we have had the same closeness—and the same support of development by government—for more than thirty years in the relationship between our Defense Department and the corporations that produce arms and their auxiliaries for the military. What is wrong with doing the same thing for peaceful economic expansion, and doing it better, without the guilt we seem to feel at not having an adversary relationship?

There is no lack of long-range planning in the United States, an impressive concentration of it within government agencies. The President's Council of Economic Advisors plans and projects, as do the

Treasury Department, Department of Commerce, Department of Energy (as long as it is allowed to last), Environmental Protection Agency, and many others. In the background, adding their massed Greek choruses warning of problems or pointing with pride, are such organizations as the National Industrial Conference Board, the Committee for Economic Development, and the various think tanks like Rand, Brookings, and the American Enterprise Institute. Very interesting plans they make. They can incubate good ideas and new projections as well or better than any of the Japanese ministries or their advisory councils.

Unfortunately, none of these agencies, government conspicuously included, can induce a single business to change its projections or shift policies, except by friendly persuasion (which is rarely attempted). No "guidance" is allowed here. Government, it is true, can have laws passed and enforce them—down to wage and price controls, various forms of rationing, and restrictions or incentives on international trade. It can regulate and control from the outside. If business disobeys, it can be admonished and punished by the law, unless its lawyers have a good day and can persuade the courts that it is the government, not they, who is the sinner. By the time these matters come to a head, however, in our grand old adversary system, the tendency has become a defect and the projection turned into a problem. What might have been a mutually profitable discussion has turned into the usual public shouting.

American business and government are generally incapable, operating under their present ground rules, of exchanging information, guidance included, early enough in the game so that by the time the course is changed, or the measure taken, most parties concerned already agree on the need for them. With us guidance becomes interference, discussion becomes argument, exchanges become confrontations. Bureaucrats are scorned. If they could make good money on the outside, the conventional wisdom still runs, they wouldn't be working in government. In fact, although dedication and competence are to be found in the U.S. civil service, the incidence of both is far lower than in Japan.

Underlying all of this is a basic difference of premise. Americans are professedly individualists, who at least by tradition regard the constraints of government as at best a necessary evil, at worst interference with a person's or a corporation's God-given right (this is about the only context in which modern Americans invoke the Deity's presence) to make their own decisions. With the Confucian capitalists it is different. They still see life in terms of relationships, among which the ties between ruler and ruled are of the first importance. As citizens of a modern democracy, they have had to abridge the old-fashioned Confucian view of authority so that "rulers" and "ruled" become their "government" and "people." The sense of personal corporate relationship, however, remains a close one.

10·People and Their Products

Productivity is a way of practicing virtue.

—Shibusawa Eiichi

The gateway to the promised land of twenty-first century capitalism may well be a flat island of reclaimed fill in Tokyo Bay, just offshore from the old industrial cities of Kawasaki and Yokohama. On the 5.5 million square meters of Ohgishima stands the Keihin Works of the Nippon Kōkan Company (NKK). Finally completed in 1979 after ten years of planning and construction—and $4 billion of investment—Ohgishima is probably the world's most modern steel plant. Almost antiseptically clean, a quarter of its area landscaped with neat lawns, shrubs, and trees, it is the antithesis of the legendary soot and smoke-grimed steel mill. It is comparatively quiet. Inside its huge plants there are very few people. Except for engineers in control towers, nobody can be seen near the furnaces. Cranes, furnaces, and transfer cars operate without visible human intervention. The huge slab, coil-cooling, and product yards are

completely unmanned. The vast rolling mill, which runs for a kilo-
meter, is operated by a shift of fifty.

When I visited Ohgishima in 1980, it was just thirty years after I
had seen my first Japanese steel mill, the old Yawata works in
Kyushu. Yawata even then had started its first postwar modernization; now part of Japan Steel, it is automated with new precision
production controls. But from the time I saw it I can remember only
a sensation of blistering heat and straining, soot-streaked furnace
crews trying to urge the most production possible out of the old
equipment they had left, most of it early imports from the United
States. The contrast between then and now, like the silence inside the
control rooms of Ohgishima, was deafening.

The Ohgishima works and the other new steel facilities in Japan
are almost totally homemade. Only the original technology was
imported. Japanese steelmakers now offer their technology and production expertise to others, including their old mentors in Pittsburgh, Gary, and Bethlehem. Works like Ohgishima are the exem-
plars of their technological adaptation, the product of constant
intricate planning and development. Each step of the steelmaking
process at Ohgishima rolls on a computer's instructions, from order-
taking in the sales office to the allocation of daily production
schedules. It is an odd spectacle to watch even the diesel carts taking
off finished pipe or rollers to delivery yards outside, without a human
in sight.

"Steel," the Japanese are fond of saying, "is a transport industry."
Raw materials come in at one side of the plant and flow in a continuous line to the shipping facilities on the other. They come from all
over the world. And the Ohgishima product goes all over the world.
Virtually every known innovation in furnace-making, antipollution,
and energy-saving techniques has gone into its making. Thanks to
the computerized energy center, which permits almost total energy
control, the Keihin Works uses about 40 percent less energy than a
conventional mill. Gases given off by the basic oxygen furnaces
(BOFs) and coke ovens are almost completely recovered and used as
fuel, supplying most of the power requirements of the works.

There are 8,000 workers at Ohgishima. A normal mill would
require almost three times that number to produce what Ohgishima
can turn out at capacity. Not the least factor in planning was the
reallocation of people from the older mills it replaced. With the
NKK union cooperating, the company was able to reallocate work-

ers to other plants, train some for new tasks, and set up a whole new manpower utilization structure before building began. It was a classic indication of the value Japan's managers set on people as one of their basic capital resources.

Ohgishima cost twice as much to build as a conventional steel plant. But its operating costs are roughly one-third that of a conventional plant. It is made for the long pull.

Not surprisingly, Ohgishima is a productivity expert's dream. In 1980 production was 1,800 tons per worker. This was more than three times that of Bethlehem Steel's relatively modern Burns Harbor plant. There are, of course, extenuating circumstances in the comparison, due to a variety of problems in the American market. Other Japanese steel mills do not show up so brilliantly against the competition. Some American mills, in particular the minimills that have sprung up in recent years, can themselves boast of significant productivity figures. And major Japanese steel companies are serviced by suppliers and subcontractors whose labor and productivity figures fall far short of the big companies'. The fact remains, however, that Japan's steel productivity has increased overall from 50 percent of American productivity in 1960 to more than 125 percent of American productivity in 1980.

The Japanese have done this by utilizing technological improvements—none of them of Japanese origin—which were available to all. These are the basic oxygen furnace (BOF), continuous casting, larger blast furnaces, and computer controls. All were put into practice. In Japan, for example, almost 80 percent of total output is produced by the BOF process, while the figure for the United States is 62 percent. Some 46 percent of Japan's steel is continuously cast, as against 20 percent in the United States. The Japanese raw steel output per worker, as of 1980, was 174 kilograms. Both American steel mills and European have a long way to go before they can equal that.

Although it is an extreme example, the man-made island of Ohgishima is a good vantage point from which to view productivity in Japan and in the United States. In each country, at this moment in history, productivity has a different face. In Japan it is an achievement. In the United States it is a problem.

Through the sixties and early seventies Japan increased its productivity rate by 8 to 9 percent annually. Even after the oil shocks between 1973 and 1978, productivity kept rising and, despite recessions, has been moving up about 4 percent annually in the early eighties. American increases in productivity, which ran roughly to 2 to 3 percent annually between 1950 and 1973, have since declined to almost nothing. In some industries the figure is negative. The level of American productivity, it is true, remains the highest in the world. But we are living off our own accumulated fat. Now that the average annual rate of productivity growth in the United States is among the world's lowest, we are doomed to be overtaken—with literally appalling consequences to our trade position and, indeed, the entire American economy—unless the downward drift is corrected. Even now, Japanese industry has surpassed American productivity in key industries besides steel, such as electric machinery and automobiles. In others, it is gaining.

This is not necessarily because American workers are less efficient than Japanese. In fact, productivity statistics may or may not measure the efficiency of labor. They are merely expressed that way, most frequently as the output of work or gross national product per worker. Obviously this is an arbitrary measuring device, and a clumsy one, which can do little better than indicate trends and offer comparisons. In the case of both the trend in American productivity and the comparisons between Japan and the United States, however, the weight of the productivity statistics is too great to be ignored.

What productivity really means is the degree of efficiency in which goods and services are turned out by an economy. How the worker produces is conditioned by how he is managed and the objectives that management gives him. This in turn is conditioned by the amount of capital that can be put in plant investment, the degree of new technology introduced, the cost of energy, the kind of labor available, and the extent to which government regulates business. We must also make allowances for how much of an economy is goods and how much is services. (Productivity in service industries is, if not lower, at least far harder to measure.)

Thus, if we are comparing Japanese and American productivity, it is not enough to talk about the shining new plant at Ohgishima and how much more steel it can turn out than any American opposite number. The purposeful-looking steelworker or engineer at a big Japanese steel complex, his latest productivity target stenciled on the outside of his hard hat (as they are at Ohgishima), may be the glamour figure of Japan's productivity surge. But others are equally important.

PRODUCTIVE MANAGEMENT

The first is the manager. As we have seen, Japanese managers, most of them wedded to a single company, tend to think in long-range terms. This is partly because of the high leverage financing of Japanese companies, which still depend heavily on bank loans and must consequently worry about the interest they will have to pay over the long pull. (Many Japanese companies are now cutting down on their proportion of bank loans and trying to increase the equity portion of their financing to avoid the drain of steady interest payments during times of fluctuating sales.) The banks rarely pressure companies for immediate returns; neither do they demand that they show consistently large percentages of profit, as happens because of shareholder (and stock market) pressures in the United States.

This emphasis on short-term profits and quick return on investment has proved almost disastrous to the American steel industry, whose leaders tell us with regularity that the need to show profits and dividends to shareholders inhibits their own investment in new plants. As a Bethlehem Steel executive put it: "The failure to implement such new technologies in American plants has not been because we do not know, but because we cannot fund. The American steel companies simply have not been able to undertake adequate capital investment programs in the 1960s and 1970s."

Here is a question of different business philosophies at issue. On paper the American rationale is sound. "What doth it profit a man," the American manager might say in a significant abridgment of the Scriptures, "if he gains the whole world [market] and loses his profit?" By contrast, the Japanese manager would prefer to gain the whole world market first and then work on the salvation of his profitability through improvements in productivity. For what, to his way of thinking, does it profit a man to have a broader *pro forma* profit on sales in a small and dwindling share of the market? All very well and good, the American may reply, but what does he say to nervous shareholders while he is getting market share—and losing money?

The very terminology used in describing American and Japanese business successes tells something about the difference of approach. In the United States, the ultimate praise for a chief executive officer is to say: "He turned the company around and increased net earnings." The impression given by these words is of some Atlas-sized president who dropped into a company and by massive injections of personal leadership managed to stop the losses and bring up the profits, in the manner of Superman pulling a train off the edge of a precipice and putting it back on the tracks. The action implied is external. It is management, that is, the CEO and his "new team" of jut-jawed vice-presidents and financial officers, who have trimmed excess personnel, sold off unprofitable divisions, and cut costs through dynamic planning, etc.

The Japanese words for successful management are quite different. They will talk, rather, of a manager "renewing the company's spirit" and making plans for "structural expansion," which resulted in greatly increasing the company's market share. Their emphasis tends to be on development and improvement from within the company—although profits, naturally, are welcome. The chief executive officer, barring a few exceptions, is praised for stimulating the total strength of the group—when he is singled out at all.

Both systems have their successes. But it is the Japanese that puts its reliance on the people in the company moving together and working out problems "through their own total efforts"—even though in fact it was the new management that may have kicked a somnolent, inefficient company into motion. In a factory populated by old-fashioned wage slaves (or young moderns with no apparent work interest besides appearing to work during certain hours and getting the weekly paycheck), the American short-lived Superman-type of leadership may indeed be best. But in the complex postindustrial world we are heading into, Japan's capitalists surely have the better long-term answer.

Why is this so? Because both the patterns and type of work done are changing, not to mention the background and expectations of the worker. Our American capitalist idea of the worker as an interchangeable part was based partly on the premise that workers did their jobs merely to secure money for support. Work was by definition (and etymology) onerous. Once the day's ration of work was over, one could have a family life, develop amusements, or go to night school to learn how to be a lawyer, depending on time, resources, and inclination.

By contrast the current generation is more apt to demand some positive satisfaction out of the work time, having been educated to think there is fun in everything. But this is not a bad thing. Indeed, by focusing one's mind on the work task and how to make it better, a person becomes an engaged participant in a group task, not merely an employee of a company. That is, as long as management encourages the idea.

Coming back to the United States to work myself, I was struck by some differences in approach. In Tokyo almost everybody in our company really thought of it as *our* company—whatever his views about the competency of management or the efficacy of the company's current objectives. In the United States most of the nonexecutive personnel I met in various businesses were only marginally interested in what they knew as *their* company. It was strictly a nine-to-five job; and many were looking for something better, where both their talents and their capacity for planning and creativity could be engaged.

The Japanese approach has been to involve workers in helping solve basic production problems inside the factory: how to make better goods and move them better. That is generally where a Japanese management starts. By contrast, American management may put its stress on financial controls, personnel cuts, or developing a "dynamic new marketing strategy"—often before the new team in the front office gets around to thinking about the basic product. Marketing gimmicks often substitute for an improved product.

There are, of course, exceptions to this rule on both sides. But the outlines of the basic differences are observable. And they have played a part in the differences between American and Japanese productivity over the past twenty-five years. The virtue of the Japanese approach lies in giving initiative to the people on the shop floor. Their voice is heard in building a product, long before it is turned over to the marketing man to sell or the financial man to sell out. Their world is still dominated by production. Their first concern, as we noted earlier, is to build practical products, not paper profits.

GOVERNMENT AT WORK

We have already indicated the exaggerations behind the simplistic idea of a Japan, Inc.—government, business, and labor—moving along in lockstep. Government help in R & D and other areas has surely smoothed the way for various Japanese industries to do better. Such aid is far from automatic. Government agencies and the Japanese automobile-makers, for example, have a long history of disputes. (Originally, the carmakers refused government advice to merge into three or four big companies—there are still eleven in

Japan—and in recent years the big ones have dragged their feet on setting up plants in the United States.) Yet government has successively helped steel, automobiles, electronics, and now the Japanese computer industry in various forms. The Kasumigaseki bureaucrats can be expected to help more than a little the semiconductor industry as well.

For while the government, except in rare cases, lacks the power to order industry or business to do a thing it is committed to support industry and urge its sensible long-range development by a variety of measures. Consultation, cajolement, incentives, and appeals to reason are all used. The great virtue of government intervention is that the bureaucrats generally take the long view, and through consultation and example encourage businesses to do likewise. It is not adversary and spasmodic regulation. It is consultative and supportive. And it is trusted.

Nowhere has the Japanese way of operating stood out more effectively than in the area of environmental pollution. In the United States, as we know, the Environmental Protection Agency, various consumers' groups, and industry fought out the pollution issue in the courts. Aside from making thousands of well-paid lawyers even better paid, this process proved costly, inefficient, and, in the case of some industries, disastrous, when what funds they had available for investment were diverted to hasty and often ineffective measures to introduce pollution safeguards, under court order or the judgments of federal regulatory agencies. The 1981 report of the Japan–United States Economic Relations Group, the blue-ribbon "Wise Men's" committee of American and Japanese business leaders, said:

> An important reason for the recent decline in United States productivity has been an antagonistic, burdensome and highly uncertain regulatory environment. While the health, safety and environmental objectives are desirable, the costs in productivity growth have been significant. . . .
>
> In addition to diverting capital from productive to non-productive investments, regulations have increased the cost of product development, added to the costs of product liability loss protection and prevention, lengthened product cycles, increased reporting requirements, disproportionately burdened small business, and raised uncertainties and risks in ultimate standards.

In Japan the problem of environmental pollution was at least as grave as in the United States. It appears even more critical when we think of the small area of the country. Nor did the Japanese public simply resign itself to industrial pollution, as the Japan, Inc. "all-for-business" stereotype would suggest. On the contrary, victims' groups and their sympathizers were organized throughout the country as a result of several serious cases of pollution, notably the Minamata sickness and similar cases of mercury poisoning in the late sixties and the pollution caused by petrochemical companies in the city of Yok-kaichi. In one of the rare cases where Japanese went to law to solve a problem, it resulted in a clear verdict against the companies involved.

As public sentiment rose against pollution, many local governments adopted antipollution measures. Finally a consensus developed in Kasumigaseki for action. After much in-fighting among ministries—for example, Health and Welfare advocated strict antipollution controls, MITI did not—a sweeping environmental control law passed the Diet in 1969. Health and Welfare Minister Suzuki Zenko, who became prime minister in 1980, was a prime supporter. In 1971 an Environmental Agency was established. It bore some resemblance to the Environmental Protection Agency in the United States.

Here, however, any similarity to the American experience in pollution control ended. Except for the round of victims' suits in the courts, the fight against industrial pollution was waged not by confrontation, but by a combination of public pressures against industry and government "guidance," heavily sweetened by tax incentives and antipollution development assistance. The bureaucracy had many weapons at its disposal and used most of them. Oil refineries were given permits and allocations that depended on a company's alertness in solving pollution problems.[1] Steel mills were assisted in desulfurization efforts by government research, then given substantial tax credits for the installation of antipollution equipment. An Environmental Pollution Control Service Corporation was set up to assist the smaller companies in their antipollution work with special loans, as well as to provide technical advice.

The bureaucracy's assistance was backed by the government's regulatory powers. These could have serious effect, especially when applied selectively to noncomplying companies in highly competitive industries. Thus, with a minimum of open confrontation, the government edged industry, by the judicious use of carrot and stick, into adopting strong antipollution controls. The carmakers were the most recalcitrant. (In Japan, as in the United States, the management of well-running automobile assembly lines seems to give executives the feeling that their interests, as they define them, are unfailingly identical with those of the country.) Here a combination of local and national government pressures and press outcry finally had its effect. And Japan's automakers grudgingly adopted the set of strict auto-emission controls that they now take credit for. The standards in Japan are indeed stricter than those in the United States. But it took a public rebuke of Toyota, the largest manufacturer, by the Environmental Agency to bring them all into line.

THE EARNEST SAVERS

When I was a small boy in modern American prehistory, a prominent radio children's program emcee, working for a savings bank chain somewhere in New York, used to push the idea that children should become "earnest savers." His commercials were vestigial remnants of the old Calvinist morality that saving was better than spending and that the family that saved together in this life might just attain salvation more easily in the next. His message was not heard for a long time. When savings were advocated in the eighties, after years of TV barkers suggesting that anything but debt financing is virtually un-American, this was by way of introducing new high interest rates, with the implication that investing at your local bank is finally a better deal than lotteries or off-track betting. When Americans heed the new commercials and save, it is probably in the context of a money market fund. In any case, it was a far cry from what we used to hear about frugal, saving characters like Benjamin Franklin.

The Japanese are anachronistic survivors of the Ben Franklin mentality. They are the last earnest savers. In 1980, Japanese families saved 22 percent of their disposable personal income. The comparable American figure was 6 percent. For many years Japan's gross domestic capital formation—the total of corporate, personal, and government savings—has approximated 40 percent, twice what it is in the United States and Europe. Actual private sector capital investment is about 20 percent of GNP, also twice what it is in the United States.

The Japanese national tendency to put yen in the bank is the product of many factors. In the Japanese family, for example, extra money comes mainly in the form of twice-yearly bonuses, which can range from three months' salary to seven or eight months' (given an awfully good profit year) on each occasion. The impulse to save this money is strong. Retirement bonuses are generally one-time lump sum payments. Government social security payments are not very large. Thus people are constantly saving for the house they hope to buy (albeit often with the company's help) or an old age with lowered income. The ingrained disposition to put money away is part of Japanese frugality, fostered since the days of Ishida Baigan and the development of the Confucian business ethic. This instinct has remained remarkably strong.

It is also supported by government policy. The government fosters the saving impulse. When a Japanese wage earner puts away some money, he has the assurance that deposits of up to 3 million yen bring him tax-free interest. Nor is it difficult—at least at present—to establish other 3-million yen accounts on the same terms.

Through this and other supportive measures Japanese have a good incentive to save, of the sort that has been hotly debated in the United States for some years. Indeed, thanks to the Japanese earnest savers, Japan offers us one example of the supply-side economics about which so much has been recently written. The Japanese earnest savers' money, through the banks, is translated into investment in capital goods. The more investment, the better productivity. Thus far at least the earnest savers in Japan, content with their tax-free interest, are a far weightier factor in Japan's economy than market analysts, worrying over quarterly percentages of earnings, leaving banks and managers free to make their long-term investments. As capital is created and the resultant product sold, the job-secured companies will dutifully put their productivity bonuses back into savings, thus ensuring what Japan's great economist statesman, Okita Saburo, calls a "virtuous circle."

THE QUEST FOR QUALITY

There are other reasons for the productivity gap between Japan and the United States. Japan's expenditure in R & D is steadily increasing, while American R & D is falling off. (In 1979, incidentally, the number of Japanese patent applicants in major countries significantly passed the American figure.) In the United States, the soaring increase in takeovers and mergers, as companies cheerfully cannibalize one another for financial reasons, continues to represent a severe loss of productivity. The billions spent on buy-outs and acquisitions, if put into new plant and product, would have significant effect. As things now stand, they represent a massive minus factor of over $50 billion yearly.

Cheap labor, incidentally, is not a compelling argument for Japan's high productivity. Both Japanese automobile-makers and steelmakers are paid by standards comparable to current *general* manufacturing levels in the United States. If anything, they are slightly above it. It is the American carmakers and steelmakers who have tended to labor-price themselves out of the market, by continually increasing pay-and-benefits packages, as the unions demanded it, but without reference to their management-worker productivity. In 1969, for example, the average worker at General Motors earned about 70 percent more than the average American factory worker. Even if we add in shipping charges, which come to about $500, we find that Japanese manufacturers are making a small car nowadays for $1,300 to $1,500 less than Detroit. Wage differences make up only a small part of this.

For the largest and most important factor in Japan's productivity lead we must return to the strong point of Japan's business: the cooperative management of its "people" capital. Management and labor cooperate in seeing that wage gains are linked to increases in productivity. And the Japanese concern for quality in manufacturing is the next thing to a passion. It is the focus of competition between companies and between work units in the same company. As Professor Robert H. Hayes of the Harvard Business School explained it:

> The Japanese believe that quality is good and better quality is therefore better than lesser quality. They will go beyond any sort of rational trade-off to achieve this. For example, if you analyze the percentage defects in a process and the costs of making that percentage less, you will very often find that it makes sense to go from five percent defects to one percent defects. If you then ask whether it makes sense to go from one percent defects to $\frac{1}{10}$ of a percent defects, the economics will generally say, "No, that does not make sense." And the American firm will not, therefore, take that step.
>
> The Japanese firm will. If you say to them, "That's silly. It makes no economic sense," they will answer, "We don't care. Better quality is better than poorer quality." Once they get to $\frac{1}{10}$ of one percent, they will go to $\frac{1}{100}$ or $\frac{1}{1000}$ of one percent. Then they will look at you with a disarming smile and say, "That's what makes us such fierce competitors. You may be satisfied with one percent defects, but we are not."[2]

The search for quality in the Japanese workplace is not merely a device ordered up by management to enhance productivity. Although planned and stimulated by management, it now amounts to a grass-roots movement among the employees of Japanese enterprises, with labor unions often participating and guiding it as well. The enthusiasm of the quest for quality is contagious. And it seems perfectly capable of traveling across the Pacific to factories in the United States.

The appearance of quality control circles in Japanese plants has previously been noted. Originating from the idea of Dr. Deming and other American engineers to eliminate substandard variances in manufacture by statistical methods, it was developed by the Japanese into a powerful instrument for increasing worker participation in setting productivity standards and ensuring worker commitment to quality goals. It is called variously quality control (QC) groups, zero-defects groups, or simply by the generic name of "self-supervisory" groups *(jishu kanri)*. Most such groups consist of from five to ten employees who are engaged in a specific activity, whether in a factory or office, although some groups are larger. Japanese companies have been encouraging such small worker groups since the mid-1960s. Workers at Japanese corporations are first taught the principles of statistical control, which amounts to learning how to study the most basic production processes, isolate their components, and decide by discussion and trial and error how they can be improved.

Workers in an auto factory, for example, may deal with the problem of changing a large stamping die in the shortest possible time so as not to hold up the production process. Workers at a camera factory set out to cut down the degree of variation in copier lamp voltage at a testing point. At a steel mill a quality control circle has the goal of cutting costs of lining material for molten steel flow conduits. Workers at a clothing factory change the production process for sewing brassieres, with a consequent saving in time and increase in output.

While engineers and technicians are helpful in these quality control operations, the system is based on the premise that the workers actually doing a job are best equipped to analyze the efficiency of the process and correct defects in it. Sometimes this takes a great deal of time. At Nippon Kōkan's Keihin Works four quality control circles worked eighteen months to assemble and test data for what became an award-winning plan for energy conservation.

The groups are constantly competing for a system of individual and group awards for good quality performance. And such competition is popular. At Nippon Steel, for example, 75 percent of all employees have volunteered for quality control work. The 55,442 participants are organized in 7,412 separate groups. Among their targets for improvement are environment pollution, energy saving, general quality and reduction of defects, safety, material savings, and labor saving.

A chain of command for quality control groups must be set up in such a way that it reinforces the normal chain of command, not interferes with it. Top management does this by setting up a committee for quality control supervision, which in turn organizes plant QC committees. These are organized into blocs, with middle management committees in charge. These see to it that the basic small unit committees get technical help, where needed, for their projects.

The precise form of these QC committees is not important. They are only one symptom of Japan's people-oriented capitalism. But they offer a marvelously convenient device for working on quality and efficiency in the workplace, at the basic worker level, without the need for putting in several layers of inspectors and supervisors to act as policemen and catch defects only after they appear. The QC system can prevent defects from appearing and minimize those which do.

A plant with a good quality control system is self-policing. In most Japanese factories, as we have seen, workers themselves are given the responsibility for good quality. Related to this self-supervision are devices that Japanese business has made well known, like cutting down on floor inventories and the practice of a worker stopping the assembly line himself, if he has a problem, and getting help to solve it on the spot—instead of leaving an imperfection for the supervisor to fix. There are, understandably, fewer levels of supervisors needed in such operations. Each worker is encouraged to be his own inspector, to take responsibility for what he does. If he has a problem, his immediate work group will help him solve it. If he has a good idea, the credit goes to him—and his workmates.

This quest for quality, along with technological innovations that now include the wide use of industrial robots, helps create new productivity records. Some thirty-five workers at a Nissan plant, for example, aided by industrial robots, produce 350 Datsun car bodies every eight hours, more than six times the productivity rate of American manufacturers. Or take the example of comparable plants

—GM's one-time showplace at Lordstown, Ohio, and Honda's at Suzuka, Japan. Honda's plant can turn out 100 cars an hour. GM's total is barely 75, with many to be recalled later owing to defects.

Modern quality control has served to reinforce the old work ethic. The old samurai Suzuki Shōzan and Confucian thinkers like Baigan and Shibusawa would recognize kindred spirits in the members of a zero-defects group at ultramodern steel mills like that at Japan Steel's Oita Works, whose slogan for some time was "001"—for zero accident, zero pollution, and No. 1 performance. Their ethic shows up in the hundreds of thousands of suggestions for better performance which Japanese workers send to management, and to which they receive a prompt response. Toyota Motor Company, for example, has about 54,000 employees. In one year it receives more than a half million suggestions from them about how to improve product and productivity.

The Japanese company is, as Yamamoto Shichihei noted, a community as well as a functional organization. The rubrics and festivals of this community are not imposed on it. They are welcomed by its people—from the company teams, the company schools, and the company matchmakers (many younger employees still prefer semiarranged marriages) to the young office ladies who ritually come to the office at the end of the New Year's vacation to show off their richly colored kimono, in the Japanese corporate version of the Easter parade.

There is more than mere groupiness here. In his search for quality, the modern Japanese worker perpetuates the same feeling of respect for the craftsman which makes Japan one of the few countries in the world to honor its artisans and skilled performers with the designation of Living National Treasures.

These workers and their managers are also telling all of us something about our postindustrial society. For them the world is something more than a series of rights and entitlements. They have been demonstrating for us all that everyone in a boat must take his turn at the oars. And Japanese management has made this possible, not least of all by accepting the fact that they, too—directors, department heads, and shop supervisors—are essentially members of the same crew as the workers' group in the quality circle.

11·Doing Business in Japan

Go ni haitte wa go ni shitagae *(when you come to a place, follow its customs).*

—Japanese "when-in-Rome" proverb

On the face of things, Japan is the perfect market for American goods. Both American workmanship and American tastes have historically been admired, along with American ingenuity and efficiency. And if American quality standards now have their critics in Japan, the general popular admiration for the American style has only intensified. Blue jeans and mass-produced high fashion, fast food emporia, Hollywood movies, the big-city hotel, American airplanes, American records, the cult of the car—the whole red, white, and blue neon of the twentieth century American life-style has been cheerfully assimilated and adapted by the Japanese, with a conspicuous lack of the intracultural resentment against it so visible in Europe. One would think Japan the perfect target for expanding American exports of consumer as well as capital goods; and fertile soil for heavy American investment of the sort that has gone on in Europe.

Such obviously is not the case. Instead almost the reverse has happened. While the Japanese export more of their goods to the United States, Americans cannot even maintain the current level of exports to Japan, still less expand the percentages of market share. From 1968 to 1976, for example, American marketing share in Japan's manufactured goods imports decreased in every category. Since the early seventies the American trade deficit with Japan has looked year by year like entries on a red fever chart. The U.S. Department of Commerce's estimates for the 1981 deficit are at the level of $18 billion, while the projected deficit for 1982 may hit the startling figure of $20 billion. How has this happened?

The explanation is more complex than the simplistic charges of "dumping" or "unfair competition" raised by would-be protectionists in the United States. Partly it is a matter of Japan's concentration in certain export areas and long-range marketing strategies, which, as in the case of the electronics industry, virtually created international markets for their products. Market shares of certain Japanese products sold in the United States rose dramatically, as these concentrated selling drives succeeded. As of 1982 Japanese automobiles held 20 percent of the American market, Japanese steel between 15 and 20 percent, cameras more than 30 percent, watches and radios more than 50 percent, machine tools 20 percent, motorcycles 90 percent.

Partly the problem is one of Japan's own historic protectionism. Although the Japanese now justly claim that they have "liberalized" tariff and many other formal restrictions, past restrictions inhibiting American and European manufactured exports to Japan gave Japanese manufacturers what amounted to a head start on their trade competitors. Similarly American business in the past was not alert to many marketing opportunities in Japan. It is far more difficult and more expensive to start a U.S. export offensive in the eighties than it would have been to spend money on international marketing in the sixties, when the Japanese were starting *their* export drives.

Other problems are involved with government attitudes, both short-term and long-term. Over the years, as we have noted, the American capitalist economy has been "market-rational," with government merely regulating industry, while the "plan-rational" Japanese have historically thought of government as actively supporting the development of new businesses and new markets. Specific economic policies of both governments also, inevitably, influence the trade balances between the countries. One result of high interest rates in the United States is to increase the value of the dollar and correspondingly cut down the value of the yen, as Japanese investment money flows out toward the United States. As a result, Japanese exports become even stronger in the American market, while American exporters have greater difficulty selling to Japan.

There is also a problem of mentality and approach. The American consumer society is just what it seems to be: a vast marketplace where the prizes go to the most appealing products irrespective of their origin. If the consumer likes them, they are good. The Japanese consumer society looks like that and once within it much the same market rules can apply. But a truly free market inside Japan remains limited by the heritage of the past and a certain built-in wariness toward accepting a totally free market in the future. Outwardly the Japanese consumer may wear the informal dress of the world's second most affluent society. But underneath the leisure styling we can still detect the armor of an economic garrison state.

It is not my purpose here to review the complex story of Japanese-American trade, a tale well told by many, but a brief outline may be of use. First consider some premises. Although Japan's total exports rarely exceed 12 percent of the GNP—less than half the percentage of big exporters like West Germany, for example—they are an important 12 percent. Japan relies on its trading partners for a great portion of its food and fuel. And it must earn the money to buy this. Fully one-third of Japan's food imports, as well as a large amount of industrial raw materials, come from the United States. The Japanese must always export more manufactured goods to the United States than Americans export to them, for they must first earn money to pay for the food and raw materials they buy from us. The fact that Japan must export to feed itself, literally, is etched on the consciousness of every Japanese, conspicuously including customs officials and bureaucrats in the economic ministries. It is part of the stored memory of scarcity which the Japanese still cherish.

Through the fifties and sixties Japan was protectionist. The development strategies that the Kasumigaseki bureaucrats worked out for the country were premised on supporting key growth industries and shielding them from competition as far as possible, until they were strong enough to fend for themselves. Business cooperated in this effort. Prodded by the government, companies in declining industries tried to change their product mix and diversify, while companies in the favored growth-potential industries tried to expand quickly. They received every encouragement to do so. This pattern was the opposite of what so frequently happened in the United States, where the government, insofar as it interfered in the marketplace, tended to favor fading labor-intensive industries in trouble, for example, textiles, and concentrated on keeping them alive (and their voters and political contributors happy) while leaving the growth area industries to fend for themselves.

Starting in the sixties, Japan began to "liberalize" and reduce its tariff barriers. This was done under heavy pressure from its trading partners, particularly the United States (whose Occupation authorities, as we have seen, had ironically been the first to put a protectionist hedge around postwar Japanese industries). Going into the eighties, we find that the Japanese have cut their tariffs to a level as low or lower than similar barriers in the United States. As the Report of the Japan–United States Economic Relations Group noted in 1981, the same development-minded government agencies that were principally engaged in pushing Japanese exports in the soaring sixties and early seventies are now trying to hold them back (with the exception of a few like computers and semiconductors). The worldwide network of JETRO (Japan External Trade Organization), for example, has since late in the seventies been concentrating on advising foreigners how best to sell their products in Japan, in contrast to its missionary work for Japanese exports some years before.

In some industries, like steel and electronics, Japanese corporations have either voluntarily reduced their exports to the United States or switched from an exports-only policy to one of plant investment in the United States. (In others, like the automobile industry, industry leaders continue to push their sales, having agreed to some cutbacks only after the most intense government pressure was put on them.) Only agriculture, owing to strong political considerations, still receives heavy tariff protection against foreign competition.

Inside Japan, the original heavy restrictions on foreign investment have largely disappeared. Liberalization is now more or less a fact. Thanks to more American pressure, indeed, the Japanese are even arranging for American companies to bid on materials for the semi-government public policy companies, for example, Nippon Telephone and Telegraph Corporation. And many of the complicated regulations on testing and inspection of foreign products, which hardly favored their entry, are slowly being revised or repealed.

Nonetheless, both American manufacturing exports to Japan and American investment in Japan are still slower than they ought to be. Part of the answer lies in the cumulative effect of past trade restrictions against them. In addition, the Japanese have been slow to clear out the thicket of complex regulations, standards, and testing and inspection procedures for foreign products, which have made life very difficult for businesses exporting to Japan. Even where restrictions on manufactured goods are eased, regulations in the service and investment sector continue to be tight, in many ways justifying American demands for "reciprocity." As Ambassador Mike Mansfield cautioned the Japanese in a January 1982 speech in Tokyo:

> When the Bank of Tokyo wanted to expand in the U.S. it bought the California First Bank. This gave it immediately over 100 branches in California with full power to accept deposits and act as any other U.S. bank. No American bank could do the same in Japan. When Fujitsu wanted American technology and a foothold in the U.S. market, it bought part of Ampahl. No U.S. company could do the same here. When Green Cross wanted access to American blood plasma, it bought Alpha, the second largest blood collector in the U.S. No U.S. company could do the same here. . . .
>
> The bilateral trade imbalance will not be solved by emergency imports alone or the restriction of [Japanese] exports. The fundamental problem will only be solved when and if U.S. and other foreign firms believe they have opportunities for access to the Japanese market equivalent to that which Japanese firms enjoy in the U.S. and elsewhere.

Part of the fault, however, lies with American companies themselves. The same emphasis on short-term profits over long-term growth and market share in American firms makes them poorly situated for the kind of long-range seeding program necessary to obtain a foothold in Japanese markets. When Nippon Telephone and Telegraph, for example, finally opened bidding to foreigners, few American firms stepped forward to compete. The U.S. government is also to blame. The same insistence on rigid observance of antitrust and other regulatory statutes by American companies overseas, as well as in the United States, has worked against their expansion.

In the sixties, also, many American businesses guessed wrong about Japan's economic prospects. Instead of establishing a corporate presence in Japan, they made money in what seemed then like the easy way, licensing patents and technology to the Japanese. This practice later came back to haunt them, as scores of Japanese companies became strong competitors, using American technology.

Later, the cost of starting a business seemed too great for most, especially since it had to be expensed. As James Abegglen and Thomas Hout have written:

> U.S. companies have traditionally entered advanced markets in Europe via acquisition, and European companies are now replaying the pattern in their U.S. entry. . . . Because acquisitions of successful companies are not possible [in Japan] the high costs of entry to Japan —acquiring land, warehouses and plant, searching out staff in a country with little job mobility, building a distribution system, establishing a brand position—all must be treated as expenses out of current earnings. . . . Few U.S. companies and few U.S. managers are in a position to undertake that sort of reduction in reported earnings for the sustained period necessary to establish a position in a highly competitive market. Further, U.S. stock prices are directly related to earnings per share, and to short-term changes in earnings per share. U.S. executive compensation is importantly linked to share price levels. The combination makes financing entry into the Japanese market by expense investment extremely difficult.[1]

The contrast between American attitudes toward exports and Japanese, over the postwar period, is revealing. For the Japanese to export has always been a necessity, if for no other reason than to earn money for the food, raw materials, and fuel that must be imported, simply to keep the society going. But in their postwar planning the Japanese, business and bureaucracy alike, went beyond this idea. Japanese businessmen were the first to think of the world in terms of a global market, in which marketing outside Japan, despite the relatively small percentage of total GNP it represented, became fully as important as marketing inside Japan. In times of recession at home, exports grow heavier, to take up the slack; and exports play a disproportionately heavy role in developing productivity and growth.

The government bureaucracy, like a military General Staff, fostered a concentration of exports in certain key industries, planning its big export breakthroughs at a few strategic positions. Industry cooperated. The whole impression of Japanese exports and, now, investments resembles that of an army on the march. The huge Japanese multinational trading companies move ahead first, testing markets, arranging local contacts, buying up available supplies of raw materials and component parts, like mobile reconnaissance units.[2] The overseas offices of the semigovernment JETRO assist in the work of intelligence and act as a backup for Japanese businesses when the main body comes in to sell. Meanwhile the government in Tokyo lays down heavy artillery barrages in the form of tax credits, depreciation allowances, and R & D assistance as artillery support.

Despite the military metaphor, there is no real high command in this army. Within it are bickerings, disagreements, and great differences of opinion about both strategies and tactics. What makes it work is the fact that both the business leadership and the government share roughly the same premises about export strategies. And so far they have been successful. Unity does not have to be imposed. Shibusawa Eiichi's idea about business serving country and public is widespread enough among Japan's present business leadership to make formal directives unnecessary. There is enough communication about objectives through the Keidanren and its allied business organizations back in Tokyo.

The garrison-state mentality behind this "offensive" export promotion lingers on in Japan even after most of the subsidies and government guidance have been expended. When a foreign business comes to Japan, a wall of "defensive" resistance goes up semiautomatically, almost without people realizing it. Nothing over the years has been so revealing of Japanese thinking about foreign business in their country than military words like *landing* and *advancing* used to describe the applications of foreign firms to do business there. Historically, this garrison-state mentality has good reasons behind it. Barely a century ago, Japanese industries were being created overnight in a desperate effort to avoid foreign domination. In the late sixties, executives of an American corporation, about to request Japanese government permission for a new joint venture, asked the advice of a veteran American businessman in Tokyo. "Just remember one thing," he said, "and take it as a basic premise. In principle, they don't want you in."

By contrast the American attitude toward export business, at least until recently, has been one of unconcern. Just as it is hard for Japanese to abandon the garrison-state mentality, it is hard for Americans to abandon the "unlimited frontier" theory of easy expansion and realize that exports and export policies are now as essential for the United States as they are for anybody. Far from developing its own kind of General Staff programs for furthering American exports, the U.S. government has, if anything, complicated the work of the exporter or foreign investor tremendously by overloading him with restrictions and regulations, and forcing him as much as possible to fight his battles against foreign competition on distant fields, while obeying regulatory standards designed for the market in America.

Nonetheless, in Europe and elsewhere, American business—export and investment—expanded dynamically in the postwar period. The successes of U.S. multinationals in Europe gave rise to books like Jean-Jacques Servan-Schreiber's *The American Challenge.* Not so in Japan. The American businessman's life there has been one of steady coping with obstacles. His struggles in Japan are complicated by a general confusion of assumptions. What is unfair discrimination to a representative of America's "market-rational" economy often seems completely logical and normal inside "plan-rational" Japan. First, to get into his market, the American businessman probably has to confront an old-boy network of Japanese companies, with interlocking support from subcontractors and suppliers—most of them apparently related—who may compete fiercely among themselves but are rarely averse to uniting against a foreigner. Japanese also tend to judge foreign businesses by more critical standards than they do one of their own.

Secondly, there is the government. Even with increasing liberalization there remain unreasonable demands for inspection and product testing. As Roy Rowan noted in a 1981 *Fortune* article on this subject:

> Japanese [automobile] exports to the United States need only a manufacturer's label certifying that the cars meet U.S. safety standards. But before an American car can be sold in Japan, its government requires six volumes of documents on standards for each model, plus local testings of nearly every vehicle—all of which adds as much as $500 to the retail price.

This example can be multiplied readily in other fields.

"Bureaucratic procedures" is an innocent-sounding phrase, but it can be used to deadly effect to destroy competition. What does it matter if the government approves entry of your product into Japan —two years after you applied?

One of the most absurd of the Japanese monopoly strongholds is the government-owned Monopoly Corporation, which imports all cigarettes into Japan. The tobacco monopoly also sells its own cigarettes, from which the government realizes heavy profits. More importantly, perhaps, it represents a living for some 38,700 embattled bureaucrats who will fight to the water's edge defending their corporate homeland. The restrictions placed on foreign cigarettes, both in quantity and pricing, represent the *reductio ad absurdum* of protectionism. Their concern is obvious—most Japanese prefer American cigarettes.

Despite all the obstacles, the history of the postwar period has shown that an American company with planning sense, patience, and a willingness to humor Japanese custom and concerns *can* establish a good lasting business in Japan. From Du Pont to Levi Strauss to Procter & Gamble, examples show how intensive cultivation of the market will win in the end, as long as a company is prepared to wait awhile for its profits. Undoubtedly there have been many failures. Most were caused by American companies' inability to abandon their own preconceptions and give the Japanese customer what he wants. Japanese trade apologists can justly point to the fact that— in contrast to their own painstaking surveys of the American market, American carmakers have never even bothered to ship cars with right-hand drive to Japan. As Michael B. Emery of Du Pont Far East explained in a 1982 *Business Week* article: "Americans try to sell products over here that sell well in the U.S. The left-hand drive car mentality is a symbol of the mentality of U.S. manufacturers."

Almost any American businessman struggling to establish his own variety of enterprise in Japan begins to think of his experience as a microcosm of a vast and infinite universe of small problems. Almost invariably he is correct. Except for the representatives of the oil majors or the bearers of coveted technology patents (who are given the status of rare protected species in Japan), most American businessmen have to cope with the same set of "givens." This is no accident. Japan's business society is so tightly centralized, despite the competition within it, that the challenge—or threat—posed by the foreign entrant, whether to government, to competitors, or to labor, is about the same.

To Americans, who are used to the windy crosscurrents of their own adversary procedures, the business climate inside Japan at first seems like that of a friendly hothouse. Everyone is really polite and genuinely solicitous about the visitor's welfare. The Japanese really seem more *sincere*. It is not hard to think this way, particularly after coming from a business world where the new president will ask smilingly after the health and well-being of your wife and family just before he fires you. In the Japanese business universe, you discover with some interest, there are no firings; or almost none. It takes the visitor a little longer incubation time in the hothouse to realize that in the ideal Japanese business society there are also no foreigners. If a visitor wants to stay, he must work hard and patiently to justify his residence.

As I have said, my own struggles in Japanese business began when I inherited management of a newly founded but flourishing sales company, Encyclopaedia Britannica (Japan), Inc., which was doing surprisingly well, with $6-million annual sales, selling English-language sets of *Encyclopaedia Britannica.* I had come to Britannica at the request of the late Senator William Benton, its chairman, and Maurice B. Mitchell, then its president. Both of them were fascinated by the Japanese market and its potential, and anxious to develop more editorial product for Japan. I was grateful for their support. Along with the late Imamichi Junzo, chairman of Tokyo Broadcasting System, who ultimately became our joint-venture partner, they kept me both productive and sane, often under severe provocation.

Given the English-language capabilities of most Japanese, it was fairly clear that the market for English-language encyclopaedias in Japan had its limits. My Chicago headquarters agreed with me. We first put together some English-language instruction books and cassettes. Then Mitchell helped me start work on a more ambitious English-language teaching course with linguists at Sophia University. I hired some editors and began translating a few ancillary products of Britannica into Japanese, also, so our new customers would have at least something immediately readable for themselves and their families.

By 1968, we were able to start selling Sophia's English-language teaching program, with an advanced type of tape recorder, which later became a fixture at "language labs" throughout the United States. This we called English Master. It proved most successful, giving Encyclopaedia Britannica (Japan), Inc. for the first time a selling alternative to the English-language encyclopaedia business. We also decided to translate into Japanese something more ambitious than the fairy stories for children with which we had started. To celebrate the 200th anniversary of Britannica, our Chicago editors had produced a set of a dozen books called *Britannica Perspectives,* single-volume treatises on the state of various arts and disciplines, for example, mathematics, religion, education, the fine arts, which were done as preliminary work for the impending revision of the *Britannica*. Their prime mover was the late Robert M. Hutchins, then chairman of the *Britannica*'s board of editors, who during successive incarnations as president of the University of Chicago and chairman of the Fund for the Republic, had led a steady, if often lonely campaign to restore balance and meaning to American education.

In Japan we separated the ungainly three-volume American set into twelve books, in the smaller size preferred by Japanese readers, and prefaced each of the volumes with an introduction by a Japanese scholar. They became a popular item in our selling package, in sharp contrast to their indifferent reception back home. This served to confirm an impression that the Japanese reading public would cheerfully purchase books that the American book buyer would reject as too abstruse, theoretical, or just difficult.

The year before, in the course of a pleasant diplomatic lunch, a Japanese friend, Kase Shunichi, the distinguished writer and former diplomat, had suggested to me that the time might be ripe for *Britannica* to translate itself into Japanese. A wealthy industrialist friend, he added, would be very interested in helping finance such a project on a joint-venture basis. At first the idea seemed farfetched. Translating anything into Japanese presents cultural as well as linguistic problems. Given the almost limitless scope of an encyclopaedia, these could only proliferate. But the idea would not go away. Providentially, Britannica at that time had been preparing a kind of simplified international encyclopaedia, designed for translation in modular form, which the company hoped to sell around the world, beginning with an Arabic version for the Middle East.

Our would-be collaborator, the late Kajima Morinosuke, chairman of Kajima Construction Company, in the end decided that publishing encyclopaedias was too far out of his line. But his initial enthusiasm and cooperation enabled us to set up a study group, commission a variety of advertising agency audience surveys, and begin planning just what shape a Japanese-language *Britannica* would take. The editors and scholars in our study group quickly concluded that, while some of our International Module may have been suitable for Middle East consumption, it was far too elementary for Japanese minds. Nor did any of us in Tokyo like the idea, advanced by some, that we first come into print with a simplified children's encyclopaedia, then—if that went well—expand to translate the whole *Britannica*. "*Britannica* has an old and good reputation in Japan," the Japanese advisers argued. "If you were to go into

Japan with anything less but the full quality adult *Britannica* itself, you would be suspect."

With a study group running in full cry and a group of editors going over our title lists to see how many *Britannica* articles needed supplement or slight revision for the benefit of Japanese readers, our small planning group pondered how we would attract a suitable Japanese partner for the project. The Kajima interests had bowed out. To find an alternative, we went, quite logically, to the local Japanese equivalent of management consultant, father confessor, marriage broker, and loan shark: the nearby branch of our leading bank. The bank, after several false starts, put us in touch with Tokyo Broadcasting System (TBS), the biggest and most prosperous of the nongovernment radio and television networks in Japan. TBS's twentieth anniversary was coming up, and its chairman, Mr. Imamichi, was anxious to commemorate it suitably. A Japanese-language edition of the esteemed *Britannica* would not be a bad way.

Why did we not go it alone? The first reason was the strong competition. A foreign company going into Japanese-language publishing would be in every sense of the word the new boy on the block. The only way to stay healthy in this role in Japan is to have an experienced local partner who knows the other fellows.

A second reason was people. To most Japanese who do not work for it (and often to many who do), a foreign company is something unpredictable and nervous-making, like a riverboat gambler who is also carrying typhoid. Japanese are often chary of joining a foreign company, however impressive its credentials. Despite the presence of both foreign and Japanese headhunters inside Japan, it is hard to induce good people to leave their jobs and join a foreign company. Like most foreign companies, we were lucky to find the employees we did. Not for us the automatic entry of elite graduates from Tokyo University. We had a mixed bag—on the one hand, dropouts from other companies, or survivors of bankrupt entrepreneurships; on the other, bright young people who were genuinely interested in being "internationalists," in learning English or perfecting it, and in studying presumably improved and refined American management methods.

Thus, while our staff was good, there was no tradition to it nor backup behind it, as there would be in a Japanese company. Salesmen would join us in droves—as the Britannica ads promised lavish incentives and reward. It was far harder to recruit the good company bureaucrats who can keep almost any set of corporate wheels greased and running. We were foreign. How big and how good we were at home was of little consequence. That was too far away. This was Japan.

Our young employees were getting better at their jobs, however. And to have the prospect of long-term planning for a Japanese-language *Britannica* encouraged them far more than I had expected. The great fear of Japanese working for a foreign company then (and now) is that the foreigners will go away. This fear has been abetted by the large percentage of foreign companies that close down their offices at the first sign of failure. In our case it was allayed by a realization that a company that began selling English-language encyclopaedias was now anxious to become a part of the Japanese-language publishing industry.

By early 1969 we had worked out the details of a partnership with TBS and Toppan Printing Company, in which Britannica was to have a majority interest. It was then that I made the acquaintance of the government bureaucracy. At the time Japan was slowly coming out of its protectionist carapace. Various industries were being "liberalized," that is, foreigners were allowed to participate and even hold a majority of the shares. The pace of liberalization was slow, almost literally a few percentage points at a time. Publishing, also, was not one of the industries in which a non-Japanese partner might be the majority management partner. So we began a slow gavotte with concerned officials at MITI and the Bank of Japan, explaining the plan of the joint venture and trying to picture for them how unique our contribution to Japanese culture would be.

In talking to the ministries, we were mercifully spared the ministrations of the home-office lawyers and consultants who normally illumine such affairs for American firms. We had engaged two well-connected Japanese firms, an accounting group and an advertising agency. While I had nothing against my own countrymen, it became ever more abundantly clear to me that a foreign company in Japan, unsupported by local friends and auxiliaries, stood as much chance of success as Custer's dismounted cavalrymen fighting unseen Indians.

And ambushes there were. The Japanese press in those days (and it has not changed much) fed on foreign companies for its exposés the way the *Enquirer* feeds on the supposed eccentricities of movie stars. Since Britannica sold its sets door-to-door, salesmen's excesses of zeal, real or fancied, were not hard to find. Although Japanese book companies sold the same way—and, unlike Britannica, barely bothered to police their more enthusiastic members—they were rarely mentioned. It was always "foreign" sales practices (for which read foreign "sharp" practices) that were called into question. When I went to remonstrate with the editor of one of the popular weekly magazines, on hearing of a scurrilous and untrue story he was about to print, he thought for a while, then said: "You may have a point. Let's see, if our writers finish the exposé on Coca-Cola's vicious sales practices in time, we'll run that and kill the story on Britannica."

In 1970 when a publicity-seeking consumers' group organized a so-called Britannica victim's league (by securing the proxies of delinquent purchasers) the press was quick to raise a hue and cry. One "activist" reporter actually participated in the "victims" league councils, then "reported" on them. Another Tokyo daily, not to be outdone, took a photograph of Britannica's then president, my successor, bowing after a meeting with the consumers, in conventional polite fashion, but ran under his picture the caption: " 'I am sorry!' Britannica's president reflects on its excesses." The matter was ultimately settled; and Encyclopaedia Britannica (Japan) went on to great things. But I had never seen such a flagrant case of trial by newspaper. By contrast, many Japanese companies had committed serious wrongs and victimized thousands in industrial pollution scandals; but the newspapers took up those matters only when forced to by the energetic protests of real victims involved.

I could hardly accuse the Japanese of outright xenophobia and racism, coming from a country where "Jap," "Chink," and "slant-eye" are still used by schoolchildren as terms of opprobrium and where the "unprovoked" assault on Pearl Harbor still arouses palpable indignation, while the detention of 100,000 American citizens of Japanese extraction during World War II has only recently become a matter of national attention. But it still hurt me to be even the temporary target of "antiforeign" mudslinging. After all, since my first book I had been considered one of Japan's friends. I kept thinking of the scout who respected the Indians in the old Western movies and kept telling the cavalry not to fire on Chief Red Feather. He was always the first to get it in the back with an arrow when the Sioux broke through.

Despite such diversions, we went ahead with building the joint-venture company to produce an unprecedented Japanese-language version of the *Britannica*. TBS would have been happy with a fifty-fifty relationship, but was prepared to accept a minority position, since it was not itself a publishing company. The Ministry of International Trade and Industry, however, was not all that ready to let a foreign interest have a majority share in *any* Japanese publishing venture. Back and forth we went to the MITI "window" for informal guidance on the shape of the company, as I have noted. Finally, a variety of compromises was accepted, two companies were formed —the second with a Japanese majority—and we were informally told our proposal was not too bad. Within a few days it was officially accepted.

There was a positive reason for the government's permission, besides our willingness to take directions. Although the *Britannica* possessed no valued technology or sought-after patents, it had long stood in Japan for knowledge and authority writ large. To translate this into Japanese, the reasoning ran, would be an asset for the country, none the less valuable for its intangibility. This judgment was seconded, albeit informally, by many Japanese intellectuals who normally were quite against almost any manifestation of American business.

The hard knocks given Britannica's corporate entry into Japan and the interested acceptance for its editorial achievement were, of course, two sides of the Japanese coin: a deep-seated aversion to a foreign (Western) presence combined with an open admiration for Western knowledge. What we lost with one, we gained with another. But the experience tended to encourage mild schizophrenia in those of us who were running the company.

One of the first things I did on arriving in Tokyo was to contribute what little public relations budget I had to help finance a meeting of Pacific area scientists at the University of Tokyo. It was appreciated. So was the long leading article we ran in the 1967 *Britannica Book of the Year* by former Prime Minister Yoshida Shigeru, the closest to a grand old man modern Japan has had. (It turned out to be the last article Yoshida wrote before his death.) These were the opening guns in what became a long campaign to make the Britannica name a household word for something other than selling.

In 1967 Bob Hutchins had visited Tokyo. During his brief stay there, we managed to have meetings and conversations with a good cross section of Japanese academia. Not long after this, with the help of Okochi Kazuo, former president of the University of Tokyo, Hiyama Yoshio, a prominent marine scientist, Nakamura Hajime, the distinguished Buddhist scholar, and others, a faculty committee of the University of Tokyo was formed to advise the editors of

Britannica on the same basis as previously formed committees at Oxford, Cambridge, and Chicago universities. This informal seal of approval was of great help to a foreign publishing company newly arrived in Japan. At the same time it symbolized and encouraged a growing contribution to the *Britannica* by Japanese scholars, as well as increased coverage of Japanese subjects in the *Britannica.* This tendency has continued. The Japanese contribution and its example played no small part in developing a spirit of internationalization in the new fifteenth edition of the *Britannica*—a monument to both Benton and Hutchins—which appeared in 1974.

From my own point of view the acquaintance of so many Japanese scholars, begun in the mid-sixties, more than repaid the struggles we had in expanding Britannica's presence in Tokyo from that of a mere sales outlet for products shipped from America to a producing editorial company whose originally Anglo-American product benefited greatly from Japanese adaptation. No one could help admiring the high standards and dedication with which so many Japanese professors infuse their various disciplines. Without their active and interested support creation of a Japanese-language *Britannica* would not have been possible.

The other element in Britannica's success in Japan was its sales force. Originally led by two gifted but temperamental sales managers (the more gifted the sales manager, the more idiosyncratic is a good rule of thumb in that business) from the United States and Canada, the Japanese salesmen developed into a well-organized organization with a dynamism all its own. They lived in a world of slogans, inspirational drives ("I hate negative thinking"), and 7 A.M. pep meetings, designed to inure them against a hard day of sales calls in a business where the rebuff is more pervasive than the sale. They developed a contagious esprit of their own, typified by a rousing company song that we would all chorus at the cyclical rallies, pep talks, and contests which are the lifeblood of any direct selling group. Once trained and organized, they soon became the best salesmen in Britannica, constantly winning the various worldwide awards given for this purpose. Their enthusiasm was catching. "Have you ever thought," one of our sales managers asked me one day, while managers, trainers, and a variety of cheerleaders were leading a hand-clapping, ear-blasting massed rendition of the Britannica song, "of starting a new religion?"

When we began selling the new *Britannica International Encyclopaedia* in Japanese, we altered our sales approach to a more innovative and more Japanese pattern. We organized the sales force into a separate company, thus to develop its own techniques and strengthen a feeling for independence. This was also in the Japanese tradition. To sell the Japanese-language set, we did away with the buy-for-your-children's-education approach and sold to young Japanese adults—teachers, civil servants, or "salary men" in Japanese companies—who wanted it as a means of self-improvement. In many cases, company "education" departments would not only permit sales canvassing on the company premises, but would also allow for group presentations and permit buyers to purchase the *BIE* through the company. This was a break with old Britannica selling tradition. It worked because it fit the Japanese environment. Probably no country in the world has such a huge population of intelligent readers or so many earnest seekers after improvement.

The encyclopaedia itself, while using basic articles from the English-language *Britannica,* was edited very carefully with an eye to Japanese reader needs and tastes. Not only did we commission new articles about Japanese persons and places—as well as a complete new version of the articles on Japan itself—but we also had to change a great many articles of a general nature to give prominent space, say, to Japanese and Asian flowers, dogs, and birds. After we had selected which articles from *Britannica* we would condense, which expand, and what Japanese-edition supplements we should use, we passed them through a process of translation, translation check, and scholarly review—for which purpose we had assembled a group of outstanding Japanese scholars. Some 5,000 different translators contributed.

We had our share of problems—the Japanese, for example, are not the world's most expert indexers—but we surmounted them, in many cases with the help of specialists generously loaned us by Warren Preece, then editor of *E.B.* But many of the problems were peculiarly Japanese. The economics department of one university, for example, was pro-Marxist, the same department at a nearby university was anti-Marxist. How could we ask for contributors from both? What, indeed, should we do with the article on Marxism? Most Japanese scholars in the field at that time were accounted too uncritically pro-Marxist, but there would be resentment among the mandarinate at having an American article (full of what came to be called "Anglo-Saxon bias") shoved down their throats. We solved the problem by having a prominent Polish student of Marxism write a quite unbiased article. Constant problems of emphasis and opinion arose, from naive editing of political science articles to an imaginative translator rendering the Articles of Confederation and the Constitution as American Constitution numbers one and two.

In the end we solved most of them. When we published the first volume in the late spring of 1972, we were confident that we were giving Japan its first really international encyclopaedia, with heavy foreign as well as Japanese input. Reader acceptance justified our hopes.

One of the original arguments in our marketing surveys for doing a full-scale edition of the *Britannica* was the extraordinarily heavy sale of various encyclopaedias produced with an almost total "Japanese bias." Our assumption proved correct that the Japanese reader had grown sophisticated enough in his tastes to demand a broader spectrum of both information and informed knowledge and informed opinion. By 1974, as the set neared completion, we were selling subscriptions at the rate of 20,000 annually. By 1975, when I relinquished the presidency of TBS-Britannica, sales were stabilizing at a level of 50,000–60,000 sets annually. Over the next few years TBS-Britannica, with its major encyclopaedia and other products, was up to a level of $80 million–$100 million in annual sales, depending on fluctuations in the yen-dollar rate, with very high profitability.

Meanwhile, Encyclopaedia Britannica (Japan), Inc., now recovered from the 1970 consumer crisis, continued to expand the basic English-language teaching courses we had started in 1967, with the help of Sophia University.

Our joint venture, TBS-Britannica, was organized as a Japanese company from the beginning (while E.B. [Japan], the subsidiary, retained a semi-American organization). Over the years we grew inescapably more Japanese in mood as well as form. Almost all meetings were held in Japanese, including board of directors' meetings, which the chairman, Mr. Imamichi—who was also chairman of Tokyo Broadcasting System—used to call "Gibney's Japanese schoolroom," as I stumbled occasionally through the approved liturgy. ("At this terribly busy time," my scripts would begin, "we hesitate to trespass on your time, but thank you for attending. . . . The past half year has been a time of serious economic problems in this country [I have yet to hear any Japanese board report that remotely suggested the national economy was in good shape] but fortunately, thanks to the dedicated efforts of our company personnel, who lent all our energies . . .")

At the end of 1973, Britannica, for reasons unrelated to Japan—

the death of Senator Benton, chairman and virtually the sole proprietor of E.B., had brought some confusion in its wake—sold its majority position to TBS. The most obvious change in procedures was that the old stream of memos and reports no longer had to be sent into Chicago. ("At last," shouted the sales director, "no more of those damn memos in triplicate.") Under my successor from TBS, Yoshida Minoru, who had first worked out the details of the joint venture with us some years back, the international character of the company continued to be stressed. Increasingly the company was becoming a factor in the world of Japanese publishing.

The foregoing is not a case history of my career as an American businessman in Japan. Still less is it a complete record of Britannica's operations in that country. What I have endeavored to show is how success in a venture in Japan can be gained by doing things the Japanese way, insofar as possible. The product must be designed for Japanese. The promotion must be designed for Japanese. The selling must be aimed at Japanese. In so doing, the visiting American must abandon any idea of built-in superiority to the Japanese, who are after all only "a race of imitators." On the contrary, they have much to tell us. A great portion of the hang-ups I observed among American businessmen in Japan were occasioned by their coming to the job with a feeling that they were somehow "superior" to the natives.

The Japanese consumer likes foreign goods. The attraction of a foreign trademark is very real. It is increasing, not diminishing, as witness not merely the success of giants like Dow Chemical, Texas Instruments, Mitsubishi-Caterpillar, and IBM, but also fast-food chains like McDonald's and Kentucky Fried Chicken. But the consumer has a mind and culture of his own. The cultural gravitational pull in Japan is probably the strongest in the world, and concessions must be made to it. Dealing with the Japanese market takes patience and induces a certain amount of humility. The left-hand drive syndrome—the naive assumption that what sells in New York or Los Angeles will sell in Tokyo, without any alterations—is doomed to fail.

12·The Japanese Factor: The Community-Company in America

Know your limits and remember that even the dew of the grass falls when it becomes too heavy.
—The Shogun Tokugawa Ieyasu

Every spring, at the new motorcycle factory in Marysville, Ohio, Honda Motors has a tree-planting ceremony for its American workers. A worker or "associate" who has been with Honda for a year plants a small pine tree on the slightly rolling ground outside the tidy factory buildings. It is a symbol of growth and long-term commitment. As one Honda employee commented: "The tree plantings concern all of us. It signifies not only that our plant is growing as far as production and the number of associates go, but that each individual's tree will grow with it. It gives a person a sense of pride—that for as long as I'm here, I'll have a tree growing there. While I'm growing with the company the tree will grow, too. . . ."[1]

The Honda pine trees are not at all a bad symbol for a new element in American business: an intensified concern for quality and workmanship, backed by a sense of company community, which we might call the Japanese Factor. It is still more talked about than exemplified, but its influence is growing, as more Japanese companies fly in their managers and business philosophies to do business in the United States. To a greater or lesser degree, depending on the circumstances, the Japanese managers are attempting to transplant their ideas of people-centered capitalism onto American soil. At the same time some American companies, more than a little interested, have started to make Japanese-style alterations in their old work patterns on their own. On the whole the transplants seem to be effective. Although hardly the surefire success formula proclaimed by a variety of management consultants—telling U.S. businesses "how-to-do-things-the-Japanese-way" is becoming a major cottage industry in business academia—the Japanese Factor has had a healthy influence on a variety of companies where it was intelligently introduced. Sometimes the effect has been spectacular.

Honda of America set up shop just outside Columbus, Ohio, in 1978 to make motorcycles. The setting and the workers are all American, but the working standards and the work ethic are largely imported from Japan. Thus far the combination has proved successful. Honda now produces 60,000 large-model motorcycles annually at Marysville to sell in the United States and twenty-four other countries. In 1982, an adjacent plant is opening for the production of automobiles. In the face of the huge exports of Japanese cars to the United States, and the correspondingly high unemployment in Detroit, the Japanese have been under heavy pressure to make some of their cars in American plants. Although Nissan Motors has started work on a truck plant in Tennessee, Honda will be the first Japanese automaker to set up an assembly line in the United States. This is significant in many ways. Hitherto, the larger Japanese automobile manufacturers have more or less publicly doubted the ability of an American work force to achieve their Japanese quality standards. This was the principal excuse for not setting up factories in the United States.

Honda has already established motorcycle plants in several countries outside Japan, part of a policy unique among Japanese carmakers to manufacture as well as sell outside Japan. Thus the motorcycle factory was in a way a test case for manufacturing automobiles. As Sugiura Hideo, executive vice-president of Honda Motors, explained:

Our success is based on our belief that we should not only sell elsewhere what we produce in Japan, but also recycle our profits by investing where our markets are. We should find a way to benefit our host countries, such as increasing job opportunities—and incidentally helping raise the level of the industry there. Our management established this policy some time ago. And I think we were correct.

Not many Japanese companies have put this policy into effect, but the number of those who do is increasing. They are moving in that direction.

At the Ohio plant, management emphasizes the two basics of the Japanese Factor: quality production and a sense of community. As Yoshida Shige, the plant manager, put it:

We believe that unless we produce a quality product, we cannot survive. And producing quality is the responsibility of everybody involved in production. It is not the inspector's responsibility to produce a quality product.

Here we all have lunch at the same cafeteria, we all use the same parking lot—and there is no reserved space—everybody shares the same locker rooms. These things create the togetherness of this plant. To maintain this togetherness is the most important issue here. . . . Everybody needs a job, but everybody likes to be treated like a human being, too. . . .

In 1974 the Quasar Division of Matsushita Electrical Company, Japan's largest electronics manufacturer, bought the Motorola color television plant at Franklin Park, Illinois, just outside Chicago. Most of the workers were retained, as were many of the same production facilities. The equipment was thoroughly modernized, however, and some functions were automated. Most significantly, Matsushita introduced its ideas of quality control in an effort to reproduce the quality standards normally attained by its factories in Japan. Although the plant's new management was largely American, every effort was made to select those elements of the Japanese system which could reverse the factory's steady decline in productivity and quality workmanship.

The changeover has had dramatic results. Under the former management, we were told, an average of 150 defects was found for every 100 TV sets produced. Employee morale was low. Absenteeism was the rule rather than the exception and worker turnover was high. As of 1981, the defects had been dramatically cut. They are now running at 5 to 7 percent—that is, five to seven defects for each 100 sets. The field failure rate is now one-tenth of what it was in 1974. There is evidently a new spirit of cooperation among the 2,000-odd employees. Quality months are celebrated, and quality slogans and posters appear on the work floors. Each week mixed groups of workers and management hold small meetings on the pattern of the Japanese quality circles. "Participation" is the key word.

How much of the improvement comes from the Japanese Factor? Richard Kraft, Quasar's president, gives a practical answer:

> You don't think in terms of taking a whole system and either using it or not. You do just as the Japanese did to us. You look, you find the things that are useful and applicable, you adopt them and apply them. Those that are not, you forget.
>
> When you visit a factory and find a quality problem, you can generally conclude correctly that the problem is not with the worker. The problem is with the management. . . . The people we have out there today are by and large the same people here under the previous ownership. But the results achieved are different. It's not because the people have changed, it's because the management has changed. The direction has changed. The environment has changed. The tools have changed. The people haven't—only their attitude. . . .
>
> We try to engender an interest in the company and a loyalty. . . . We try to generate an environment that makes the employees interested in the success of our company. And part of that is seeing the total product and understanding what the total result of their effort is. Part of it is feedback about their performance, not in a critical way, but in an informative way. Part of it is generating a family atmosphere through the employee activities that we support. . . .

Westinghouse Electrical Corporation is all-American, but in 1979, concerned with the need to raise productivity, Thomas J. Murrin, president of Westinghouse's Public Systems Company, decided to try an experiment: introduce the Japanese Factor. In 1980, after a visit to Japan, Murrin decided to test Japanese-style participative management at Westinghouse. To run the test he picked the company's construction group, headed by William A. Coates. Coates then set out, after considerable study, to see if he could replace the built-in adversary relationship of management versus union at his plants with something of a consensus spirit, a mode of decision making that he also injected into meetings on the executive floor.

As Coates explained his purpose:

> When you go into Japanese factories, and you look at their assembly lines, you find many of the workers doing the same kinds of tasks American workers do. . . . But those employees feel a pride and a responsibility and management feels a respect for that employee that's a little different than it is in America. This mutual respect and responsibility between management and the employee—that's the kind of thing we're striving to copy from the Japanese.
>
> Here at Westinghouse we are fostering this mutual respect through quality circles, another Japanese idea. At these meetings, employees share productivity ideas and problems. The company benefits because a "use" sort of experience is tapped and employees benefit because they can play an active role in shaping their work-lives.
>
> When you leave a quality circle meeting as a participant, you go back to your job, hopefully, with the idea in mind that Westinghouse is concerned about quality.
>
> It's been very difficult for me personally to change my management style. I'm like everybody else. I expected to be told when I was the employee and I expected to tell when I was the boss.
>
> It's difficult, but Westinghouse believed we had to learn from the Japanese in this switch to participative management.

One testing ground for Coates's ideas was the old Sturtevant plant at Hyde Park, Massachusetts, just outside Boston. A metalworking plant turning out industrial fans, Sturtevant would appear to be a classic example of a dying American factory. Thoroughly unionized, it had a long history of labor-management suspicion and dispute. From 1976 to 1981 its market declined 19 percent. Under the new participation program, this trend seems to have been reversed. At first suspicious, the workers—union leaders included—have now pitched into the quality circle program with some energy. David Smith, Sturtevant's operations manager, added: "We see this whole issue of participation and involvement as maybe the single most important key ingredient that we can bring to bear to improve the operating effectiveness of the business."

The foregoing comments are those of management. Yet in the case of all three companies, the rank and file seemed to react with similar enthusiasm. There were interesting parallels in their comments. From Honda:

> From past jobs I've always just come home and moped around. Now every day my wife asks me what happened—I tell her all the eventful things that happened. She knows it's a very big change. I've been here about two years and it's the best two years of my life so far. . . . Yeah, I mean it's not just a forty hour a week job. You go there and you can express your ideas all the time. Like I said before, they're always encouraging new ideas and better ways to improve. . . .

From Quasar:

> Well, just about everything changed. They took out all our old belt-lines, we used to run our chassis on a belt and you kept up with that line and kept going. When the Japanese came in, they brought in all their new lines and each chassis stopped in front of the girl. She inserted the parts, stepped on the pedal, and the chassis moved on. . . . You didn't have to lean over to chase the chassis if it went by too fast. . . .
>
> Everybody is quality-conscious now. Because every operator who runs a machine or does any operation is held responsible for that job and they're almost like a full-time inspector on that job. . . .

From Westinghouse:

> Well, first I think that the employee has more input now into the product he is building. He has a greater say into how things should be done and as a result of having some input into his workplace, I think he will make a greater effort to see that a better product is made.
>
> I think if everybody—if everybody does the job properly, we could compete with anybody. It's not competing against the Japanese or the Italians or any other countries. It's doing your job properly. Once you do your job properly, you can compete with anybody.

Such appreciative comments about the Japanese Factor in American business are typical of many others. For as Japanese business expands in this country, the idea of people as capital will doubtless expand with it. Before going on to review why Japanese investment has increased in the United States, two comments are appropriate:

The Japanese idea of the company as a well-knit, quality-conscious community can profitably be transplanted to the United States. Those who caution that cultural barriers of some sort prevent this should recall how deeply present-day Japanese business has been influenced by American models and the leavening effect of the American Occupation. Ironically, the ideas of putting human relations into business and leading by example were preached to the Japanese by U.S. businessmen on loan to MacArthur's occupation forces.

Obviously the mystique of Japanese business cannot be exported as is. For one thing, the stresses, challenges, and opportunities of America's multiracial society, with our clear consciousness of regions, minorities, and special interests, make business-cultural tree-planting of the Japanese order a complex bit of horticulture. But the basics it teaches are as valid for American life as they are for Japanese.

This is especially true of present-day Americans. The young worker's grandfather may have been satisfied either with totally impersonal relationships at the workplace or a cozy but demanding paternalism generally more profitable to the company than to its filial employees. He had other ideals and foci for his interest and loyalties —his church, his country, or a variety of highly participatory community activities, from lodges to volunteer fire departments. The young worker of today either does not share these old ideals at all or subscribes to them nominally, in a very weakened form.

By contrast, he is acutely conscious of immediate gratifications and satisfactions and most concerned about the quality of life. He has if anything an overdeveloped sense of his rights, as opposed to fairly hazy ideas of what responsibilities are. As a member of the "me" generation, whose ego is daily massaged by what amounts to a cult of personal satisfaction, he likes to speak out—and is concerned that his ideas and thoughts be heeded and acted upon. The idea of participating in the company-as-community may be more congenial to him than to past generations. It may be necessary if a company wants to develop in him anything like a commitment to his work.

This raises another point. *Why in the first place did Americans have to learn or relearn such obvious things as the value of cooperation and the appreciation of quality in the products or systems that we make?* That is something to ponder. The United States of America as of the early 1980s is for better or worse the best example of democracy that exists. We are still the freest people and a considerable number of us worry constantly that all of us are not equal enough. Politically speaking, we have participatory democracy, perhaps to a fault. Government, even under the presidency of Ronald Reagan, sees to it that we keep our society egalitarian. Through the rampant criticisms and comment of the press, the lawsuits and protests of hundreds of single-issue constituencies, and the well-intentioned directives of tens of thousands of judges, we ensure that, politically and socially speaking, practically every American enjoys his God-given right to be heard.

Why is it then that at so many of our workplaces we perpetuate an economic authoritarianism: a division between bosses and workers, between vested managers and temporary sellers of their services, between rulers and ruled? Why is it that we continue to think that business life consists of taking it on the chin as an underling until you can get loose from your particular relationship, work hard (for yourself), and end up telling someone else what to do, as you yourself were told? If you have a problem with your workers, so the old philosophy ran, fire them. If you have a problem with your bosses, quit and work for the competition. Or call down on their heads the sanctions of a national union or a court. But don't try to talk it out and see what management and workers might do if they communicate with each other and strive for a community of objectives.

In a 1981 issue of *Fortune,* Bernard Krisher, one of the best American journalists in Japan, interviewed several Japanese top executives whose companies have established plants in the United States about their experiences with American workers. Here are some samples of their reactions:

Yoshida Tadahiro, senior managing director of YKK, the world's leading zipper manufacturer:

> The most severe shocks I experienced in the U.S. came when people in whom we had confidence suddenly quit and when companies in our own industry scouted our people away. When we hire people we expect them to stay with us for five years at least, but we had some people leaving after only three years. Some of our trusted employees have gone so far as to recruit others in the plant to join them at another company. I still find this very difficult to understand, and I don't know how lower-ranked employees can be motivated or imbued with a sense of company loyalty under such circumstances.

Iwama Kazuo, president of the Sony Corporation:

> I have no intention of criticizing American manufacturers, but take the Zenith or the RCA factories, where each worker's job on the line is clearly set and defined. He need only follow his specific function.

If an incomplete component reaches his place on the line, it's not his responsibility, so he won't be blamed for all the defects. It's management's responsibility. In Japan, however, the worker is part of the overall cooperative set-up that achieves the quality.

Nakai Hajime, executive managing director, Sanyo Electric Company:

American workers maintain a much looser relationship towards their company, compared to Japanese. . . . In Japan the union lives with the company and never pulls the trigger unless it finds itself in an extremely serious situation. It tries as much as possible to work with us on the same ground, because its members' future and prosperity are directly linked to ours. The important question for us right now is how to instill this concept in our American workers.

Mogi Yuzaburo, general manager, International Division, Kikkoman Foods:

I'd like to dispel the myth that Japanese management is really all that good and will produce wonders if transplanted abroad. We should be very careful about applying either so-called Japanese-style management to America or American-style management to Japan. Take the Japanese seniority system: while it offers security and creates a more harmonious atmosphere conducive to good results, it may also serve to reduce incentives to do good work.

A well-publicized difference is Japan's so-called human-oriented management, contrasted with America's efficient-style management. Ten, fifteen years ago many American management books of the Peter Drucker genre were being translated and widely sold here in Japan because we felt we were leaning too much towards the human-oriented side. We thought that in order to compete with America we ought to learn to be more efficient. Today, on the other hand, Americans feel that they've been perhaps too preoccupied with efficiency and are trying to learn something from us about human relations. A good balance between the two seems the best answer.[2]

The companies these four men represent all came relatively early on the American scene. Sony began turning out TV sets at its San Diego plant in 1972 and later opened a tape manufacturing plant in Alabama. Sanyo now manufactures in Arkansas as well as San Diego. Kikkoman's soy sauce plant at Walworth, Wisconsin, was one of the pioneers in American investment. YKK has plants in Illinois, California, and New Jersey, in addition to its original installation in Georgia. A variety of Japanese industries have now established themselves on American bases. Kawasaki runs a motorcycle plant in Lincoln, Nebraska. Alumax, an aluminum manufacturer, has plants in fifty American cities; and subsidiaries of Dai Nippon, Inc. and Suntory, Ltd, are similarly geographically diversified. Four Japanese firms make microwave ovens in the United States. Fujitsu, the Japanese computer giant, has joined NEC, Toshiba, and Hitachi in setting up semiconductor manufacturing units.

Although Japanese direct investment in North America is still only a fraction of European, it has grown very quickly in the space of a few years. In 1978 it totaled $2.7 million; by the end of 1979 this was up to $3.4 million. As of March 1981, Japanese investment in the United States and Canada had reached $9.8 million, and was steadily increasing. Estimates suggest the total will exceed $20 billion by 1985. Of this total only a quarter has been in manufacturing. Wholesale businesses accounted for almost half. But manufacturing is on the increase. More than 200 U.S. companies are under Japanese control.

At that the rush to invest came late. Had Japanese companies started investing and building in the United States earlier in the seventies, much of the later protectionist agitation against Japanese goods would have been blunted. This is particularly true in the case of automobiles, whose makers, with Honda the principal exception, have shown as little sensitivity to the problems of American workers as the Detroit carmakers seem to have previously shown to the concerns of American consumers. The electronics manufacturers started coming to America in force when it became clear that restrictions would be put on the endless import of consumer electronics from Japan. The bearing manufacturers did likewise. The very concentration of Japanese exports to the United States—more than half of them in automobiles, electronics, and steel products—made them peculiarly vulnerable to the threat of protectionism.

In any case, a basic reason for Japanese manufacturing investment was defensive. It was the inevitable result of the success of the export drives and a trade balance heavily adverse to the United States.

In fairness to the Japanese manufacturers, it must be said that until 1971 Japanese government restrictions on overseas investment made this a chancy proposition at best. The last restrictions on such investments, in fact, were not removed until 1978.

Some companies had special reasons for moving a plant to the U.S.A. The soybeans for Kikkoman's basic product came mostly from America. A capricious embargo on soybean exports during the Nixon administration, later revoked, had suggested to Kikkoman's executives the value of manufacturing close to the source of their raw material. Similarly, plastics companies began moving plants to the United States, owing to the low price of American petroleum feedstocks.

Two important cost factors were involved. The appreciation of the yen against the dollar was one of them. This happened throughout the seventies. Not only did the stronger yen erase the competitive advantages of many Japanese exporters to the United States; at the same time it made investment across the Pacific far cheaper than it had been.

The second cost factor was labor. In 1970 the average hourly earnings of Japanese manufacturing workers were slightly more than 30 percent of what Americans earned for similar tasks. By 1979, Japanese hourly wages had climbed to 90 percent of American. By now in some industries the Japanese workers are higher paid. Ironically, in view of the still heard American argument that Japanese exports do well here because of low-cost cheap labor at home, the United States is becoming for Japanese manufacturers in the eighties an abundant reservoir of cheap and available labor.

Another general reason for Japanese investment was to effect economies of scale in manufactures, so important to the Japanese, by developing the American market further. In addition, many Japanese businessmen regarded the American market as a good testing ground, where the experience in marketing and selling would in the end make their products better and more competitive elsewhere.

Against these pluses were two built-in drawbacks, deficiencies that still tend to make Japanese firms hold back on American investment. One is the obvious cultural and social differences between the pluralistic, open, and regionally distinct society of America, as contrasted with the hothouse "one-family" atmosphere within Japan. Inside Japan, with business, government, and the banks generally cooperating, the market sometimes seems to be controlled by thermostat. American market conditions are far less manageable. The American consumer is far more volatile.

The second drawback was people. It is one thing for Japanese management to establish offices and sales headquarters in the United States, where contact with real-life Americans is basically restricted to buyer and seller relationships. The trading company representative in a city like New York or Los Angeles can create around him a microcosm of the society he has left at home. There are Japanese clubs, Japanese restaurants, Japanese golf clubs, and even schools where children can keep up on their Japanese and their national team spirit. Wives, many of whom barely speak English, can live secure within the perimeters of what became in many cases Japanese colonies in big-city suburbs. The businessman himself need not practice his English too assiduously. "Business English" and an abundant supply of young interpreters would do.

To set up a factory was another matter. There the Japanese would have to cope with a wholly different society and a wide variety of foreign people problems for which the average Japanese is notably unprepared.

It has been argued, therefore, that Japanese managers in multinational companies export badly. The same qualities of Japanese management which make them so effective at home—the sense of company community, the frequent face-to-face meetings with colleagues and superiors, with both decisions and evaluations coming from long exposure—they lose when they are transferred to an overseas subsidiary. Unable to communicate well with their employees—whether in the United States or Thailand or Indonesia, although for different reasons—they do far worse than they would do in a comparable job in Japan. The period of their overseas job is thought of like a prison term. Many do not bring their families or, if their wives come along, older children are left at home "to continue their education," so that they will not miss the atmosphere of all-Japanese schooling, or endure the stigma of returning to Japan, to fight the university exams, with only a "foreign" education.

All this happens, I concede. Along with other Japanophiles in the United States, I have winced at the diffidence of so many Japanese managers among us and their insularity from the life of American communities around them, not to mention their American employees. Many managers and their wives give the impression of earth visitors camping on an unfriendly planet (or from a more American perspective, of Martians temporarily locked out of their spaceships).

The stereotype, if widely based, does not always hold true, however. It depends on the man, on his temperament and attitude as much as his competence, just as with American managers who go to Japan. Many Japanese managers—probably the most talented and imaginative of their breed—experience as much suffocation as gratification within the warm embrace of the company at home. Such men will welcome a foreign assignment, with all the perils of home office isolation noted above. It gives them a chance to be their own persons, while staying within the system, and build their own social world selectively for a change. Younger people, who have had more of an "international" education, are understandably ever so slightly more relaxed in foreign living than their fathers. This trend, I believe, will continue. It will be fostered by the obviously increasing importance of building up productive and happy subsidiaries or joint ventures outside Japan.

In my own experience first living in Japan, then commuting to and from Japan and the United States and meeting a great many American-based Japanese businessmen, I have noticed a considerable change in their makeup over the past ten years. The new breed is indeed more internationalist. They are apt to speak good English. More than that, they are relatively at ease in American surroundings. Many have attended American graduate or business schools and to a great extent are clued into the ways of American business thinking. These really accomplished people are still rare, but their number increases.

Nonetheless, most Japanese businessmen are still nervous about opening plants in America. They are working hard at it. Some fail or only partially succeed. (Failures are often disguised by Japanese management's reluctance to give up quickly.) But the successes are there. Japanese business has given Americans an example in their midst of how better personal relationships can help productivity.

We have seen how the Japanese Factor might improve or even transform an American workplace. There is no doubt about the efficacy of the Japanese "community" approach to work, especially with people doing assembly-line jobs. By giving workers a sense of participation, by informing them and rotating them in different tasks, some of the deadening aspects of factory work are lessened. For the blue-collar man, therefore, the advantages of the Japanese way are often measurable. After decades of being treated like a cog in a machine, a worker will naturally respond to a system that consciously attempts to humanize. The result, as we have seen, is greater efficiency as well as better spirits.

With white-collar employees, however, the Japanese approach may not always be so effective. Along with their job security policy and cooperative spirit, Japanese businessmen have a tendency to be sticklers for form and status. Although the workforce may be one big family, it is one in which papa and elder brother demand a great deal of respect, in the finest Confucian tradition. Precisely graded titles and positions mean a great deal to Japanese. So do proper channels, which are all-important when navigating the bureaucratic waters of any Japanese corporation. The rites and ceremonies of a Japanese organization include a great deal of protocol, meetings, and paperwork that even veteran American memo writers and meeting callers would find unnecessary. For all their technological innovation and management modernity, the twenty-first century capitalists of Japan are still at heart more than a little Confucian.

This is good and bad. While the strong Confucian sense of relationships holds companies as well as families together, it also engenders a certain stuffiness, unnecessary concern for one's dignity, and procedures that are needlessly rigid.

Many Americans find the atmosphere in the offices of Japanese companies too formal and authority-laden for comfort. American women, in particular, given the comparatively stratospheric level of the liberation society in America, are shocked to discover vicariously the relatively low estate of working women in Japan. Japanese executives, in turn, are unaccustomed to well-qualified female executives who would rather play a speaking role themselves than listen to what the menfolk have to tell them. Some women employees of Japanese company branches in the United States have indeed sued their companies for what they feel is discrimination against them.

In Japan the protocol and the hierarchical rankings are softened by the constant communication that goes on around the company society—the department head hosting dinner at a Chinese restaurant, the company tours, the weekly meetings of the company tennis club, volley ball team, or flower arrangement group, or for that matter, the members of the quality circle getting together to talk about new ways to increase productivity. At the new plant in the United States it will take a good bit of time to get such activities started—and more time to get American employees interested in them. Meanwhile the newly hired American finds the atmosphere around him heavy and not a little oppressive. He is apt to move on before really giving the company a chance, in the process fulfilling the prophecies made to his branch manager by his old friends in the Tokyo office that Americans are too restless to stay with one job very long.

If Japanese managers are more formal than their American counterparts, they are less apt to look over people's shoulders to make sure that they are doing their work properly. They like to let people do their separate jobs without interference, an attitude that should be welcome. On the contrary, it often results in curious misunderstandings, especially in the more creative areas of a business, like planning, promotion, or public relations. A classic confusion of this sort occurred at a meeting I attended at a large Japanese subsidiary in California. The purpose of the meeting was to work out a plan for a new promotion campaign. It had been called by one of the Japanese executives, who told his American colleagues in the promotion department that the vice-president, newly arrived from Tokyo, would sit in on the meeting.

The Americans on the staff had been complaining that Tokyo management was giving them little or no direction about what kind of campaign would be acceptable. Now at last, they said, some guidelines would be given them. They went into the meeting prepared to be instructed, and after hearing the outlines of one plan, simply marked time until the vice-president arrived. He said very little. When asked whether there was any new policy to guide them, he replied that there was not, but that he was interested to see what they were developing. The meeting, needless to say, ended on a note of wild inconclusion.

Had this been Tokyo, the people in the department would have prepared several alternate plans and been well on in the process of discussing them when the vice-president joined them. He could then get the sense of the group, help rally sentiment behind one of the proposals or a modification thereof, and adjourn the meeting with a new promotion campaign in the making. There would have been no need to explain any company guidelines, since everyone in Tokyo knew pretty well what they were and how far they could be stretched.

Nothing happened at the meeting in California because neither of the parties knew what was expected of them. The Americans wanted more obvious direction from their vice-president than he was normally prepared to give, even in a Japanese situation. He in turn had wrongly assumed that his promotion group, without waiting for any guidelines, had worked out a variety of acceptable approaches. So much for international business intuition at the western edge of the Sun Belt.

Relations with American unions represent another problem area for Japanese-run businesses in the United States. While most large Japanese companies are unionized, their unions, as we have seen, are apt to be the single-enterprise union, not an affiliate of a strong national union like the UAW or the Teamsters. Japanese executives fear that the American union organizer thinks first of the national union's interests, with the particular local's concerns only secondary. This is the exact opposite of most Japanese union thinking. American union leaders, who have grown up under the adversary system, are frankly leery of the Japanese company's community-harmony approach. As an organizer for the AFL-CIO's International Brotherhood of Electrical Workers observed during the course of an organizing battle with a Japanese-owned electronics manufacturer: "There's a big difference between a company handbook and a union contract."

Neither this nor the other problems mentioned above are insoluble. Basically Japanese investment in the United States is good for everybody. Both by employment and by example, it has much to contribute to the American economy; and it will further the already strong ties between America and Japan. There is, however, one big incipient barrier to the future expansion of Japanese business here which can be breached only in Japan. That is the continuing restrictions against Americans having the same economic freedom in Japan which Japanese enjoy in the United States. Restrictions are often unwritten; but they are no less strong for that. Japanese businesses in the United States will be operating under a cloud as long as Japanese lawyers can be admitted to the bar in most American states, while Americans are barred from appearing in a Japanese court; as long as Japanese bankers can buy out or merge with banks in the United States, while American banks in Japan are rigidly restricted; as long as Japanese firms can join the New York Stock Exchange and manage a wide variety of financial services in the United States, while American firms are carefully excluded from doing such things in Japan. And Japanese businessmen run the risk of incurring reciprocal sanctions. Japanese are justly assertive in their defense of free trade, but they must realize that free trade is a two-way street.

13·The Hare in the Jungle: Japan's Difficult Future

Pride is a very transitory thing (Ogoru Heike hisashi karazu).
—*Japanese proverb*

In the late summer of 1979, I sat down in a conference room in San Francisco with a group of Japanese businessmen, young to middle-aged, to offer an introduction to some of the ideas and attitudes they might encounter in their tour of American business and financial centers, just beginning. We spoke in Japanese. My command of that language is far from perfect, but I find that I can talk more freely and frankly with most Japanese in their language, and more importantly, encourage those who are talking to me to do the same. Although there are outstanding exceptions to this rule, the average Japanese businessman sounds somewhat like a programmed robot when he speaks English. In Japanese the stuffy and apparently tongue-tied visitor from Tokyo, freed from the stilted phrases of overly correct English, can marvelously transform himself into an interesting neighbor who can be variously warm, witty, or angry, and who is apt to be acute in his observations and understanding rather than "polite" and noncommittal.

The talk quickly ranged far afield from a simple introduction to American politics. The most interesting of my questions came from a banker, who taxed me with my choice of a title, *Japan: The Fragile Superpower,* for my last book. "Exactly what," he asked, "is so fragile about Japan?"

In answer I mentioned the obvious fragilities of Japan: the almost total lack of raw materials and any significant military power, with which all present, of course, agreed. I went on to describe the fragility implicit in the defensive unity that the Japanese present to the outsider. Other nations may show a stone face to the world because of artificial political imperatives, as in the Soviet Union, or because of aroused feelings of racial unity and indignation, as in black Africa's attitude to South Africa or the Arabs' hostility to Israel. One even meets survivals of the once assertive insularity of the traditional British. But the Japanese do not merely hide behind feelings of insularity and apartness. They project the attitude of a nation society which continues to look contentedly in on itself, its classic national inferiority complex transformed by success into a confidence bordering on arrogance.

Such a unity of feeling is praiseworthy in a sense. But how long can Japan afford it? How long can the Japanese persist in keeping the rest of the world, spiritually and psychologically, at arm's length, when they have become the world's greatest trading nation, to many the world's banker, by their own very remarkable achievements condemned—whatever their wishes—to play an increasingly active part in the world's conversation? "Internationalist," to be sure, has become a good word in Japan. But how often does it mean anything? How often does "internationalist" mean little more than reading foreign books (mostly in translation), buying Japanese versions of foreign products, developing familiarity with foreign movies, or buying an expensive English-language course to collect dust in the closet.

Every Japanese at the table knew exactly what I meant, and some had given the matter a good deal of thought. "Yes," the consensus of their comment ran, "we must do better here." An internal unity of thinking that expresses itself so poorly to outsiders *is* a national weakness. It can be called a mark of fragility. How much separateness, how much aloofness is permitted to a nation or a people so important to the world?

The internal unities of Japan are to a foreigner awesome. All but the most superficial observers see these unities on a visit to Japan. More precisely, they sense them. The unity of race is, of course, obvious. The foreigner who has lived long in Japan cannot escape feeling like a piece of alien flotsam tossed on a Japanese sea. The unity of nation is less obvious, but it, too, gradually strikes one as unique. The Japanese say words like "our country" or "the government" in a very special way. Deeper than respect or ostentatious patriotism, it bespeaks a sense of inescapable possession. We are here, the Japanese seem to say, because we have always been here and we have no choice but to work, act, and decide in unison. Besides, we like it that way.

The unity of culture is less apparent in a people who have partly earned their reputation as the world's great borrowers and adapters, but it exists. It acts like a powerful undertow beneath the tides of foreign influence—whether Chinese, American, or European—an undertow that is not as free-flowing as it seems. In the end Japan accepts or rejects selectively, adjusts and channels according to its own caprice.

There is even a unity of humanitarianism among the Japanese. They have a genius for seeing to it that as few wounds as possible are mortal. They know in their bones that mutual survival is what counts. In none of the world's societies are human abrasions so controlled, the casualties of life's battles so sedulously minimized. Diluted, altered, criticized though it be, a pervasive principle of "responsible duty and human sympathy"—*giri-ninjo* in Japanese—still orders Japanese behavior, but it is a homegrown product, like straw sandals and fish liver and sake. Duty may indeed be practiced outside, to a limited degree, as international commitments and business contracts are observed, but not that special kind of human sympathy—that storied people-adhesive—which has sufficed in Japan to do for the Christian virtues of love and mercy. It is *ninjo* (human sympathy) that evaporates at the water's edge. A communal bond of sympathy inside Japan looks quite different to an outsider.

Let us consider the case of the Vietnamese boat people and their fellow fugitives from Cambodia. These refugees from varieties of victorious Indochinese Communism have courted appalling hardships in an effort to flee a country where they see no hope for the future. As of January, 1982, some 477,000 of them had been taken into the United States as permanent residents. France accepted 80,000 for residence there, Australia 61,000, Canada 80,000, West Germany and the United Kingdom about 20,000 and 15,000, respectively. Some 200,000 are now in Thailand and 250,000, mostly ethnic Chinese, have been received in China. Some 70,000 are in transit camps in Malaysia, 30,000 in Indonesia, and 5,000 in the Philippines.

Japan, as of January 1982, had qualified exactly 1,419 Vietnamese for resident status. This was under pressure from other democratic countries to open its doors to more, since the best the Japanese government had done by 1979 was to admit three.

Japan, it is true, has pledged more than $100 million of the $300 million total already put up for Vietnamese resettlement, the United States having provided most of the balance. But in the eyes of other nations, at least, it costs little for the rich man to offer money. What is more important is the evidence of sincere charity—in a literal way, a demonstration—if not of international brotherhood, of the sense of international responsibility that an offer of resettlement implies. Here the Japanese response has been so small as to be laughable. When the first groups of Vietnamese managed to get to Japan, deposited on its shores by their rescuers, they were kept from staying more than the briefest time—not to mention gaining residence in Japan— by a protective screen of administrative regulation and red tape at which the veteran bureaucracy of the Japanese immigration department so excels. They fared little better than the shipwrecked foreign sailors in the Tokugawa days of Japan's self-seclusion. At least the procedures were better formalized.

The money, at that, might reasonably be regarded as interest payback on the $3-billion trade surplus that Japanese businessmen accumulated during a successful decade of exporting to Vietnam, in support of a war that Japan managed to use as a handy profit center. It was, so to speak, plus business.

Like many highly vocal American antiwar activists who were conspicuously silent in criticizing the killings in Cambodia, the spear bearers of Japan's well-publicized antiwar crusades said little or nothing about this violence from the other side. That is probably to be expected. But unlike the case in the United States or the Western European countries, there were few calls from the Japanese public to help these people in need—hardly a murmur. Japanese politicians were unusually quiet on this issue. Whether the Vietnamese refugees were highly skilled or unskilled, the Japanese made it clear that they were not wanted. Those who were accepted will be allowed to stay for cosmetic reasons.

The problem is certainly not the old Japanese dilemma of too-many-people-on-too-little-land. To admit 5,000 or 50,000 or 100,000 would pose no great hardship to a prosperous, industrialized nation of 117 million. The problem, of course, is that the Vietnamese are outsiders. There is no room for them inside the hothouse atmosphere of Club Japan, the world's largest fraternal and social organization, with its millions of dues-paying members. Indeed, one will not envy the few Vietnamese who are allowed to settle in Japan. Even more than the Koreans, Chinese, or other Asian nationals who are in Japan, they will run the gauntlet of a tight community's collective stare—because they are, of course, different. One recalls the portrait, etched in acid indignation, that Kurosawa has given us in his great film *Waga seishun nikui nashi (No Regrets for Our Youth)*, where the family of the antiwar "traitor" was watched by hundreds of half-hidden hostile eyes from the roadside, as they tried to eke out a living in the remote farming village. It was not so much that they were traitors. They were watched with such hostility because they were *different*.

Japan's record of assistance to the developing countries is notably poor. At least until recently, direct development assistance has amounted to .002 percent of Japan's GNP. (The figure for France, by comparison, is .006 percent, for the Federal Republic of Germany, almost .004.) This is thin gruel in view of Japan's huge trade with developing countries throughout the world. "This is not aid," a statesman from one of the ASEAN countries remarked, "it is sales promotion." Ambitious plans like that of former Foreign Minister Okita Saburo for a $20-billion Japanese Marshall Plan for Southeast Asia may have been discussed, but little effort was made to implement them. Although more recently the amount and scope of Japanese aid and assistance programs have grown, the total, as a percentage of total Japanese GNP, has decreased.

Japan's defense commitment is similarly small, although expanding. Indeed, Japanese popular attitudes toward national defense and increased military cooperation with the United States have changed significantly in the opening years of the eighties. Yet American pressures for a greater Japanese contribution are understandably increasing. When a country spends almost 8 percent of its own GNP for the military, part of which is deployed to support obligations for another nation's defense, it is irritating to find the protected party limiting its expenditures to less than one percent of its own GNP. It is doubly irritating to many Americans, when we observe that American taxpayers who help support Japan's defense are losing jobs because of economic competition from that country, happily unencumbered

MIRACLE BY DESIGN

with the heavy military burdens shouldered by the United States.

Many of the complaints against Japan are unjust. But some of them are valid and demand attention. The time has long gone when the Japanese could keep an aloof posture, taking their profits from the world outside without the need to involve themselves in the world's problems, except selectively. We all live too closely together. Right now, the fragile superpower need worry less about its lack of natural resources, energy, or armaments than about a basic matter of its communications with all those other people outside the Japan Club.

Most of the comment on Japan and its society running through this book is favorable. It is meant to be. Not only do I admire the Japanese for their modern achievement, but I also think what they have done is worthy of our most humble and searching study. Their economic achievement has indeed been something of a modern miracle. The Japanese have added a new dimension, also, to our old ideas about capitalist free enterprise; and they have pointed the way for a twenty-first century capitalism that by being deliberately people-centered, if not humanist, in structure and tone seems to fit a level of rising expectation among us all, about improving the quality of life and participating in the day-by-day decisions that affect us most. This is particularly true for Americans. The Japanese have shown us how a modern economy can move toward agreed social and economic goals, without the need for enduring the regimentation and government dictation of the kind of society that goes with socialism.

Yet there are flaws as well as question marks in the Japanese model. Their insularity, as I have noted, is flaw number one. Another flaw, possibly, is the extent to which Japanese youth may change. Thus far, the Japanese have gone on to success after economic success because they had a direction they could agree upon, a goal for which all were willing to work, and careful managers—managers rather than leaders—in both government and business who always made sure that the crowd was with them. Changing values could disturb this fine balance.

Demography now works against Japan. One reason why the Japanese miracle fulfilled itself was the relative youth of the Japanese workforce. A flow of young people, at the bottom of the wage and seniority scale, makes smooth running for a business economy founded on full employment and the seniority system. Now the shape of the pyramid in Japan's workforce is changing. By 1985, 17 percent of the Japanese population will be over the age of sixty. While new

202

high school graduates, the basic sinew of Japanese industry, are growing scarcer, there is a traffic jam of sorts in most businesses at the level of department head or lower. Chances for steady regular promotion, once assured, are now getting worse.

Meanwhile Japanese industry is changing its own structural shape. Both business and government managers are emphasizing the shift from basic heavy goods production to the more knowledge-intensive industries. Having virtually exhausted the supply of borrowable and adaptable technologies, the Japanese must invent their own. The great question mark in Japan's future planning will be the ability of young Japanese to innovate as well as engineer.

The Japanese people as a whole, still enjoying the cumulative euphoria of the economic miracle, and (as of mid-1982) less affected by the depression trend than any other major economy, are not noticeably concerned about these clouds on the horizon. But Japan's business and government planners are very concerned. The problem of international relations is uppermost in almost everyone's mind. In the Ministry of International Trade and Industry's basic planning document—at least the one that is circulated—"contributing positively to the international community" is listed as the first of three major goals. (The others are: [2] to overcome the limitations of national resources and the shortage of energy; and [3] to improve the quality of life, but without slowing the momentum of economic growth.)

"In the 1980s," the report began, "Japan will be increasingly called upon to contribute to the harmonious development of the international community. . . . Interdependence among nations is expected to deepen further in this decade. Politics and economics will become more closely related to each other, making the world even more complex."

This kind of statement is something of a milestone for MITI, the government agency that originally charged the engines of the high-growth society, its spokesmen insisting for many years that Japan's economic growth had nothing to do with international politics whatsoever. It is a milestone in another way, for in it MITI formally announced, as it were, the fulfillment of past objectives. "Since the Meiji Era," the report continued, "Japan has struggled to achieve a level comparable to that of Western countries by modernizing and developing an industrial society. Japan has today achieved the goal it set for itself. . . . Japan in the 1980s will have to seek new directions and face new challenges."

Amaya Naohiro, formerly MITI's vice-minister for international trade, is one of the many responsible Japanese who have worried about the problems of putting an aloof and introspective Japan fully into the international conversation. In a 1980 article titled "Japan as a Mercantile Nation," he chided his fellow countrymen for their aloofness and self-confidence, when their international position was in reality such a precarious one.

> Mao Zedong is said to have remarked that a revolution is not a ball. Borrowing his metaphor, one might say that international society is not a ball; it is a semi-jungle. And Japan is a plump hare living in this semi-jungle. We should not delude ourselves into thinking that bears and wolves will say to us, "My dear hare, we sympathize with you for not having claws and teeth." For hares to multiply in the jungle, and for merchants to prosper in the warriors' society, it is necessary to have superb information-gathering ability, planning ability, intuition, diplomatic skill, and at times whining sycophancy. Mere mouthing of pretty phrases about justice, peace, freedom, non-discrimination, and other niceties will never guarantee a prosperous life for merchant or hare.
>
> When we look dispassionately at Japan's conduct as a mercantile state, we find that Japan is hardly as earnest and meticulous as Tokugawa merchants were in providing for a well-oiled business environment. To cite an example, the reaction of the Japanese government and public to the refugees from Vietnam and Cambodia is lacking in humanism and unresponsive to international society. Japan's economic assistance to developing nations falls short in earnestness and the degree of attention paid to the distribution of efforts and funds. Whereas the outside world is forcefully directing such criticisms at Japan, neither public officials nor private citizens are responding with anything like the agility of the old-time merchant or the hare. . . .
>
> If Japan chooses to continue treading the path of a mercantile nation in international society, it must apply itself wholeheartedly to the merchant's trade. This means that, when necessary, Japan must go begging to the oil-producing nations; that, if circumstances compel, Japan must grovel before the military nations. Japan also must be wise enough to calculate the strengths and weaknesses of oil-producing and military nations, to perceive correctly the trends of the world and of history, and to choose risk-minimizing options. And when money will be helpful, Japan needs the gumption to pay handsomely.
>
> Perhaps most important to life as a shrewd merchant is a major shift in national consciousness. First, the Japanese as a whole must change their stance from an inner-directed posture to an outer-

directed one. Instead of watching their feet to spot pennies, like a peddler, they must stride confidently forward as would a merchant prince.

Second, merchants control their emotions in order to calculate benefits dispassionately. They develop the ability to resist wishful thinking, to be thorough in information gathering and analysis, and to judge their surroundings accurately. In Japan this implies putting particular stress on the important role of the mass media. . . . If the people have the right to know, the newspapers should have the duty not to misinform them. . . .

Third, the merchant must beware the spirit of dependence. There must be no excessive expectations of or illusions about the benefits that will accrue from protectionist policies implemented by the government or from the good will of peace-loving nations. . . .[1]

He went on to say that the Japanese people might want to rearm and become again a "warrior nation." This point of view could be defended. Rearming to any considerable extent, however, would cost a great deal of money and pose a whole new set of problems. If the desire is to maintain the status quo with minimal defense forces, then Amaya feels that the Japanese must take a very low posture indeed. He speaks with some authority, since he was the ranking government official who negotiated with the United States both on Japan's purchases of Iranian oil and the agreement to have certain voluntary limits on the export of cars to the United States.

In fact, Japan's economic plans for the rest of the century suggest that very considerable accommodations be made to the wishes, concerns, and protests of other nations. Japan, as former U.S. Ambassador James M. Hodgson is fond of saying,

gained its economic ascendancy not by exploiting its natural resources, but by converting its picturesque archipelago into a huge industrial processing plant. Each day bulk raw material arrives in volume at Japanese ports in huge new special purpose ships. There Japanese technology, capital, and skill take over to turn the material into high quality products.

In the new grand design of Japanese government planners, Japanese businesses would speed up their investment in overseas plants and in effect farm out the more elementary, labor-intensive kind of industry to these outposts. They would retain in Japan the more complex higher-technology type of manufacture. The Japanese in their high-growth period have not exactly been short of labor, but there is no surplus. As the population ages, there will be fewer hands still. Thus the "huge industrial processing plant" will delegate some of its tasks to overseas outposts, much in the way that Japan's big industrial corporations farm out many of their production processes to subcontractors and regular suppliers.

There will probably be ample Japanese capital to invest. Thanks to a long period of fast growth and heavy exports, many Japanese corporations are veritably awash in liquid assets. Bank loans have been repaid on a big scale, and to the extent that many large Japanese corporations have no higher leverage than their American counterparts. In his book, *The Developing Economies and Japan,* Okita Saburo unfolded a variety of cogent plans for a world of "interdependence" in the eighties, where Japan acts not merely as a supplier to developing countries, or Newly Industrializing Countries (NIC), but also as a stimulus to further development in those countries.[2] This will require not merely technology export but also investment in offshore factories. We have seen how this kind of Japanese investment is gathering momentum in the United States.

Like other aspiring "post-industrial" countries, Japan cannot afford to stand still. The spectacular success of other Confucian capitalists in the NICs of Taiwan, Hong Kong, Singapore, and Korea has been partly at the expense of Japanese business. The Koreans in particular, with their expanding steel and ship-building capabilities, are now pushing Japanese industries the way the Japanese have been pushing the Americans.

To invest successfully, however, Japanese must really become "interdependent" with others and shed the thick shell of insularity they have retained up to this time. It will be good for the world and for Japan if this can be done. A critical factor in the accomplishment of any sweeping development plans is the ability and attitude of Japan's younger generation. The generation of Japanese management which succeeded to top posts in the Occupation or post-Occupation era is now passing from the scene. They are the last of the traditionally minded "Meiji men," that is, people who were born in the Meiji era, which began with Japan's modernization and ended in 1912. A new generation of formerly middle management is now taking over from them. Within a decade or so these people will be retiring or, as is more likely in the case of Japanese chairmen or chief consultants *(sodanyaku),* leaving the company when death do them part. From the late 1980s onward, Japanese industry and the government's

The Hare in the Jungle: Japan's Difficult Future

economic ministries will be in the hands of the postwar generation.

It has often been suggested that the work ethic is far weaker among this new generation in Japan than in the past. The reasons given are that the younger generation tends to prize individualism more, and aspires more to personal satisfactions and a better quality of life for the individual, in the manner of its American counterpart. I find little real evidence to support this view. Although young Japanese workers *are* more concerned with vacations and trips and private lives than their elders, this is a matter of degree, not a qualitative change. In some ways the younger generation is even more faithful to the ideal of "corporate family consciousness." A study was made in 1979 of representative Japanese and American companies fifteen years after an identical sampling of opinion in 1962. Its authors concluded that the present generation is, if anything, more committed to the work society than was the group studied fifteen years ago. Some 73 percent of workers questioned felt that the company was "a part of my life at least equal in importance to my personal life." The figure for American workers was 21 percent.[3]

In other respects the young workers gave more or less traditional Japanese responses to questions. Sixty-four percent of them, for example, felt that low rent or free company housing was a good idea, as opposed to only 8 percent of the Americans. In a speech summarizing the survey, Arthur M. Whitehill noted the almost opposite reactions of American and Japanese workers to an employee asking his work superior for advice about a marriage partner. "Seventy-four percent of the Americans," he noted, "said that one's superiors should not be involved in such a personal matter compared with only five percent in Japan—a really striking cross-cultural difference in values."

These percentages I cite not necessarily as evidence of differences between Japanese and American workers, but merely to underline my point that the younger generation of Japanese workers is not all that different. One hears constant complaints among Japanese businessmen that the young people coming into companies lack proper "spirit," they are not dedicated, they think too much of themselves, they are "cheerful and carefree," "clever rather than bright," and not very tough. I myself made similar observations when I was in Japan —but I am not at all sure that such complaints are not merely signs of advancing age. That Japanese young businesspeople tend to be more self-centered than before, with wider interests, worse manners, and deplorable handwriting, is probably true. There are few signs, however, that they are about to cast off the Japanese work ethic or start changing jobs, in the American manner.

The fact that the young are more relaxed and less "tight" than their elders may indeed be a very good thing, if they are expected to go forth into the outside world and run textile mills in Indonesia, shoe factories in Brazil, or semiconductor plants in the United States. In the present generation of Japanese managers only a small minority of talented and overworked executives have proved themselves capable of dealing with foreigners far from the comfort of their hothouse society at home.

Overseas management problems are not the only thing that Vice-Minister Amaya's Japanese hare has to worry about as he deploys his long-eared family into the world's semijungle. Japanese may have decisively checked the growth of industrial pollution in their narrow islands, but the dangers are still with them. The social security bill in Japan, as in the United States, is growing ever higher, although the government in Japan supplies far smaller payments to its people, who rely more on company benefits, postretirement jobs, and indeed, their own substantial savings. And the effects of an aging population will make itself felt more and more.

Now that so much has been "liberalized" and government licenses and permissions are no longer necessary for Japanese companies, the government ministries' "administrative guidance" is not quite the formidable instrument that it once was. There remains a basic political consensus among the Japanese people in favor of the ruling conservatives in the Liberal Democratic Party, creaking and faction-ridden instrument that it may be. It would require a major act of faith on the part of millions to resurrect the moribund Japanese Socialist Party, which threw away its opportunity to take power time and time again by its loud fidelity to Marxist "revolutionary" solutions to economic problems in the face of the obvious success with which the capitalists were solving them.

If there were a major depression, if the complacent society were rudely jolted, if the factories had to close down—scholars of Japan have been toying with such scenarios for the past decade, wondering what might happen then to the storied Japanese consensus. But the resiliency of Japanese business after the staggering oil shocks of the seventies gives us some evidence that the capitalism of Japan can cope with a great many unexpected problems. Its margins are admittedly thin. What would happen to the Japanese in the face of a universal protectionism is something to conjure. Yet the new internationalism of the Japanese planners suggests that they are well aware of this possibility and are working to avoid it. A concept like the Pacific Basin idea, for example, has already developed some sense of community among the countries bordering the vast ocean. It was originally a Japanese idea, powerfully supported by the late Prime Minister Ohira.

There is another great advantage that the Japanese have: the advantage of demonstrated success. The development-centered ideals of the twenty-first century capitalists have a wide appeal. They appeal both to developing countries like the ASEAN nations and to overdeveloped economies like that of the United States. In their stress on worker participation, their accent on quality, their insistence on free cooperation between different elements in a nation's society, the Japanese are pointing the way.

14·Some Lessons for Americans

We must not forget that a phoenix rises only from its own ashes and that it is not a bird of passage, neither does it fly on pinions borrowed from other birds.

—Nitobe Inazo

In the foregoing chapters I have attempted to show how the post-war brand of Japanese capitalism has made a success of things, the premises on which it operates, and the kind of people who make it work. I have compared aspects of the Japanese success to American shortcomings in many areas, work ethic, labor-management relations, productivity-consciousness, legal activity, bureaucracy, and export strategies included. This is not to advocate instant imitation. It is hardly possible to set up an American Ministry of International Trade and Industry, staffed with elite university graduates, to institute subtle "administrative guidance" on the conduct and strategies of our corporations. Neither would our "full-disclosure" society tolerate the quiet maneuverings of Japan's establishment. The Japanese combination of formalized hierarchies and middle-level decision making would not take hold easily in most American companies; and I fear that it is rather late in the game to think of introducing Mr. Shibusawa's Confucian work ethic in Detroit.

And yet there are striking parallels between the Japanese situation and our own. We have many common problems. Their solutions are impeded very little by cultural differences. Japanese and Americans share both a certain native pragmatism and a hard, competitive approach to business. We have studied from the same books, learned the same technologies, and worried about similar market problems. Here the similarity between Japanese and Americans is far closer than it is between Americans or Japanese and our European counterparts.

So we are in a good position to learn a lot from Japan's business success and to apply the lessons we learn to our own activities. At the very least, a look at the workings of Japanese capitalism will help correct some errors and distortions in our own brand.

Having learned some harsh lessons from their past, the Japanese are busily marching past the guideposts of the present, on their way to building an ever bigger future. They may not succeed, but they are trying hard. Their economic planners, in government and business alike, are already well past the eighties in their thinking, as they devise products, markets, and strategies for the year 2000 and after. Now investing as well as exporting, they are preparing a network of factories and trading centers scattered over the world like pro-consular outposts. Their builders are siting new factories. Their inventors are patenting new processes faster than their engineers and technicians can adapt them. Government and their industrial establishment are working on the transfer of people and plant into new industries from old ones, supported by a popular consensus founded on the confidence of past successes.

The modern heroes of Japan, in the best tradition of free enterprise societies, are mostly builders and doers and people who run things. There is the engineer in the testing laboratory, the quality control leader on the factory floor, the manager who has doubled his sales, the company president who orchestrates it all, the dedicated bureaucrat in his narrow Kasumigaseki office, the elder statesman, the scientist, the always respected professor behind them all, who taught most of them to think in an orderly fashion.

By contrast, who are the heroes of American business society? Or, put another way—for we are suspicious of heroes, like establishments, P.R. men, and teachers—who stands in the forefront of

American business and makes the headlines as well as the big profits? We too have our builders and scientists and dedicated managers. But our cast of "heroes" would also include some dubious new categories. We have the financier who cuts costs and closes factories, the merger specialist who swallows up companies, the lawyer who alternately sues and settles, the accountant who tailors the sharply creased annual reports, the Wall Street analyst who points with pride or views with alarm the slightest fluctuations in quarterly earnings, the lobbyist-lawyer who peddles influence in Washington, the ubiquitous consultant who receives large fees to make managers' decisions for them, the gimlet-eyed young M.B.A.—his or her portfolio bulging with new studies in motivational psychology and management controls—out to make the first big million. And there is always the latest father figure in the White House who makes everyone feel good and upbeat about our economy for at least his first year in office. It is not hard to find numerous role models in this collection.

If this sounds like mere fulmination, consider some of the facts. Of every 10,000 Japanese, 400 are engineers and scientists; of every 10,000 Americans, only 70 are engineers and scientists, but there are 20 lawyers and 40 accountants. The Japanese figures for these professions are 1 and 3, respectively. The American business schools, as we have seen, graduate some 50,000 M.B.A.'s annually. (Only a handful of M.B.A. students are currently studying in Japan.) Only a small percentage go into production or sales, once widely regarded as the pillars of business. By far the great M.B.A. majority elect to work in financial management, analysis, controls, or consulting.

Unlike the Japanese with their almost obsessive planning for the future, American businessmen seem absorbed in the present, heedless or contemptuous of the past, and interested in the future only in the near-term and only insofar as their own individual profits are concerned. They are judged by peers and superiors on current performance, and compensated on that basis. From the chief executive officer down, the dollars one earns for the company this year or next determine the bonus and the raises. The American manager seems only minimally interested in building a sound company to last for the future. He may well change jobs within the next two years, and the effort would be wasted. He is, however, marvelously schooled in the present ramifications of tax shelter savings, depreciation allowances, and the near-term risings and fallings of price-earnings multiples. He is well aware of the values of technological development and professes a keen interest in research and development, but not if it interferes with the immediate profits on which he is judged. To paraphrase a famous American business leader's message to his corporate troops: "I want all the R & D we can get as long as it doesn't interfere with our 15 percent profitability goal."

Consider the dismal record. American productivity increase has virtually stopped, the legacy of years spent ignoring both capital investment and worker involvement, granting automatic raises without reference to productivity and routinely passing on the ensuing high prices to the customer. By contrast, as we have seen, Japanese productivity continues to increase, and wage increase levels are closely linked to it. Inflation in Japan has been appropriately contained. Japan had its last big bout of double-digit inflation after the energy crisis of 1974. The lesson was learned by both labor and management. Since then it has been well controlled. From 1975 to 1982 the wholesale price index rose from 100 to 136. In the United States we have only recently pulled back from double-digit inflation —and at a very heavy cost.

American personal savings are the lowest of any major economy, ranging between 21 and 25 percent.

Despite recent increases American capital investment continues to be the lowest of any major economy. In 1981 it was not quite half that of Japan.

Despite our proclamations of free enterprise, we continue to subsidize industries, generally sick ones. From Richard Nixon's protection of textiles in 1971 to the Chrysler bailout in 1979, the record has been a dismal one. In 1980 outlay in subsidizing sick industries came to more than $300 billion.

Federal regulation of industries has been spasmodic, costly, and almost punitive, with countervailing tax credits or other incentives given as an afterthought, when given at all. In 1979, according to estimates prepared for the Joint Economic Committee of Congress, the bill for this came to $100 billion. In Japan, as we have seen, the cost of industry's compliance with antipollution regulations has been amply cushioned by planned government assistance. Productivity was not impaired.

R & D expenditures, continually rising in Japan, are proportionately dropping in the United States. We have noted the striking difference in the rise of patent production in Japan and the falloff in the United States. In Japan, furthermore, most R & D comes from the private sector. Where government intervenes with money and support, as in the case of the semiconductor industry, it does so only selectively. For research we continue to be dependent on defense needs—a double-edged sword indeed.

Consider the trade figures of the two nations—a good if rough index of economic strength. Between 1975 and 1982, Japan's trade surplus generally increased, to a level of $30 billion in 1982. America's trade deficit increase suggests that 1982 figures will be even worse than the record deficit of $42.4 billion in 1978.

The comparison is so dismal as to be almost a caricature. Where the Japanese save we spend. Where Japanese companies invest our companies divest. They conserve, we conspicuously consume. Where the Japanese find new jobs for people in depressed industries, we fire them and close the plants. Where the Japanese tighten the standards of their education, we loosen ours, with predictable effect. Where the Japanese keep zealously expanding their total product, we fight over what we have left.

Japanese capitalism is a study in growth, growth agreed upon and growth pursued. The American economy seems by contrast a vast Brownian movement. All its particles are wildly in motion—suing, arguing, firing, and denouncing—but going nowhere.

In making these comparisons I am not rendering any value judgments about relative virtue. The Japanese trading company man buying up stores of raw materials in Africa or Southeast Asia or South America—or the United States—is hardly an altruist. He is out to enrich his company (by beggaring his neighbor, if necessary) in support of an import-export pattern to which his company and his government give broad acquiescence. The Japanese engineer may be only cleverly adapting patents or inventions that others have discovered. The bureaucrat may be rigging unfair restrictions on imports from Europe or the United States. The elder statesman may have handled more dubious political payoffs within the last ten years than most American politicians see in a lifetime.

Nor am I blindly congratulating the Japanese on a pervasive foresight. In the area of world politics—and most particularly in their relationship with the United States—most of the Japanese establishment—business and government—has displayed a shortsighted selfishness and absorption in their own profits that make American money manipulators or European cartel-makers look like altruists. They have evoked a storm of protectionism which may yet devour them.

The arrest of six Japanese businessmen from Mitsubishi and Hitachi in San Francisco in June 1982, caught red-handed apparently in an effort to steal IBM computer secrets, is hardly an ad for international good citizenship. Granted that the FBI "sting" operation which caught them was virtual entrapment, an attempt to pay $600,000 for industrial espionage, at a time of anti-Japanese protectionism in the United States, suggests not merely bad morals, but appallingly bad judgment. Nothing so well dramatizes the dark underside of Japanese business—the tunnel vision of the insensitive company man interested only in the enrichment of his group. Collective avarice is just as bad as individual greed.

Our theme here, however, is the effectiveness of Japan's economy, not of its business follies or political policies. Indeed, whether the Japanese economy goes on to greater triumphs or falls the victim of its own political shortsightedness is irrelevant to the discussion here. The lesson for Americans lies in what Japan has done. The Japanese have constructed a future-oriented, people-centered, dynamic form of capitalism which is demonstrably more successful than anything seen in America for the last twenty years. They have done this because they were smart, they were patient, they worked together, and they responded to the precious stimulus of adversity.

To a greater or less degree, any free enterprise society must use the lessons of this capitalism and adopt some of its practices if it expects to survive into the next century. What the Japanese have done amounts to a work of collective business brilliance. As members of that society which originally contributed so much to their success, it behooves Americans to see Japan's accomplishments, evaluate them, and apply what we can of our findings at home—before it is too late. Above all, we must think in the long-term. A capitalist is a person who invests money, plant, and manpower for the purpose of lasting, long-term gain. What we have become in the United States is less a society of capitalists than a loose association of quarreling traders, speculators, and promoters. That is something quite different.

There is no better way of comparing Japanese and American solutions than in their handling of old-age pensions, social security, and various beneficiary programs. Both countries are in the process of "graying." In the 1930s less than 5 percent of Americans were over sixty-five years old. In 1982 that figure is 11 percent. It will double itself over the next half-century, causing a massive shift in productivity as we know it. As former Secretary of Commerce Peter G. Peterson wrote recently: "For the next several decades, our elderly population generally, those who receive the benefits, will grow at 20 times the rate of our labor force, those who contribute the benefits."[1]

The figures in Japan are similar. In 1982, 10 percent of Japan's population is over sixty-five. By the year 2020, the figure will have reached 19 percent.

The solutions proposed for the graying problem, however, are vastly different. One looks to the future; the other is mired in the present. In Japan the government payments for social security are not great. Beginning at the age of sixty, each Japanese retiree receives roughly only between $6,000 and $8,000 annually, with certain medical benefits appended. Retirement ages in companies, however, which were originally set at fifty-five, have been moved up to sixty, and may possibly go higher. But in the Japanese business tradition, retired employees are generally hired again on a contract basis—and at reduced salaries—or given employment opportunities with subsidiary companies. By the time retirement comes, it is presumed they will have already bought their houses and educated their children. It is time, the reasoning goes, for the next generation to take over. Yet the tendency in Japan is for older people to keep working, even at humbler jobs than they had before. They contribute something, as they would wish. The old men working as watchmen or as modestly paid advisers, the old women picking up around the offices, like the ubiquitous tea ladies so often denounced by foreign visitors to Japan as superfluous, are working because they want to—and because they belong to an ethic of work. They feel useful, and their modest government pensions or allowances are supplemented by the basic support received from their employers. It is wages, not charity. And they are working for it.

Not so in the United States. Here people tend to retire for good —and they are supported in their retirement largely by the federal government, with pension funds coming close behind. The social security checks come whether they are needed or not. The money is an "entitlement." These payments, like the pensions of federal employees, far from being subject to inflation, are carefully indexed in such a manner as to anticipate inflation. Where the average income of wage earners rose by only 2 percent in real terms, for example, during the seventies the checks from social security went up more than 50 percent higher than the increase in prices.

As Peterson's article makes clear, the payments for such benefits and the number of people paid is increasing in a geometric progression, at a rate vastly higher than the increase in numbers and compensation of the wage earners who must support them. He wrote:

> In 1960, Federal outlays for the elderly constituted only 13 percent of the budget. Today, that figure is 27.5 percent. In the last two years alone, outlays for the elderly increased by almost 30 percent, or almost $50 billion. Joseph A. Califano, Jr., former Secretary of Health, Education and Welfare, has predicted that spending for the aged will constitute an unsustainable 35 percent of the budget by the turn of the century, and an unthinkable 65 percent by 2025.
>
> . . . The country must learn that pensions can grow over the long term only if the economy is growing as rapidly as the retired population. To produce the needed real economic growth, we must transform both our pension systems and the tax systems surrounding them so that instead of encouraging spending and consumption they will encourage savings and investment.

In his article Peterson suggested some good solutions for this and other problems.[2] This is a classic case where the American approach to an economic problem works against the future, in fact sacrifices the future economic health of the country, simply to preserve and enhance the benefits and gratifications of the immediate present. In contrast, the Japanese way of handling this problem, although it has its defects, in the long run works for productivity, present and future, rather than against it. We act in response to political pressure and in the direction of that pressure. The Japanese control their pressures better.

Peterson's thoughtful article echoes the concern of economists like Lester Thurow and politicians like former Senator Adlai E. Stevenson III over what Daniel Bell has termed the "revolution of rising entitlements." At a point in history where economic growth, the lifeblood of the free enterprise system, is badly clotted; every conceivable pressure group imaginable—old people, minority interests, special business interests, civil service employees—is trying to squeeze one last benefit or special entitlement for itself, through the constant exercise of political pressure. Everyone seems to feel that he or she is entitled to more, but has no particular interest in working harder for it. The Japanese have their own versions of special interest groups, although of course far less than in the pluralistic society of the United States. But the Japanese, pressure groups included, are prepared to work for what they get. They are still close enough to the tradition of scarcity and the recollection of common need to think of duties in the same breath as rights.

Not so with us. *The Washington Post* put our national problem well early in 1982 in a half-facetious editorial commenting on an alleged offer of Japanese aid to the United States. Noting that we are accustomed to giving aid to the LDC—less-developed countries—the paper commented: "What is needed is a new concept; the ODC —or over-developed country. These are nations in which the majority of citizens have become so involved in their personal prosperity that they have lost the will to devote their energies and resources to the commonweal. . . ."

There are a few good signs on the horizon that Americans can still work for the common interest and set aside the adversary positions (for example, labor versus management, government versus business) which have been allowed to harden among us. Ironically, it has been the pressure of Japanese competition which finally forced at least a few steps toward labor-management cooperation in the American automobile industry, a traditional battleground. It is good news for this country when UAW leaders can talk about helping management solve its problems and when a Ford vice-president can note that "the wave of the future . . . is greater participation by our workforce in the business process." The agreement made in February 1982 between the Ford Motor Company and the United Auto Workers was justly called historic. The union accepted a thirty-month freeze on wages, and deferred cost-of-living increases and reductions in paid time off. In return the company guaranteed a base income for veteran workers until they retire—on the analogy of Japanese industry's lifetime employment principle—a profit-sharing plan (reminiscent of the Japanese profit-based bonus structure), and a two-year moratorium on certain plant closings. The subsequent General Motors contract made these historic changes a widespread reality.

While "historic" for American labor-management relations—and the product of Detroit's present adversity—the agreement was even more significant in that it reflected Japanese ideas of labor-management cooperation. A great many American managers and union leaders have been making the pilgrimage to Japan lately, and doing some learning in the process. When Ford's chief negotiator, Peter J. Pestillo, said that "we aren't willing to treat our hourly people as the most variable cost we have," he was using the language of Japan's people-centered capitalism. Similarly, when the semiconductor firms of Silicon Valley in California set out to keep their employees permanent with impressive benefit and worker participation plans, in the Japanese manner, they are recognizing what Japanese business found out many decades ago: lifetime employment makes good business sense. The truth of this axiom will become ever clearer as we go further into the postindustrial age. For this new era leads us to the kind of knowledge industries where people count more than assembly lines and worker participation in achieving company goals is essential, not merely a nice thing to have.

Our lack of a work ethic centered on people—or, if you will, our neglect of the ethic that was once so strong within us—is not only pulling down our industrial productivity statistics. It shows up in other areas of our national life and in much the same manner. In his 1981 book, *National Defense,* James Fallows eloquently pictured the flaws of a military that has exalted technological development and managerial skills at the expense of the soldiers who must use the weapons and fight the battles, if they come. His comments remind us how deeply our defense establishment is in thrall to the "more bang for a buck" theory, that is, the constant obsession with ever more sophisticated "managerial" techniques and ever more lethal weapons development, with shockingly little thought given to the people involved in the armed forces—their education, their training, and their esprit de corps. "The machines," Fallows writes, "are merely tools. Through the history of combat they have been far less important than the strategies under which they are employed and the bonds of mutual trust, shared sacrifice and recognized leadership that give coherence to the forces who use the weapons."

Something like this can be said of our approach to workers and factories and offices. Our business, or so much of it, uses people as mechanical pawns or counters in its numbers games. Managers deploy them in pursuit of various business strategies, concerned mostly that certain numbers of people with certain job qualifications be available to perform certain tasks, useful only as long as the tasks performed can bring back a return of certain percentages on investment. The workers react accordingly—and build their lives and expectations outside of the workplace as much as possible. They despair of ever participating in decisions, even small ones that affect so much of their daily lives. If they find conditions too hard to bear, they can also move on. That is freedom.

The United States is the classic democracy of modern times, the home of "of the people, by the people, for the people." "Why," a Japanese economist once asked me, "do you not inject some of that 'people' principle into your economic institutions?" Instead we are content to leave their governance to managers and their calculators. If real problems arise, we can always, it appears, go outside of the workplace and seek help or sustenance or redress from the government and its laws.

Japan has proved that a free enterprise democracy can plan for its future and move toward commonly accepted goals without slipping into statism, violating individual rights, or dismantling the free marketplace. In their business planning Japan's twenty-first century capitalists and their opposite numbers in the government ministries have made their share of mistakes. They have often had to wait a long time for a popular consensus on some subjects. But they have kept their people working together for the national prosperity. A variety of different motives—the pursuit of the good life, national self-respect, international association, improved living standards—have been harnessed to the same goal. Risks have been taken. Crises have been faced. For all the fragilities of their economy—and the political consensus that supports it—they have carried off their plans.

It is time for Americans to take the long view ourselves. We pride ourselves on our capitalist tradition. We preserve the image of a nation of individualists—entrepreneurs and risk-takers—whose national specialty continues to be realizing dreams and expanding frontiers through daring and know-how. Yet in fact we are mired in a present of warring interests and inept compromises between them, where self-interest has replaced individualism and risk-taking is professionally minimized. We are not entrepreneurs but cautious committeemen. We are mortgaging the future of ourselves and our children to the demands of instant gratification. "Enjoy now, pay later." Many have come to accept the advertising promise of the installment plan as an article of faith.

The last real national goal we had was the exploration of space—at least at its beginnings. It is surprising how much that space effort accomplished in its first flush of enthusiasm. Educational standards were raised. A heartening popular consensus was formed. And not least of all, the economic payoff from the engineering and scientific work of the space pioneers was staggering in its scope. It created, for example, the successful miniaturization techniques on which so much of our modern technology is based.

It is time we developed some similar long-term goals and set out to work in support of them. To remodel our economy for future productivity is a good start. It cannot be done merely by talking supply-side economics and relying on the goodwill and risk-taking proclivities of American business to start the boom going. Nor can we restore our ailing industries by renewed doses of protectionism. In the mid-seventies, when both the automobile and the steel industries were given valuable respites (in the case of steel at least, through protectionist trigger price devices aimed at Japan and European competitors), a surge of new long-term investment in these industries was conspicuous by its absence. It is highly doubtful that a business world whose principle characteristic in the early eighties is take-over cannibalism will be moved by exhortation to plan for future productivity.

For better or worse, government must play a part in developing a new industrial and economic policy for this country. While supply-side tactics are admirable, as a corrective to past demand-feedings of the consumer economy, they will be ineffective unless supported by a most carefully planned program of tax and other incentives that reward saving and productive investment and penalize the opposite. As Adlai Stevenson III pointed out: "The new supply-siders, like the old demand-siders, advocate macro-economic measures which assume an efficiently working market. They do not get at the roots of our competitive difficulties, such as wage and price rigidities, or the sheltering of declining [economic] sectors which squeezes off growth and employment opportunities elsewhere in the economy."

The Reagan administration has doubtless made some useful contributions to future economic health, in that it has shown the way to reevaluating and cutting government aid and subsidies that were given not wisely but too well. But it has shown little inclination to go after the big problems, like the swelling social security burden on the country—and for the usual political reasons. It has been easier to take away benefits from the poor. There are few signs of any real macroeconomic policy appearing.

A new industrial policy would recognize the need for government to assist the work of industry, without overwhelming it. However rosy is the dream of a small-town Coolidge America, we cannot escape the fact that in a modern economy government cannot afford to be a mere bystander or referee. Behind the economic success of Japan and Germany lies neither *laissez faire* nor centralized economic planning. On the contrary they combine the strengths of government and the marketplace.

A new industrial policy would encourage savings and capital formation with every device at government's disposal. The means are there, by rewriting the tax laws alone. It would promote investment in research and development by similar methods. But industrial policy does not end with tax concessions. To succeed it must provide a stimulus to greater national competitiveness, and an incentive for wider growth.

Among the steps that many have advocated are an industrial development bank; government support for high-technology industries on something more than a random basis; education programs for retraining and reeducating workers, as some industries fade and others swiftly grow; a greatly strengthened Export-Import Bank; a new government patent policy; revision of banking and antitrust laws to permit better American competition in exports, with the chance of using trading companies for this purpose, on the Japanese model; and a greatly strengthened Department of Commerce, Trade, and Technology to spearhead government support of U.S. industry.

I would suggest also that we give serious and consistent attention, both on a national and community level, to the problems of our declining educational standards. We seldom stop to consider that the premise for the successful cooperative worker in the Japanese quality control circle is a rigorously administered system of primary and high school education which teaches a few basic disciplines well. Conversely we give little attention to the effect which poor education, loosely administered, has on our national productivity. On one side we have the bright graduate, whose "enrichment" curriculum, with its stress on individuality above all, ill suits him to work easily with others. On the other side we have children who have been promoted and graduated without learning elementary reading and mathematics.

These are not revolutionary ideas. They will not lead to socialism or statism. Far from it, they will powerfully strengthen American capitalism and turn its energies toward future productivity. There are few things Japan's Confucian capitalists have accomplished in building a "plan-rational" economy that cannot be usefully adapted by Americans. There is no mystery of an alien culture in what they have done.

But they have done it with a will. And that is our problem in America. As long as we wallow in the Age of Entitlement, obsessed by dreams and goals of a dubious "self-fulfillment" which no one can define, we are incapable as a nation both of conceiving a new twenty-first century economy and of making the hard political decisions necessary to put long-range plans into effect. Republics live by virtue.

It is a collective virtue, based on the shared aspirations, ethics, and morality of their citizens. The Japanese have retained their work ethic because, albeit in a modest way, they have retained the Confucian and some of the Buddhist ideals of service and mutual support which created it. If we continue to disparage our own work ethic and ignore the noble and demanding ideals on which it is based—religious in their roots—we shall go the way of Rome, Athens, and the rest, a monument to our own contentiousness and greed.

Notes and Sources

Chapter 1: The Twenty-First Century Capitalists

1. In his brilliant study *Capitalism, Socialism and Democracy* (New York: Harper, 1942) Joseph Schumpeter warned about "the obsolescence of the entrepreneurial function." He held that the entrepreneurial spirit which gave capitalism its vitality would pass away as risk-taking entrepreneurs were replaced by cautious managers. All of Schumpeter's social, if not his economic conclusions in this book are based on observations and examples in Europe and the United States. The possibility of a Japanese contribution to capitalism does not seem to have crossed his mind, an understandable lapse at that point in history.

2. Yamamoto Shichihei, *Nihon Shihonshugi no Seishin (The Spirit of Japanese Capitalism)* (Tokyo: Kōbunsha (Kappa Books), 1979). The English translations given here and in later passages quoted are my own.

3. Although less than 30 percent of the Japanese work force enjoys secure lifetime employment up to retirement age—mostly those working for the 34,000 odd major companies employing more than 300 people—small and medium-sized companies attempt to provide similar security as their means permit.

4. *MITI and the Japanese Miracle: The Growth of Industrial Policy, 1925–1975* by Chalmers Johnson (Stanford: Stanford U. Press, 1982) is a fascinating, seminal work on the Japanese economic bureaucracy.

5. From a speech by Miyoshi Masaya, Managing Director of the Keidanren, delivered at Denver, Colorado, in June 1981.

6. The name recalls Japanese military tactics in World War II. While American infantry doctrine was, for example, to take the top of a hill and fortify it, the Japanese Army preferred to entrench on the reverse slope, just over the crest,

so as to take the opposition by surprise, firing on them just as they seemed about to gain their objective on the summit. Or so the theory ran.

7. Daniel Bell, *The Cultural Contradictions of Capitalism* (New York: Basic Books, 1976).
8. From a speech by Hanamura Nihachiro, vice-chairman of the Keidanren, delivered at Denver, Colorado, in June 1981.

Chapter 2: The Work Ethic and How It Grew

1. As quoted in *The Development of Japanese Business 1600–1973,* by Johannes Hirschmeier and Tsunehiko Yui (London: George Allen and Unwin, 1975).
2. The exception, "The Japanese and the Jews," was originally published under the pseudonym of Isaiah Ben Dasan and became almost instantly a Japanese bestseller. Ostensibly written by a longtime Jewish resident of Japan, the book set out to examine the many interesting similarities and differences between the two singular and unique cultures, Japanese and Jewish. In fact Yamamoto used the device of comparison as a vehicle for a gentle but acute self-analysis of his fellow Japanese.
3. Notably Nakumura Hajime, one of Japan's great Buddhist scholars, and the American Robert Bellah, author of the classic *Tokugawa Religion.*
4. The quotations from Baigan and Motoori are taken from Bellah's *Japanese Religion.*
5. When asked to define the origin of his teachings, Ninomiya remarked: "One spoonful of Shinto and a half-spoonful each of Buddhism and Confucianism."
6. As quoted by Johannes Hirschmeier, in his article on Shibusawa in *The State and Economic Enterprise in Japan* (Princeton, N.J.: Princeton U. Press, 1965).

Chapter 3: The American Factor

1. Charles "Engine Charley" Wilson, onetime president of General Motors, who later held Cabinet office in the Eisenhower administration, made the often-quoted comment "What's good for General Motors is good for the country." The union leader Walter Reuther, then head of the UAW-CIO, on hearing of Wilson's remark commented tartly that one reason for GM's having developed the automatic shift was to enable Wilson to drive "with both feet in his mouth at the same time."

Chapter 4: Management and Human Capital

1. Excerpted from Frank Gibney, *Japan: The Fragile Super-Power* (New York: Norton, 1975).
2. When Nagashima Shigeo, the popular manager of the Tokyo Giants, was unceremoniously booted out of his job in 1980, a real wave of protest came up from the country. In America such a firing would have been routine, particularly in

baseball, where managers' heads roll almost seasonally. But in Japan, even conceding that a severance was necessary, it should have been preceded by several rounds of quiet conferences, a period of "self-reflection" for the manager, after which he would announce his resignation (to give those under him a chance) and simultaneously receive a showy position in the club offices. When the Giants' management did not observe this rubric, they were roundly criticized.

3. Keynes's definition was cited in R.H. Tawney's *Religion and the Rise of Capitalism* (London: Penguin, 1980), the memorable work on religion and business ethics in the West, which concludes with Tawney's prophetic concern with a civilization "which has brought to the conquest of its material environment resources unknown in earlier ages, but which has not yet learned to master itself."

4. William J. Abernathy and Robert H. Hayes, "Managing Our Way to Economic Decline," *Harvard Business Review,* July/August 1980.

Chapter 5: The Integrity of the Company

1. There are, to be sure, "groups" of companies, like Mitsui or Mitsubishi, that communicate closely with one another and often formulate general policies in common. Almost all of them are survivals of the prewar *zaibatsu* combines. Many have interlocking stock relationships, a device that Japanese companies of like mind often employ. Yet each company retains its independence; and there is no overall holding company controlling the entire group. Thus the group is quite different from the conglomerate.

2. Japan is, however, a democracy; and the Commercial Code gives stockholders a right to be heard, even at such ceremonial occasions. According to the code, the board of directors is a "decision-making" body. So we have the phenomenon of the *sokaiya*—literally, the "meeting-man" (from the words *kabunishi sokai*— "general meeting of the shareholders"). Originally the *sokaiya* was a free spirit, possibly, who came to the board meeting of a large public company to utter some complaint on behalf of small stockholders against current company policy or the state of the balance sheet. Quite possibly, the complaint was justified. As time went, *sokaiya* turned themselves into a kind of underground cottage industry. Purchasing just enough shares of various companies to qualify for attending board meetings, the *sokaiya* would make nuisances of themselves. They would not only ask embarrassing questions about management's program, but also try to disrupt the whole meeting—if they were not bought off in advance.

Japanese management's answer was predictable. To guard against the intrusions of these "offensive" *sokaiya,* it was only natural to hire the company's own *sokaiya,* whose "defensive" job was to serve as a claque for constantly applauding management's proposals, drowning out the opposition.

Chapter 6: Company Unions That Work

1. The yen figures are given to make the comparison more accurate, since the relative value of the yen and the dollar changed during this period. The dollar

equivalents of these Japanese raises in 1972 and 1980, at the exchange rates then in use, were $1.39 and $4.81, respectively.

2. For purists: *Me ni aoba yama hototogisu hatsu gatsuo.*

Chapter 7: How to Be Law-Abiding Without Lawyers

1. According to a preliminary survey made by the American Bar Foundation and reported at the general meeting of the American Bar Association in 1981, the total number of lawyers was 535,000, as of the end of 1980.
2. A noted defender of the common law and dean of Northwestern University's law school, Wigmore also taught law at Keio University in Tokyo during the closing years of the nineteenth century. Portions of his *Law and Justice in Tokugawa Japan* (Tokyo: University of Tokyo Press, 1967) have been reprinted in recent times.
3. From Kawashima Takenori's article "Dispute Resolution in Contemporary Japan," included in A.T. von Mehren, ed., *Law in Japan* (Cambridge, Mass.: Harvard U. Press, 1963). Twenty years after this was written, however, one must concede that the degree of distrust in judges and their decisions has been decreasing.
4. Kawashima Takenori, *Nihonjin no Hōishiki (The Consciousness of Law Among the Japanese)* (Tokyo: Iwanami Shinsho). The translation is my own.

Chapter 8: Our Contracts, Their Consultations

1. I followed his advice and made a cautious statement. The union was organized the next day, before my written exhortations had been typed.
2. From *The Consciousness of Law Among the Japanese.* (This particular passage was translated by Charles R. Stevens.) I am indebted to Professor Kawashima for other points made in this section.

Chapter 10: People and Their Products

1. In this section on antipollution measures, I have relied heavily on the authoritative study *Environmental Law in Japan* by Julian Gresser, Koichiro Fujikura, and Akio Morishima (Cambridge, Mass.: The MIT Press, 1981).
2. Taken from an interview in the film *People and Productivity: Learning from Japan,* which was planned and edited by Maurice B. Mitchell and myself at the Pacific Basin Institute and produced by Chuck Olin for the Encyclopaedia Britannica Educational Corporation. All the quotations are used here with the kind permission of Encyclopaedia Britannica Educational Corporation, Chicago, Illinois.

Chapter 11: Doing Business in Japan

1. James Abegglen and Thomas Hout, "Facing Up to the Trade Gap With Japan," *Foreign Affairs*, Fall 1978.
2. For a concise and informative discussion of the trading companies' function see Yoshi Tsurumi, *Sōgōsosha: Engines of Export Growth* (Montreal, Canada: The Institute for Research on Public Policy, 1980).

Chapter 12: The Japanese Factor: The Community-Company in America

1. This comment, along with the other quotations from executives and workers at the Honda, Quasar, and Westinghouse factories mentioned in the following pages, was taken from the film *People and Productivity: Learning from Japan*, prepared by the Pacific Basin Institute and distributed by the Encyclopaedia Britannica Educational Corporation, Chicago, Illinois.
2. Bernard Krisher, "How the Japanese Manage in the U.S.," *Fortune*, June 15, 1981, © 1981 by Time, Inc. All rights reserved.

Chapter 13: The Hare in the Jungle: Japan's Difficult Future

1. Amaya Naohiro, "Japan as a Mercantile Nation," as translated and abridged in *Japan Echo*, Vol. 7, No. 2 (1980). The original article appeared in *Bungei Shunju*.
2. Okita Saburo, *The Developing Economies and Japan* (Tokyo: University of Tokyo, 1980).
3. The study was conducted by Arthur M. Whitehill and Shinichi Takezawa. Their earlier survey was analyzed in their 1968 book, *The Other Worker*. Both sets of findings are compared and discussed in their current book, *Workways* (Tokyo: The Japan Institute of Labor, 1982). Whitehill is professor of international management at the University of Hawaii; Takezawa is dean of the School of Social Relations at Rikkyo University in Tokyo.

Chapter 14: Some Lessons for Americans

1. Quoted from Peter G. Peterson, "No More Free Lunch for the Middle Class," *The New York Times Magazine*, January 17, 1982.
2. Among his solutions: raising the age level at which social security payments begin, to conform with modern life expectancy standards as well as to add needed labor to the workforce; and removing the practice of automatically indexing social security and similar payments, a device adopted originally to check the effects of inflation, but which in fact has become in itself a bad inflationary factor.

Index

INDEX

Index

INDEX

Index

INDEX

Index

INDEX

Index